# DIGITAL COPYRIGHT LAW

CAMERON HUTCHISON

# DIGITAL COPYRIGHT LAW

Digital Copyright Law
© Irwin Law Inc., 2016

All rights reserved. No part of this publication may be reproduced, stored in a retrieval system, or transmitted, in any form or by any means, without the prior written permission of the publisher or, in the case of photocopying or other reprographic copying, a licence from Access Copyright (Canadian Copyright Licensing Agency), 1 Yonge Street, Suite 800, Toronto, ON, M5E 1E5.

Published in 2016 by

Irwin Law Inc.
14 Duncan Street
Suite 206
Toronto, ON
M5H 3G8

www.irwinlaw.com

ISBN: 978-1-55221-424-4
e-book ISBN: 978-1-55221-425-1

**Library and Archives Canada Cataloguing in Publication**

Hutchison, Cameron, 1963–, author
Digital copyright law / Cameron Hutchison.

Includes bibliographical references and index.
Issued in print and electronic formats.
ISBN 978-1-55221-424-4 (paperback).—ISBN 978-1-55221-425-1 (pdf)

1. Copyright and electronic data processing—Canada. 2. Copyright—Electronic information resources—Canada. 3. Copyright—Canada. I. Title.

| | | |
|---|---|---|
| KE2779.H88 2016 | 346.7104'82 | C2016-902809-7 |
| KF2994.H88 2016 | | C2016-902810-0 |

Printed and bound in Canada.

1 2 3 4 5   20 19 18 17 16

# SUMMARY TABLE OF CONTENTS

PREFACE AND ACKNOWLEDGEMENTS  *xiii*

INTRODUCTION  *1*

CHAPTER 1: **Interpretive Dimensions**  *13*

CHAPTER 2: **Authored Works**  *43*

CHAPTER 3: **Neighbouring Rights and Collective Management**  *85*

CHAPTER 4: **Ownership, Licensing, Registration, and Infringement**  *103*

CHAPTER 5: **Technological Protection Measures and Rights Management Information**  *123*

CHAPTER 6: **User Rights**  *145*

CHAPTER 7: **Internet Intermediaries**  *175*

CHAPTER 8: **International Dimensions**  *191*

TABLE OF CASES  *215*

INDEX  *221*

ABOUT THE AUTHOR  *233*

# DETAILED TABLE OF CONTENTS

PREFACE AND ACKNOWLEDGEMENTS  *xiii*

**Introduction**  1
A. The Interests That Copyright Law Is to Advance  1
B. Towards a Balancing of Interests  2
C. The Digital Disruption  4
D. Rebalancing Copyright in the Digital Age  7
E. How This Book Addresses Copyright Issues  8

CHAPTER 1:
**Interpretive Dimensions**  13
A. Introduction  13
B. Digital Facts  13
C. Statutory Interpretation  16
    1) Approaches  18
        a) Ordinary Meaning  18
        b) Dynamic Intentionalism  19
        c) Purposivism  22
D. Evolving Principles of Law  25
    1) Legitimate Economic Interests and Separation  27

      2) Technological Neutrality  30
         a) Non-discrimination  31
         b) Non-interference  34
E. Neutralizing Digital Facts  39
F. The Future of Technological Neutrality  41

CHAPTER 2:
## Authored Works  43

A. Introduction  43
B. Requirements for Copyright in Authored Works  44
      1) Literary, Dramatic, Musical, or Artistic Work  44
      2) Fixation  48
      3) Expression  49
      4) Originality  51
      5) Authorship  54
C. Economic Rights  56
      1) Reproduction and the Status of Non-consumptive Copies  57
      2) Substantial Taking  64
      3) Telecommunication  71
      4) Distribution and Exhaustion  73
      5) Authorization  78
D. Moral Rights  82

CHAPTER 3:
## Neighbouring Rights and Collective Management  85

A. Introduction  85
B. Neighbouring Rights  86
      1) Performers' Performances  86
      2) Sound Recordings  89
      3) Equitable Remuneration  91
      4) Broadcasts  92
C. Collective Management of Copyright  93

CHAPTER 4:
## Ownership, Licensing, Registration, and Infringement  103

A.  Introduction  103
B.  Ownership  103
C.  Licensing  105
   1)  Assignments, Exclusive Licences, and Non-exclusive Licences  105
   2)  Contract Law Issues  108
   3)  Open-Source Licences  112
D.  Copyright Registration  114
E.  Infringement  116
   1)  Identifying Infringers on the Internet  118

CHAPTER 5:
**Technological Protection Measures and Rights Management Information**  123

A.  Introduction  123
B.  Technological Protection Measures: Section 41  124
   1)  The International Legal Context  124
   2)  Purpose  126
   3)  "Effective" Technological Protection Measures  127
   4)  Circumvention  130
   5)  Is There an Access Control Right?  131
   6)  Manufacturers and Intermediaries  133
   7)  Remedies  136
   8)  Exceptions  136
C.  Rights Management Information  140

CHAPTER 6:
**User Rights**  145

A.  Introduction  145
B.  Fair Dealing  146
   1)  Allowable Purposes  146
   2)  Criteria for Assessing Fairness  149
   3)  Fair Dealing in the Digital Context  154
C.  Exceptions Outlined in Sections 29.21 to 32.2  157

1) User-Generated Content 158
2) Private Copy Exceptions 161
3) Educational Institutions 164
4) Libraries, Archives, or Museums (LAM) 167
5) Computer Programs 168
6) Incidental Use/Temporary Copy 169
7) Ephemeral Copies 170
8) Retransmission 170
9) Perceptual Disabilities 171
10) Statutory Obligations 171
11) Miscellaneous Exceptions 172

CHAPTER 7:
**Internet Intermediaries** 175

A. Introduction 175
B. Background 176
    1) The Issues in *CAIP* 177
        a) Safe Harbour Considerations 177
        b) The Authorization Right 179
    2) The US Notice and Takedown Regime 180
C. The *CMA* Amendments 181
    1) The Notice and Notice Regime 181
    2) Network (or Connectivity) Services 183
    3) Digital Memory Providers (Hosting) 184
    4) Information Location Tools (Search Engines) 185
    5) Services That Enable Infringement (Peer-to-Peer Sharing) 186
D. The Status of Authorization Liability for Internet Intermediaries 188

CHAPTER 8:
**International Dimensions** 191

A. Introduction 191
B. Public International Law 191
C. Private International Law 193
    1) Jurisdiction 194

    2) Choice of Law  *202*
    3) Recognition and Enforcement of Foreign Judgments  *206*
D.  Ubiquitous Infringement  *208*

TABLE OF CASES  *215*

INDEX  *221*

ABOUT THE AUTHOR  *233*

# Preface and Acknowledgements

About a year ago, it occurred to me that with all the changes, and sometimes controversy, surrounding the recent digital amendments to the *Copyright Act*, as well as the relative surge of digital copyright law cases, it was time for someone to write a book on *digital* copyright law. It is my hope that the legal community will find this book useful both as a roadmap of potential legal issues in this area, as well as a competent analysis of those issues. I am indebted to Zaid Jivani, JD (class of 2015) for his excellent research assistance, and to the University of Alberta for the EFF/SAS grant that funded him. Thank you to the University of Alberta Faculty of Law for granting me a half sabbatical during which time I wrote most of this book. I would also like to express my appreciation to Irwin Law for its editorial assistance and for publishing this book.

I was motivated to write this book as a mark of achievement that might someday inspire my children — however far off in time that might be. My six-year-old boy, Kenji, loves to draw books about Batman. He will sit down at our dining table with his coloured markers, draw up several pages, staple them together, and then read to his parents from his book, all in the span of ten or fifteen minutes. About six months ago, during my sabbatical, he asked me, "What do you do at work all day?" "I am writing a book" I replied. He looked at me skeptically and said, "I've never seen you make a book." Here is the proof, Boost! Sorry, there are no pictures.

## DEDICATION

*For Carol, Kenji, Maya, and Naomi*

## NOTE

In this text, whenever "the Act" is used or a section number appears without its corresponding Act title, the reference is to the *Copyright Act*, RSC 1985, c C-42.

# Introduction

## A. THE INTERESTS THAT COPYRIGHT LAW IS TO ADVANCE

Copyright law is best understood as a policy tool whose overarching purpose is to promote the generation of knowledge and culture in society.[1] It is generally accepted that copyright law does this by advancing certain interests. These are (1) *authorial incentive* (to ensure an adequate level of monopoly rights protection for authors so that they have incentive to create "works," such as music, books, and computer programs, through commercial exploitation), (2) *user rights* (to ensure that downstream authors and users of such works can benefit from using those works in new or productive ways during the term of the monopoly), and (3) *dissemination* (to promote the widest possible dissemination to the public of these works and their uses). In so doing (and possibly as a fourth interest to consider), copyright law should not unduly burden technological uses and innovation.

The concurrent advancement of these interests is often not possible, and conflicts between them must then be reconciled, ideally so as to further copyright's overarching purpose. The persistent tension

---

1   Patricia Aufderheide & Peter Jaszi, *Reclaiming Fair Use: How to Put Balance Back in Copyright* (Chicago: University of Chicago Press, 2011) at 16: "Copyright policy is the collection of ways that a government provides incentives to create culture. And we mean culture broadly — building, aggregating, and sharing knowledge. Progress is grounded, as policymakers know, in the growth of culture."

within this group of interests is between the monopoly rights of authors in their works, on the one hand, and the unauthorized exploitation or dissemination of these works in some form during the term of the monopoly, on the other hand. For example, the price to be paid for stronger downstream-user rights of copyrighted works is that the authorial incentive may in some way be reduced. These conflicts, and their reconciliations, happen during the drafting of statutory rules, and, when such provisions are ambiguous at the point of application in disputes, the interpretation of these rules.

## B. TOWARDS A BALANCING OF INTERESTS

Given the purpose of copyright, we might best be served by seeking "to measure, empirically, whether this policy or that policy increases or decreases the output of cultural products, assists in the promotion of knowledge, or otherwise promotes the public's interests, including authors' interests."[2] It is hard to refute the desirability of this approach and, indeed, empirical evidence should be relied upon, at least at the level of policy, to inform legislative change. The problem, in many cases, is that the data are either unavailable or incomplete.[3] The next best solution is to study the arguments for and against a certain policy, and seek out the views of affected interests.[4]

In this endeavour, legal discourse idealizes "balance" between copyright's competing interests as the laudable goal of copyright law. However, interest balancing is an elusive concept. For example, there

---

2   William Patry, *How to Fix Copyright* (New York: Oxford University Press, 2011) at 135. See also Ian Hargreaves, *Digital Opportunity: A Review of Intellectual Property and Growth* (London: Intellectual Property Office, 2011) [Hargreaves Report].

3   Hargreaves Report, *ibid* at 2.13, notes three main obstacles to using evidence on the economic impacts of intellectual property (IP).

4   Studied efforts into the expected impacts of a policy choice should lead to better policy recommendations and avoid clearly suboptimal choices. Sometimes, these poor choices are, nonetheless, made for other reasons. See Michael Geist, "The Great Canadian Copyright Giveaway: Why Copyright Term Extension for Sound Recordings Could Cost Consumers Millions" (22 April 2015), *Michael Geist* (blog), online: www.michaelgeist.ca/2015/04/the-great-canadian-copyright-giveaway-why-copyright-term-extension-for-sound-recordings-could-cost-consumers-millions. The reasons for pursuing poor policy choices may be due to political ideology, unsupported rhetoric on the need for longer and stronger intellectual property protection, lobbying efforts of powerful industry groups, the implementation of international commitments, or some combination thereof.

are many methods for the legal treatment of Internet intermediaries as conduits for infringing activities: we might impose on them proactive duties to use content surveillance measures to monitor for copyrighted works, or we may assign them to a more passive role of acting only upon actual notice of an infringement. Either approach is arguably "balanced." It is the exact calibration of the balance that is open to debate, thus rendering the balance concept pliable. Still, the balance metaphor serves as a heuristic for achieving the overarching purpose of copyright. In the absence of evidence or even the availability of some other heuristic, the idea that we should seek a balance, in the sense of simultaneously advancing all interests (and concomitantly not overly advancing any one interest) affected by a rule or regime, might be the safest choice.[5] When drafting or interpreting a rule, policy-makers and judges should consider the various arguments as to the right calibration of the impacted interests before rendering judgment as to the right balance.

The rhetoric of balance appears prominently when courts interpret the Act. The Supreme Court has, generally speaking, been adept at reaching results that seem to properly calibrate the advancement of copyright's interests. These (mostly) "right" interpretations are often cloaked in the technical language of law. But they are at least as convincing at the policy level as they are at the legal level, and often even more so. For example, there was no way to know whether the majority's interpretation in *Théberge v Galerie d'Art du Petit Champlain inc*, which favoured purchaser over authorial rights, advances the goals of copyright except that we may sense that such an interpretation likely has significant positive implications for downstream uses of duly purchased copies with little impact on authorial incentive.[6] This may or may not be empirically true, but it appeals to our logic and judgment as most likely the right result in terms of furthering the goals of copyright.

---

5   Over-advancing any interest, to the exclusion of others, is antithetical to the notion of balance in copyright law. As Abella J put it in *Canadian Broadcasting Corp v SODRAC*, 2015 SCC 57 at para 145:

> To tilt the balance too far towards protection of creators' rights would undermine the right of users to access and work with creative materials. To tilt it too far towards access, on the other hand, would fail to provide a just reward to creators, leading authors and their supporters to under-invest in producing and distributing their works. At both ends of the spectrum, the public loses some benefit of creative works.

6   2002 SCC 34 [*Théberge*].

The rhetoric of balance in the copyright context has been with us since the beginning of the new millennium, and it has been routinely applied in both the analogue and digital contexts. The emergence of the principle of technological neutrality is, in part, a reflection of the desire to maintain balance in the face of a new digital reality. The challenge has been, and continues to be, maintaining the right balance as new digital technologies evolve.

## C. THE DIGITAL DISRUPTION

*Digital technologies* have been defined as "technologies that allow information and processes to be created and stored in digital form, with the possibility of distribution over electronic networks."[7] There are two fundamental attributes of digital technologies implied in this broad definition that have had transformative implications for copyright law. First, the digital format, as a technology, makes the creation, copying, and transmitting of content exceptionally easy.[8] Second, the Internet is a vehicle through which content in the digital format can be disseminated on a prodigious scale.[9] This digital format for displaying and processing content and information, and the Internet platform of its dissemination, has jettisoned copyright from a domain of limited concern only to the creative industries into a matter of primary interest in the knowledge economy.[10]

The attributes of digital technologies fundamentally disrupted copyright law which, in turn, prompted legal change. The main response in the United States and internationally (and much later in Canada) was twofold: first, the legislation of anti-circumvention measures to protect content owners against illegal copying and access; and second,

---

7   David Poole with Sophie Le-Phat Ho, *Digital Transitions and the Impact of New Technology on the Arts* (June 2011), online: Canadian Public Arts Funders www.cpaf-opsac.org/en/themes/documents/DigitalTransitionsReport-FINAL-EN.pdf.
8   The advent of Web 2.0 — in particular, the proliferation of mobile devices, the interoperability of software/hardware, and the rise of user-generated content — makes the creation and sharing of content a taken-for-granted fact in most people's daily lives.
9   No less significant has been the rise of cloud computing and broadband distribution that permits seemingly unlimited digital storage space (where copies are stored) and easy access to content.
10  See Hargreaves Report, above note 2 at 1.18.

the creation of a regime of knowledge-based infringement for Internet intermediaries so as not to impede use and development of the Internet.[11] In the opinion of some, this policy response resulted in the "destruction of creativity."[12] Anti-circumvention measures did not effectively stem the tide of illegal content sharing on the Internet, while the knowledge-based infringement regime incentivized the creation of intermediaries, such as YouTube, that facilitate the illegal sharing of content, rather than the creation of content.[13] There is no doubt that the economic pie for authors and intermediaries has shrunk as much content is available either illegally or at highly reduced costs for those willing to pay. However, it remains unclear what impact, if any, this has had on the incentive to create.

The focus on the negative implications for copyright holders tells only half the story about digital technologies and copyright law. Digitization has facilitated the efficient and economical *production, use,* and *legal dissemination* of copyrighted content. The production of movies and music is generally much easier, of higher quality, and less expensive due to advances in digital technologies. Works can be more easily (and more frequently) commented upon or recast through fair dealing uses of copyrighted content. Moreover, new platforms of content delivery that have emerged in the digital age have massively increased the legal dissemination of (and markets for) works.

Some see enormous opportunities in these developments, which copyright law seems only to inhibit. According to Patry, the social and economic foundations of copyright law are unsuitable in this new age. He argues that artificial scarcity, upon which "old" copyright law was premised, now conflicts with modern digital abundance:

> The new markets created by the Internet and digital tools are the greatest ever: Barriers to entry are low, costs of production and distribution are low, the reach is global, and large sums of money may be made off of a multitude of small transactions. This contrasts dramatically with the world of analog artificial scarcity, which base sales on small number

---

11  Other measures — more apparent in US law than in Canada — have been to make copyright law "stronger and longer": Patry, above note 2 at 11. Patry also refers to it as "copyright inflation."

12  Robert Levine, *Free Ride: How Digital Parasites Are Destroying the Culture Business, and How the Culture Business Can Fight Back* (New York: Anchor Books, 2011) at 11.

13  Ibid at 16.

of expensive transactions, a situation that favored gatekeepers over individuals.[14]

We might see shades of truth that the old copyright law has not fully adapted to meet the new digital reality. : For example, liability may be imposed for non-perceptible copying that facilitates the creation or distribution of a work, even though the purpose of copyright is to protect against the unauthorized copying of the *expressive content* of a work. At the same time, entirely dispensing with old copyright law might be an overreaction.[15]

In a similar vein, James Boyle argues that the response to the "Internet Threat" of zero-cost copying has been for copyright law to impose "perfect control," including the inappropriate resort to anti-circumvention measures within the domain of copyright law. But this reaction was premature, according to Boyle:

> What the Net takes away with one hand, it often gives back with the other. Cheaper copying does not merely mean loss, it also means opportunity. Before strengthening intellectual property rights, we would need to know whether the loss was greater than the gain and whether revised business models and new distribution mechanisms could avoid the losses while capturing more of the gains.[16]

The law, at least in Canada, has not remained impervious to facilitating the potential of digital technologies in positive ways. Incrementally, the law has favoured new ways of creating and disseminating culture on the Internet even at the expense of traditional content industries. Consider, for example, the user-generated content exception in the *Copyright Act* or Supreme Court interpretations of the Act that give paramount importance to the Internet as a means of disseminating copyrighted content and its legitimate uses.[17] Still, much of the old copyright law remains with us.

---

14   Patry, above note 2 at 3.
15   See Hargreaves Report, above note 2 at 4.11: "The challenge is to respond to the turbulence which this technology has caused for copyright in a way that facilitates the emergence of new businesses, without undermining the basic model of copyright, which has sustained creative businesses for more than three centuries."
16   James Boyle, *The Public Domain* (New Haven, CT: Yale University Press, 2010) at 62.
17   *Society of Composers, Authors and Music Publishers of Canada v Canadian Assn of Internet Providers*, 2004 SCC 45 [*CAIP*].

These larger debates provide important context and shed some light as to how, and why, particular legal rules have been implemented or interpreted to meet the perceived needs of the digital age. The implications of any of these views for copyright policy and law, if any are indeed true, are enormous. To the extent that copyright law frustrates the advancement of its intended purpose in this new reality, there is discordance between law, as written, and the policies it is meant to further. Questions about the efficacy of rules (or the regime as a whole) in achieving copyright law's purpose in the digital era seem destined to remain one of the known unknowns that will fuel much debate about copyright policy in the immediate future.

## D. REBALANCING COPYRIGHT IN THE DIGITAL AGE

The legal response to the digital disruption in Canada was painfully slow. Only in 2012 were digital amendments made to the Act, through the *Copyright Modernization Act*.[18] Before that, courts were forced to adapt (sometimes awkwardly) copyright doctrine to the new digital reality. Thus, for example, the Supreme Court had to pronounce on the liability of Internet intermediaries for acts of infringement without the benefit of specific legislative direction on the issue.[19] The *Copyright Modernization Act* codified some of these judicially created rules while, in other cases, new regimes were put in place to deal with new problems created by digitization, or to implement international treaty obligations. But even after the amendments, key ambiguities and gaps remain.

This book will focus on legal adjustments demanded by digital change: (1) the creation of distinct digital-only regimes in the Act and (2) the adaptation of legal doctrine to digital technologies. For some legislated regimes, such as the anti-circumvention rules in section 41, policy choices favouring authorial incentive over other interests are apparent. This illustrates two points. First, the balance metaphor is as pliable at the regime level as it is at the more granular level of analyzing specific rules. Anti-circumvention measures, or digital locks, even when they hollow out user rights, may be justified as efforts to reassert lost authorial incentives and, therefore, restore balance back into the copyright regime. The second less obvious point is that whatever the legal response,

---

18  SC 2012, c 20.
19  *CAIP*, above note 18.

if any, to digitization, there often is no returning to a pre-digital era balance. Copyright has been disrupted not by legal change but because the nature of content generation and dissemination has changed. We are now in an era of recalibrating, not resetting, the balance.

Perhaps less obvious is that the same is true for the adaptation of copyright law doctrine to digitization. Despite constant efforts to give new life to old doctrine, and to recruit new interpretive principles such as technological neutrality to the cause, the best that can be said is that digital technologies and their implication for copyright can be accommodated in the law, but not neutralized in their effects. For example, when the Supreme Court interpreted authorization infringement, in the Internet intermediary context, to mean *actual knowledge* of infringing activities and not *control* over infringing activities (as it does in the analogue context), it favoured technology providers as instruments of dissemination to the detriment of the authorial incentive interest. There is, in other words, consequences for the interests involved notwithstanding the attempt to legally neutralize differences.

## E. HOW THIS BOOK ADDRESSES COPYRIGHT ISSUES

My aim in this book is to offer a concise analytical treatment of Canadian copyright law, with an obvious focus on the digital dimension. As the first book of its kind in Canada, *Digital Copyright Law* has the important goal of introducing to the legal community and educated laypersons the full range of legal issues, big and small, that animate this novel area of Canadian law and of doing so in an accessible manner. I generally adopt an objective approach to the issues for two reasons. First, I view this book as a resource for the legal and policy communities and, as any lawyer knows, it is critical to understand all sides of a given issue. Second, many of the key ambiguities and gaps require further study and considered analysis before I could responsibly take a position on them. There are times, however, when I strongly advance a position that I believe to be correct.

Chapter 1 discusses the general factual attributes of digitization and the Internet that make any legal adjustment difficult. Most of the chapter deals with interpretive *legal* approaches and principles applicable to this area of law. Although something of a primer on statutory interpretation, it is, I hope, much more than that. An effort is made to illustrate the critical relevance of choice of approach and technique to the interpretive outcome in difficult cases. More than that, certain principles have emerged in copyright law to guide interpretive results. One of these—technological neutrality—is a principle of complex dimensions which has arisen specifically to deal with the immense challenges posed by digital technologies.

Chapter 2 highlights the core subject matter of copyright and its accompanying rights. Section B discusses the requirements for copyright to subsist in an artistic, literary, dramatic, or musical work. In typical cases, digitization is easily accommodated within these rules, though one need not venture too far into the realm of unusual "digital" cases to find doctrinal uncertainty. The same is also true of Section D which deals with moral rights. The core of the chapter—Section C—is concerned with the nature of the rights granted to authored works: these rights pertain to reproduction, telecommunication, distribution, and authorization, and they may take on complex dimensions when considered in the digital environment, sometimes leading to confused results. For example, judicial treatment of copying for non-consumptive use, as in technical copies made in an Internet transmission or as a way to facilitate data mining, has been inconsistent due, in large part, to a failure to understand copyright law in a purposive sense. Moreover, fundamental and important questions, such as whether exhaustion of rights doctrine applies to digital products, remain unresolved.

Chapter 3 analyzes the neighbouring rights and collective management provisions of the Act. Neighbouring rights consist of sound recordings, performers' performances, and broadcasts and are given a unique set of rights under the Act. These sections of the Act are dense, and there is little to no interpretive guidance offered by caselaw. Rather than duplicating the technicalities of these provisions, the chapter focuses on the essence of the rights offered and their practical significance. It also includes a short section on collective management of copyright since many neighbouring rights are administered in this way. Collective management is the administration of a catalogue of works and/or neighbouring rights by a single collective society on behalf of its owners. Essentially, these collective societies help to set and collect fees for uses of their catalogues of works or neighbouring rights. There are four regimes of collective management under the Act, which are briefly discussed at the end of this chapter.

Chapter 4 explains the rights and incidentals of copyright ownership. At the heart of copyright is the ability of the owner to license or sell an interest in the copyright to others. The law is generally permissive about the numerous ways in which a copyright can be divided and sold (or licensed) by way of contract. Contract is intimately tied to the copyright licensing though it remains unclear to what extent provisions of the Act may be contracted out of. Included in the discussion on licensing is a consideration of website terms of use and their enforceability. The open-source licensing scheme, which has become a critical means of promoting productive collaborative outcomes, is also discussed. The nature and kinds of infringement actions, as well as the remedy of statutory damages (which was modified in an important way by the *Copyright Modernization Act*) is addressed. Finally, the caselaw on when, and on what terms, Internet service providers (ISPs) must disclose the identity of purported infringers — and the manner in which alleged copyright trolls must communicate with would-be defendants — is given special consideration.

Chapter 5 explores the most digital-specific and controversial aspect of the Act as instituted through the *Copyright Modernization Act* — the protection afforded to anti-circumvention measures (or digital locks). It is essential to understand these anti-circumvention measures in light of the international context in which they arose. Despite the many theoretical and practical problems that have arisen in the United States, Canada appears to have instituted even stronger measures than those that are offered under the *Digital Millennium Copyright Act* (DMCA),[20] for example, an apparent intent to give copyright holders an access right. Still, the scope of protection afforded to these measures will hinge, in many important ways, on the interpretation given to key language under section 41 of the Act, for example, what constitutes a "circumvention" of an "effective" technological protection measure (TPM)? This chapter also considers the protection of rights management information (RMI) attached to a work. Although less controversial, there are important interpretive issues here, as well.

No area of copyright law has seen such a seismic shift in the interpretation of its provisions than fair dealing, discussed in Chapter 6.

---

20   Pub L No 105-304, 112 Stat 2860 (1998) (codified in scattered sections of 17 USC) [DMCA].

Beginning in *CCH Canadian Ltd v Law Society of Upper Canada*,[21] with the re-conceptualization of fair dealing as user rights rather than as narrow exceptions under the Act, to *Alberta (Education) v Canadian Copyright Licensing Agency (Access Copyright)*,[22] and *Society of Composers, Authors and Music Publishers of Canada v Bell Canada*,[23] which lowered the threshold of allowable purposes to a minimal level, fair dealing has been a key mechanism for advancing the non-authorial interests of copyright law. This is apparent even more so in the digital environment where the scale of dissemination of use of a work, potentially fatal to a fair dealing analysis, was neutralized in *Bell Canada*.[24] These developments augur well for new technological uses of works, such as Google Books or HathiTrust, that have yet to be considered by Canadian courts. A number of exceptions in the Act are much more specific than fair dealing and will be discussed in the second part of the chapter. These pertain to uses made of works or other subject matter by entities such as educational institutions or libraries, to name just a couple. In fact, these exceptions are not comprehensive treatments of the activities they address, but rather should probably be characterized as best practices for ensuring that certain acts do not constitute infringement.

In Chapter 7, various Internet intermediary functions — for example, network services, hosting, and search tools — are assessed for their exposure to copyright infringement liability. The basic thrust of the *Copyright Modernization Act* was to continue to protect such activities against liability to the extent that they are passive and content neutral. More surprising perhaps was the legislature's choice to adopt a less onerous (for intermediaries) "notice and notice" regime rather than the "notice and takedown" regime in the United States. This reflects a policy choice to remove intermediaries from the pre-court judgment copyright dispute process. Significant, too, was the inclusion of section 27(2.3), which establishes a new ground of infringement for host services that exist primarily to enable acts of infringement. The obvious target of this provision is BitTorrent file-sharing sites although it will be interesting to see what other content-sharing websites are also caught (and for which reasons).

---

21   2004 SCC 13 [*CCH*].
22   2012 SCC 37.
23   2012 SCC 36 [*Bell*].
24   Ibid.

Intellectual property protection has long been regulated by international law, most notably, through the WIPO (World Intellectual Property Organization) "Internet" treaties.[25] Many treaty commitments, including anti-circumvention measures, have been implemented into Canadian law. After a brief consideration of public international law issues, most of Chapter 8 will discuss private international law aspects of copyright infringement. When there is a purported cross-border infringement of a copyright, which jurisdiction's court should hear the case, and which jurisdiction's law should be applied to resolve the dispute? These have always been difficult questions though they have been magnified by the scale of cross-border activity facilitated by the Internet. The question of when a foreign court's judgment against a defendant can be enforced in a Canadian jurisdiction will also be examined. The chapter concludes with a consideration of the problem of ubiquitous infringement — that is, where a single activity (infringement) on the Internet may give rise to liability in multiple jurisdictions. Model rules have been developed to address this kind of problem in a way that modifies the application of traditional private international law principles.

---

25   *WIPO Copyright Treaty*, Can TS 2014 No 20 [*WCT*] and *WIPO Performances and Phonograms Treaty*, Can TS 2014 No 21 [*WPPT*].

CHAPTER 1

# Interpretive Dimensions

## A. INTRODUCTION

This chapter begins with a discussion of the attributes of digital technologies (referred to as "digital facts") and the challenges these pose for copyright law. These attributes are both familiar and strange. They relate to issues that are not wholly unfamiliar to copyright law but in a way that is radically different. In this sense, it is unclear whether to classify them as differences of kind or of scale though they have surely profoundly changed copyright. Section C considers the approaches to statutory interpretation used in response to these challenges. Finally, in Section D, on principles of law, special attention is given to technological neutrality as an interpretive tool for adapting copyright law to the new digital reality.

## B. DIGITAL FACTS

The advent of digital technologies and the Internet brought with it the uncertain spectre of whether existing legal regimes were capable of regulating this groundbreaking technology. The early legal commentary split into two camps: those who doubted the ability of law to respond to a game-changing technology[1] and those who viewed the Internet as

---

1   See, for example, David R Johnson & David G Post, "Law and Borders — The Rise of Law in Cyberspace" (1996) 48 *Stanford Law Review* 1367 at 1370 [emphasis in

merely the latest phenomenon demonstrating the law's ability to adapt to new technology.[2] A quarter century later, we know that the latter view prevailed and that the law has shown remarkable facility for adapting existing doctrine to this disruptive technology. It has done this through two principal means: the creation of entirely new regimes to offset the potentially disruptive effects (e.g., anti-circumvention measures), as well as the accommodation of digital differentness within existing legal doctrine (e.g., tiered meanings of the authorization right)[3]

But what was so different about the Internet that it precipitated this debate? And what is it about this differentness that remains relevant today and continues to present challenges to the interpretation of copyright rules? There are four *factual attributes* of digital technologies in response to which policy-makers and courts have struggled to make adjustments. It is hard to classify these attributional differences as being of kind or merely scale. The problems they presented were certainly not unheard of prior to the Internet. Illegal copying and sharing of content, for example, is as old as copyright. But the scale of the problem caused by digitization has been colossally magnified.

---

original], who argued that the paradigm for legal regulation in the real world does not fit with cyberspace. They argued that the effects of Internet communications are global such that states lack power or legitimacy to regulate them.

> The rise of the global computer network is destroying the link between geographical location and (1) the power of local governments to assert control over online behavior; (2) the effects of online behavior on individuals or things; (3) the legitimacy of a local sovereign's efforts to regulate global phenomena; and (4) the ability of physical location to give notice of which sets of rules apply.

Instead, Internet behaviour must be addressed through means that are unique to the features of the technology, for example, online communities or passwords. See also David G Post, "Against 'Against Cyberanarchy'" (2002) 17 *Berkeley Technology Law Journal* 1365; and Mark A Lemley, "Place and Cyberspace" (2003) 91 *California Law Review* 521.

2   See, for example, Jack L Goldsmith, "Against Cyberanarchy" (1998) 65 *University of Chicago Law Review* 1199 at 1218. (It is feasible and legitimate for real-space law to regulate online behaviour. The challenge lay in applying traditional legal doctrine to the novel Internet context. This is manageable, however.)

3   See discussion in Section E, below in this chapter, about the authorization right as interpreted in *CCH Canadian Ltd v Law Society of Upper Canada*, 2004 SCC 13 [*CCH*] (as a control test in the analogue environment) and in *Society of Composers, Authors and Music Publishers of Canada v Canadian Assn of Internet Providers*, 2004 SCC 45 [*CAIP*] (as a higher-threshold knowledge test in the digital environment).

## CHAPTER 1: INTERPRETIVE DIMENSIONS

The attributes of primary significance that are responsible for disrupting copyright were discussed in the Introduction: *ease of creating and copying content* through digitization technology and *widespread dissemination of content* facilitated by the Internet network. Digitization makes works easily, instantly, and perfectly reproducible at zero marginal cost. The creation of user-friendly software and peer-to-peer networks (most recently, BitTorrent sites) facilitates the copying and downloading of music and other content files for free. With Web 2.0 — and, in particular, broadband connectivity — the concern expanded from the downloading of files to the unauthorized streaming of content over the Internet. In addition, the Internet created a vehicle for dissemination of works on a massive scale. Now, content could not only be copied for free, but also transmitted and shared through a readily accessible and global network. These two attributes worked in tandem to facilitate large-scale, unauthorized (and uncompensated) sharing of content, striking at the very core of authorial incentive for creators.

There are two further attributes of digitization that have presented profound challenges for copyright law: these are referred to here as *copy dependency* and *ubiquitousness*. Digitization, whether in the production process of content creation or in the transmission of content over the Internet, is dependent upon the creation of temporary and imperceptible copies. To perceive a copy of work on one's computer may involve the making of one or more of these non-perceptible copies along the way, for example, on the RAM (random access memory), or for the purpose of caching. Do these copies implicate the copyright holder's reproduction right and thus are compensable, or should they be viewed as irrelevant? From a jurisdictional perspective, information on the Internet defies conventional notions of location and, more particularly, state sovereignty. Even the most basic Internet communication involves the travelling of packets of information across multiple locations, frequently crossing borders without detection. How then is it possible for individual states to regulate the trans-boundary dimensions of Internet communication? And when is it appropriate for a legal system to assert jurisdiction over multi-jurisdictional transmissions?

On its own, each factual attribute may, depending on the issue, cause complications. Sometimes, all of them work synergistically to compound and complicate any given issue. For example, the problem of illegal file and content sharing results from the first two attributes and raises concerns with respect to the last two. As we turn to interpretive methodologies, we will see that many complications emerge from the application of vague legal rules to these factual attributes. Generally, the purpose behind the rule will highlight which of these attributes become relevant; how they are resolved in specific cases is a much more difficult question.

## C. STATUTORY INTERPRETATION

Courts often assert that copyright law is a creature of statute.[4] In other words, there is no copyright law but that which is found, or at least has some basis, in the *Copyright Act*. In fact, this assertion is only partly true. There are doctrines of copyright law that are unanchored in, or even appear contrary to, the language of the Act. For example, there is no statutory basis for excluding an interviewee's expression from copyright protection, yet this is what courts have decided.[5] Be that as it may, the vast majority of copyright is based on the language of the Act.

Statutes prescribe *brief, incomplete,* and sometimes *poorly drafted* rules, leaving ample room for the judicial interpretation of their meaning in specific cases. Each of these problems should be briefly discussed. First, as legal thinkers such as Hart and Fuller long ago observed, statutory rules offer *brief* prescriptions relative to the complexity of human affairs they are designed to regulate.[6] As such, they do not precisely dictate answers to anticipated matters, much less offer guidance to unforeseen or novel cases. Consider, for example, *Théberge v Galerie d'Art du Petit Champlain inc*.[7] The section 3 right to "reproduce" is directed to an abstraction, that is, activities and technologies that create copies of a work. Although we may presume that the right was intended to apply to photocopying of works or new activities such as digital downloading, there is nothing in the language of section 3 that might tell us whether creating canvas-backed posters out of paper posters implicates the right, the issue in *Théberge*.

The Act is replete with such vague rules that are to be applied to a myriad of factual circumstances, many of which are complex or unan-

---

4   *Compo Co v Blue Crest Music*, 1979 CanLII 6 (SCC).
5   See, for example, *Gould Estate v Stoddart Publishing Co*, 1996 CanLII 8209 (ONSC).
6   See discussion of HLA Hart and Lon Fuller in Cameron Hutchison, "Which *Kraft* of Statutory Interpretation? A Supreme Court of Canada Trilogy" (2008) 46 *Alberta Law Review* 1.
7   2002 SCC 34 [*Théberge*].

ticipated. Although there are obvious challenges to the interpretation of vague language, it does facilitate the adaptation of statutes to new circumstances, technological or otherwise. So, for example, the Act refers to the "right to communicate to the public by telecommunication" without identifying any particular medium or method by which that might occur. In other words, the statute does not say "communicate to the public through broadcast by TV or radio" which, at the time of the adoption of that language, was its intended meaning. The word "telecommunication" allowed this provision to be adapted to a new technology that emerged shortly after this language was adopted: the Internet.

Some language in the Act is explicitly drafted to account for technological change: consider, for example, to produce or reproduce a work "in any material form whatever," which is in section 3. Even when such language is not present, courts generally proceed on the unstated assumption that the Act is to be interpreted in a dynamic manner: to accommodate, within the parameters of the language used, the advent of new technologies. The willingness of courts to adapt the Act to new technologies is crucial for developing copyright law in a coherent and sensible fashion. One can imagine, for example, the silly interpretations that might result if rights were limited to technologies in existence at the time of their proclamation into law many decades ago, for example, if the reproduction right covered analogue, but not digital technologies.

Vagueness is not the only problem associated with legislative drafting. Statutes may be *incomplete* by failing to offer any guidance on a particular issue. Here, it may matter whether a legislature anticipated the issue but chose not to address it. If it did, one can argue that there was no intent to regulate the matter and, therefore, that which is not prohibited is allowed. A prominent example of this, discussed in Chapter 2, is the apparent intent to apply an international exhaustion rule to digital products. If it is an unforeseen issue, courts may choose to fill in the gap left by the statute. Most problematic is where the legislation is *poorly drafted* such that provisions conflict or do not make any sense. Unfortunately, there are examples of this problem in the Act, and courts are forced, with some help from interpretive techniques, to make the statute harmonious or at least coherent.[8]

---

8  See, for example, the relationship between the computer program exception in s 30.6 of the Act and the right to make backup copies in s 29.24, as discussed in Chapter 6.

## 1) Approaches

The approach to statutory construction chosen to find or develop meaning of statutory language usually has a determinative impact on the interpretive result. Consider the following pre-Internet zoning bylaw: "no offering of adult entertainment to members of the public."[9] Let us say that pornographic content is streamed from a private house located in a neighbourhood with this bylaw restriction. Is this in violation of the bylaw? The provision is broadly worded — in particular, the meaning of "offering" — and a court could reasonably find streaming of such content in violation of the *ordinary meaning* of the *language* of the bylaw. Alternatively, a court might take a different approach and consider the provision in light of the *intention* of the lawmakers. If city council debates disclose that the provision was specifically directed to public establishments such as strip bars (and moreover, the Internet did not even exist at the time of the bylaw's drafting), then a court might reach the opposite conclusion. Or, a court may try to discern the *purpose* behind the rule by looking at the legislative record or identifying some mischief that gave rise to the rule. Different interpretive results would likely ensue if the purpose was to ban the offering of public adult entertainment to neighbourhood patrons, as opposed to preventing a decrease in property values.

There are three main approaches to the interpretation of Canadian copyright law, which loosely track the discussion in the above example: (1) ordinary meaning, (2) dynamic intentionalism, and (3) purposivism. These are outlined below.

### a) Ordinary Meaning

To be sure, all statutory interpretation approaches consider the primacy of the plain or ordinary meaning of the language, that is, the natural meaning or connotation of the words that arise when one reads the provision. Dictionaries are usually consulted as non-authoritative aids to determining word meanings. But judges who consider ordinary meaning to the exclusion of context, purpose, or intention run the risk of overly broad interpretations of a rule, as illustrated in the above example. In the copyright context, for example, is the differing interpretations of the section 3(1)(f) right "to communicate to the public by

---

9   Based on the case *Voyeur Dorm, LC v City of Tampa*, 265 F3d 1232 (11th Cir 2011).

telecommunication" offered by the Supreme Court of Canada. In *Society of Composers, Authors and Music Publishers of Canada v Canadian Assn of Internet Providers*, the downloading of a copy of a work was held to constitute a communication to the public by telecommunication:

> At the end of the transmission, the end user has a musical work in his or her possession that was not there before. The work has necessarily been communicated, irrespective of its point of origin. If the communication is by virtue of the Internet, there has been a "telecommunication."[10]

Eight years later, in *Entertainment Software Association v Society of Composers, Authors and Music Publishers of Canada*,[11] the Court reversed itself, holding that section 3(1)(f) is a performance right based on a consideration of the legislative intention, thus capturing Internet streaming activities, and not downloading. The point is that the broad wording of the provision is capable of capturing both activities — downloading and streaming — and the Court was able to provide a more exact meaning only by looking beyond the language of the section — in this case, by considering legislative history and intent.

### b) Dynamic Intentionalism

Better interpretive results ensue from a consideration of ordinary language in light of context, purpose, and intention. These added considerations may suggest a more precise meaning of the language in question. In *Entertainment Software*, for example, the majority determined, from a reading of the legislative history of section 3(1)(f), that the right was initially conceived as a *performance* right directed at radio and then later, television broadcasts.[12] As a performance right, "communication" under section 3(1)(f) captures activities functionally equivalent to TV and radio such as Internet streaming but not permanent copies through downloading — more appropriately caught by the reproduction right.[13] Unlike the kind of static or originalist intentionalism discussed in the pornographic website example above (what specifically did the city council have in mind), this form of intentionalism is dynamic: it allows new activities to be included under the rule so long as they are

---

10   *CAIP*, above note 3 at para 45.
11   2012 SCC 34 [*Entertainment Software*].
12   *Ibid* at para 20.
13   *Ibid* at paras 27 & 28.

similar in material respects as those in contemplation at the time of drafting.[14] In other words, by analogizing new technologies with media known to be covered as revealed in the legislative history, courts are able to update or modernize the rule.

Despite the effectiveness of its use in *Entertainment Software*, legislative history is often unavailable, unreliable, or simply unhelpful in resolving specific interpretive ambiguities. Records of debate or discussion during the legislative process about specific provisions are typically sparse to non-existent in Canada. When found, they are unlikely to have much probative value to the specific fact configuration under consideration. And even when relevant, their authoritative value may be in question: for example, who speaks on behalf of the legislature, and what is the motivation of an individual legislator who opines on the meaning of the text?[15]

The intentionalist approach more typically considers textual indicia of legislative intent, usually on an inferential basis. For example, if there is an indication that the legislature was aware of an issue in one part of the Act, but failed to address that same issue in another part of the Act in the same way or at all, there is a strong inference that it chose to treat the issue differently. For example, the fact that "dramatic work" is defined in section 2 of the Act refers to works which are "fixed," whereas that word is absent in the definitions of "artistic work," "literary work," and "musical work," implies that the fixation requirement only applies to the former, but not the latter, works. This example also illustrates that courts may choose to ignore such inferences since the fixation requirement, has, in fact, been interpreted to apply to all works. Many inferences about the intent behind statutory language are made through the application of maxims of interpretation. The maxim

---

14  Analogizing new facts with cases that the court knows were intended by the legislature to be covered by a rule is a form of legal reasoning advocated by Henry Hart and Albert Sacks' legal process school: see, for example, Henry Hart & Albert Sacks, *The Legal Process: Basic Problems in the Making and Application of Law* (Cambridge, MA: Harvard University, 1958). It is thought that this approach ensures the development of statutory meaning on a principled basis: see William N Eskridge, Jr, *Dynamic Statutory Interpretation* (Cambridge, MA: Harvard University Press, 1994) at 1.

15  Politicians may advance interpretations of a provision in the legislature in the hope that courts will consider them indicia of legislative intent. Although the minister responsible arguably speaks for the government when speaking to legislation, the value of representations made by other legislative members is less clear.

*ejusdem generis* states that a more general word, at the end of a phrase, should be informed by the more specific words that precede it. For example, the "otherwise modify" language of the right of integrity in section 28.1 should be interpreted within parameters of meaning consistent with the words "distort" and "mutilate" that precede it.

Inferences by their very nature are far from exact; indeed, sharply opposed inferences of legislative intent are sometimes contested in legal arguments. For example, the maxim *expressio unius est exclusio alterius* (which means roughly "that which is not included is deliberately excluded" and is illustrated in the fixation example above) makes the following inference: if a statutory provision states that apples, oranges, and mangoes grown in a jurisdiction are to be taxed, we make the inference that peaches are not to be taxed since they are not mentioned on the list. This may be countered with either of two arguments that might lead to a different result: that peaches were not included since the legislature for some reason did not direct its mind to this particular fruit (maybe because no one grew peaches in that jurisdiction until only recently); or that the specified fruit was identified to ensure that these were, for greater certainty, subject to the tax but not necessarily to the exclusion of other fruit. In either case, a court may construe the provision as also applying to peaches.

A similar battle of inferences surfaces in the relationship between copyright infringement and the specific, condition-laden exceptions that appear after the fair dealing provisions in the Act. In *Canadian Broadcasting Corp v SODRAC 2003 Inc*, which addressed whether incidental copies of a work made in the production of a broadcast implicated the reproduction right, the majority and dissenting judgments took very different views on the meaning of these specific exceptions, in particular, sections 30.8 and 30.9. According to Rothstein J, for the majority, these narrow exceptions were a "specific and deliberate" response (via a 1997 amendment to the Act) to efforts by broadcasters to shield them from infringement for broadcast incidental copies. In his view, "Parliament could have adopted broader provisions. It chose not to. It is not for the Court to do by 'interpretation' what Parliament chose not to do by enactment."[16] The inference is clear: Parliament comprehensively considered the matter and set out the applicable rules for the exception;

---

16   2015 SCC 57 at para 53 [*CBC*].

actions committed beyond these rules are intended to be treated as infringement.

Justice Abella, in her dissenting opinion, viewed these exceptions as a response to the decision in *Bishop v Stevens*,[17] in which reproducing a single work for the purpose of effecting a broadcast was found to have infringed copyright. In her view, these were "discrete legislative responses to a specific judicial interpretation" and reflect an "effort to provide greater judicial certainty that certain classes of ephemeral recording are not to attract liability."[18] Moreover, these provisions are "*not a comprehensive statement on the content of the reproduction right, or which kinds of copies will trigger it.*"[19] Implicit in this reasoning is that these "discrete" exceptions were made in response to the single-copy-for-broadcast-type situation in *Bishop* and were not intended to regulate (nor could the legislature foresee) the kind and degree of copy-dependent technology that would emerge almost twenty years later. In the absence of an exception addressing this kind of activity, the Court was forced to consider whether the copying in question triggered the reproduction right based on the principle of technological neutrality. To analogize with the tax on fruit example above, the incidental copies in question were the new peach farms that did not exist when the legislation was first drafted.

### c) Purposivism

Almost every Canadian court cites the "modern rule" in adopting a purposive approach to statutory interpretation:

> ... the words of an Act are to be read in their entire context and in their grammatical and ordinary sense harmoniously with the scheme of the Act, the object of the Act, and the intention of Parliament.[20]

This is an ecumenical approach to interpretation as various sources are consulted to shed light on the ordinary meaning of the words in the statute. Typically, the most accessible and helpful additional sources of meaning are context and purpose. *Context* refers to a number of fac-

---

17  [1990] 2 SCR 467 [*Bishop*].
18  Justice Abella in *CBC*, above note 16 at paras 174 & 175.
19  *Ibid* at para 175 [emphasis in original].
20  Elmer Driedger, *The Construction of Statutes*, 2d ed (Toronto: Butterworths, 1983) at 87, quoted in *Rizzo & Rizzo Shoes Ltd (Re)*, [1998] 1 SCR 27.

tors. First, it may refer to the meaning to words that may be suggested by surrounding language or a reading of the Act as a whole. We know that in the copyright context, for example, the section 3 right to "reproduce" means copying, not procreation. Furthermore, we also know that the surrounding language "in any material form whatever" suggests an intention that the reproduction right applies to new technologies. Second, it may refer to a broader conception of the legal context, for example, rules in the common law or international law that may shed light on the meaning of certain language. Third, though rarely acknowledged by courts as a source of meaning, is context in the sense of the law reflecting and maintaining relevance to the society in which it operates.

*Purpose* may refer either to a reason behind a particular statutory provision or, more globally, the general aim of the Act. In Canada, the purpose of a statute is often judicially determined based on a reading of the Act as a whole. The most commonly referenced statement of purpose of the *Copyright Act* is that of Binnie J in *Théberge*:

> The *Copyright Act* is usually presented as a balance between promoting the public interest in the encouragement and dissemination of works of the arts and intellect and obtaining a just reward for the creator (or, more accurately, to prevent someone other than the creator from appropriating whatever benefits may be generated).[21]

While somewhat abstract, purpose can serve as a useful aid by identifying the interests to be balanced in cases where the ordinary language of the provision, even after a consideration of all other sources of meaning, remains ambiguous.

Returning to *Théberge*, for example, the Court was asked to decide whether converting duly purchased paper posters to canvas-backed posters, without creating any additional copies, constituted infringement of the reproduction right. The majority's reasoning was strongly influenced by the above statement of purpose:

> The proper balance among these and other public policy objectives lies not only in recognizing the creator's rights but in giving due weight to their limited nature. In crassly economic terms it would be as inefficient to overcompensate artists and authors for the right of reproduction as it would be self-defeating to undercompensate them. Once an authorized

---

21  *Théberge*, above note 7 at para 30.

> copy of a work is sold to a member of the public, it is generally for the purchaser, not the author, to determine what happens to it.
>
> Excessive control by holders of copyrights and other forms of intellectual property may unduly limit the ability of the public domain to incorporate and embellish creative innovation in the long-term interests of society as a whole, or create practical obstacles to proper utilization.[22]

The interest of the copyright holder was set off against the interest of dissemination of the work (via the purchaser's right to do as she wished with the duly purchased copies) in a way that, in the Court's judgment, achieved the right balance.

There are three interests, identified as forming the purpose of copyright, that may need to be balanced when interpreting the Act.

First, there is a public interest in offering an incentive and just reward for an author to create works. Given that works are informational goods not excludable to the public once they are released and able to be consumed without depletion, there is a need to commoditize copyright creations to properly compensate authors. Copyright does this by giving a property right (a right of exclusion) to authors by way of a limited monopoly protection. Most, if not all systems of copyright are premised on the need for incentive: artistic works will be under-produced if society does not provide incentive for authors to engage in these activities. Less universal is the concept (referred to in *Théberge*) of "just rewards" for the author. This is an entirely different justification than the means-to-end utilitarianism just discussed. Rather, *just rewards* implies that an author is fairly entitled to the benefits of her creation, perhaps even indefinitely. This rationale may augur for stronger and longer monopoly protection than the incentive justification: benefits to a creation may accrue long after the incentive needed to create that work has "expired." Due to other interests at play in copyright, however, the scope of just rewards for the author cannot be overly expansive.

A second interest is that of user rights, most notably captured in the fair dealing provisions of the Act. In *CCH*, these erstwhile "exceptions" to copyright were recast as "user rights" integral to the Act and to be given a broad and liberal interpretation.[23] This means that existing works can be used for legitimate purposes, such as criticism and educa-

---

22  *Ibid* at paras 31–32.
23  Above note 3.

tion, so long as the dealing with the work by the user is fair. User rights also refer to those elements that are in the public domain and are not protectable by copyright, for example, ideas and insubstantial borrowing and other limiting mechanisms. User rights often compete, or at least are in tension, with the rights of copyright holders.

A third interest is that of maximizing the dissemination of works to the public. One great concern about monopoly rights over intellectual creations, be it copyright or patent, is accessibility. The fact that we must pay monopoly prices to access works frustrates the widest dissemination possible for a work. The tension here, of course, is that the monopoly is needed to compensate authors (to permit incentive and just rewards). The exhaustion doctrine suggested in *Théberge*, namely, not allowing copyright holders to control the use of copies of a work once duly purchased, is a manifestation of the importance of the dissemination interest. More significantly, the importance of the Internet as a tool of dissemination is a recurring theme in copyright law. For example, citing from *CAIP*:

> The capacity of the Internet to disseminate "works of the arts and intellect" is one of the great innovations of the information age. Its use should be facilitated rather than discouraged, but this should not be done unfairly at the expense of those who create the works of arts and intellect in the first place.[24]

This passage reminds us of two things. First, the dissemination interest is intimately tied, in the digital age, to the development of the Internet. Second and more generally, even at the level of interpretation, conflicting interests need to be calibrated.

## D. EVOLVING PRINCIPLES OF LAW

The use of judicially created principles of law as a reasoning tool in resolving difficult interpretive issues is a recent trend in Canadian copyright and intellectual property law jurisprudence. These principles, when they arise in particular contexts, can assist in making the law coherent by sensibly resolving uncertain or absurd statutory meaning in the face of novel facts. Like a purposive analysis of the law, principles

---

24 *CAIP*, above note 3 at para 40.

have certain objectives. The objectives of principles tend to be more specific in advancing matters of fundamental importance in the law; they may include recalibrating the balance of interests that underlie the purpose of copyright law in a particular context.[25] For example, one might conceive of the principle of technological neutrality as an instantiation of a purposive approach to statutory interpretation. It is a discretionary principle that courts could use to "break ties" between competing interests that underlie the purpose of copyright, in the face of ambiguous statutory language or unclear legislative intent. Thus, in considering whether broadcast-incidental copies are reproductions under the Act as in *CBC*, the principle might be invoked to favour a stronger claim of unencumbering technological innovation over a weak and less legitimate assertion of authorial incentive or just rewards.

The role and pedigree of legal principle was most famously theorized by Ronald Dworkin. To him, rules dictate "in an all or nothing fashion. If the facts a rule stipulates are given, then either the rule is valid . . . or it is not . . . ."[26] Principles, on the other hand, do not operate in an all-or-nothing fashion nor do they explicate the conditions of their application; rather, they offer a reason to argue in one direction but without necessitating a particular decision. Furthermore, in situations where the literal application of a rule may lead to an otherwise straightforward, though unreasonable result, Dworkin insists on a mediating role for legal principle:

> Instead, we make a case for a principle, and for its weight, by appealing to an amalgam of practice and other principles in which the implications of legislative and judicial history figure along with appeals to community practices and understandings. There is no litmus paper for

---

25   For a view of technological neutrality as preserving copyright's balance, see Carys J Craig, "Technological Neutrality: (Pre)Serving the Purposes of Copyright Law" in Michael Geist, ed, *The Copyright Pentalogy: How the Supreme Court of Canada Shook the Foundations of Canadian Copyright Law* (Ottawa: University of Ottawa Press, 2013) 271 at 299: "Taking seriously the idea of copyright as balance between authors and the public reveals the principle to be ultimately concerned with the *preservation* of this copyright balance in the digital environment. As such the technological neutrality principle . . . is part and parcel of that balance."

26   Ronald Dworkin, *Taking Rights Seriously* (Cambridge, MA: Harvard University Press, 1977) at 24.

testing the soundness of such a case — it is a matter of judgment, and reasonable men may disagree.[27]

As an example, Dworkin presents the case of *Riggs v Palmer*, in which a court was faced with a grandson seeking to inherit from a validly enacted will made by the grandfather whom he had murdered. Since the will was validly enacted according to statute (and further, there was no mention that a beneficiary could not inherit as a result of murdering a testator in that statute), a straightforward application of the rule should have permitted the grandson to inherit. Yet, the court found that it is a fundamental maxim of the common law, as reflected in contract and property law, that no one should profit from his own wrongdoing; as such the grandson was denied the inheritance.[28]

## 1) Legitimate Economic Interests and Separation

Other than technological neutrality, there are two other principles of intellectual property law that have emerged in Supreme Court jurisprudence in recent years: the principle of legitimate economic interests, which first appears in *Théberge*,[29] and the principle of separation, which debuts in *Kirkbi AG v Ritvik Holdings Inc*.[30] Both of these principles were applied by Bastarache J in *Euro-Excellence Inc v Kraft Canada Inc*.[31]

In *Théberge*, the issue was whether an ink transfer of a print from one substrate (paper) to another (canvas), without creating more copies in the process, engaged the copyright holder's right to "produce or reproduce" the work under section 3 of the Act. This language is broad and non-specific to a particular result in this factual context. Justice Binnie, for the majority, reasoned:

---

27  *Ibid* at 36.
28  *Ibid* at 23. But how do we know when, as in *Riggs v Palmer*, 115 NY 506 (1889), a rule should be changed by a principle? Dworkin's answer in *Law's Empire*, when he revisits this question, is as follows: "[i]t is only because we think the case for excluding murderers from a general statute of wills is a strong one, sanctioned by principles elsewhere respected in the law, that we find the statute unclear on the issue." Ronald Dworkin, *Law's Empire* (Cambridge, MA: Belknap Press of Harvard University Press, 1986) at 352.
29  Above note 7. My brief treatment of the cases in this section, in particular, reflects an assumption that most readers of this chapter are familiar with these judgments.
30  2005 SCC 65 [*Kirkbi*].
31  2007 SCC 37 [*Euro-Excellence*].

> But in what way has the legitimate economic interest of the copyright holder been infringed? The process began with a single poster and ended with a single poster. The image "fixed" in ink is the subject-matter of the intellectual property and it was not reproduced. It was transferred from one display to another.[32]

The principle of legitimate economic interests offered a reason to limit the copyright holder's reproduction right in favour of the purchaser's interest to engage in this activity with validly purchased copies. As this case illustrates, a principle may refine the balance between the competing interests inherent in the purpose of copyright law.

In *Kirkbi*, the makers of Lego blocks attempted to extend their monopoly after the patent expired by claiming the design of the blocks as unregistered trademarks. The doctrine of functionality, which disallows such utilitarian features to be used as a trademark, prevented them from doing so. The only problem was that *Kirkbi* had a strong statutory interpretation argument that negated the doctrine of functionality in respect of unregistered marks.[33] That result, however, would have been absurd in that unregistered marks would be treated very differently in this respect than registered marks. Instead of struggling with the sloppy legislative drafting that led to such a result, the Court began its analysis with what seemed to be an organizing principle of intellectual property regimes:

> The economic value of intellectual property rights arouses the imagination and litigiousness of rights holders in their search for continuing protection of what they view as their rightful property. Such a search carries with it the risk of discarding *basic and necessary distinctions between different forms of intellectual property and their legal and economic functions*. The present appeal is a case in point. It involves the distinction between patents and trade-marks. In order to understand the role and relevance of the doctrine of functionality in the law of trade-marks, some comments on the nature and function of patents and trade-marks will be useful.[34]

---

32   *Théberge*, above note 7 at para 38.
33   See Hutchison, above note 6 at 13–15.
34   *Kirkbi*, above note 30 at para 37 [emphasis added].

This separation principle in *Kirkbi* essentially overrides an otherwise absurd application of the statute.

In Bastarache J's judgment in *Euro-Excellence*,[35] both "legitimate economic interests" and "separation" were applied as principles (though not referred to as such) in a way that avoided an unpalatable result suggested by the legislation. The facts and law in the case are complicated and, for present purposes, it is enough to know that the copyright in trademarked logos was asserted as a means of preventing the otherwise legal importation of chocolate bars. In holding that copyright should not be misused to frustrate legitimate trade, Bastarache J reasoned that both the copyright holder's legitimate economic interests,[36] as referred to in *Théberge*, and the separation of intellectual property regimes,[37] as articulated in *Kirkbi*, meant that "incidental" works of copyright, for example, logos on chocolate bars that functioned as trademarks, are not actionable in this context. It is important to note that the two other judgments in that case either rejected the application of these concepts as having any bearing on the dispute or did not consider them. Nonetheless, Bastarache J very much applied these principles in a Dworkinian sense.

It is not unusual that the meaning of a principle — indeed, its very existence — may be judicially debated. Reasonable people may, as Dworkin tells us, disagree about such things. Decision makers must look to the judicial and legislative history, together with community understandings and practices, to ascertain whether a concept has achieved enough traction within the legal corpus that it has persuasive value as

---

35   Above note 31.

36   *Ibid* at para 85:

> The Act protects only the legitimate economic interests of copyright holders. It protects the economic benefits of skill and judgment; it does not protect all economic benefits of all types of labour.... In particular, if a work of skill and judgment (such as a logo) is attached to some other consumer good (such as a chocolate bar), the economic gains associated with the sale of the consumer good must not be mistakenly viewed as the legitimate economic interests of the copyright holder of the logo that are protected by the law of copyright.

37   *Ibid* at para 87:

> While it is certainly true that one work can be the subject of both copyright and trade-mark protection (see s. 64(3)(*b*) of the Act), it is equally certain that different forms of intellectual property protect different types of economic interests. To ignore this fact would be to ignore the "basic and necessary distinctions between different forms of intellectual property and their legal and economic functions," as noted by LeBel J. at para. 37 of *Kirkbi*.

a fundamental organizing principle of the law. There should be future opportunities to test the status, application, and scope of these tentative principles. For example, a possible future application of legitimate economic interests of copyright holders might be to prevent the use of copyright as a means of censoring expression.[38] It is debatable whether either legitimate economic interests or separation has attained the level of principle. However, as the next section shows, the principle of technological neutrality has permeated the caselaw such that it is an established, though still developing, principle of copyright law.

## 2) Technological Neutrality

The principle of technological neutrality has played a central role in the interpretation of key issues in copyright law jurisprudence over the past dozen years. The principle embraces two different objectives: (1) non-discrimination in respect of technologies and activities endogenous to copyright and (2) non-interference in connection with activities and technologies exogenous to the Act. The primary purpose and effect of *non-discrimination* is to ensure that copyright doctrine evolves in a way that embraces new technologies. This can operate to extend the rights of both owners and users of copyright. The main concern of *non-interference* is that copyright not unduly restrict the use of existing technologies or the innovation and development of new technologies. Sometimes, the two objectives of technological neutrality coincide. For example, technological neutrality in in *Society of Composers, Authors and Music Publishers of Canada v Bell Canada*,[39] was both non-discrimination (in extending user rights into new technologies) and non-interference (in not attaching copyright liability to a new and potentially infringing activity).

Judgment is to be exercised to determine whether either or both manifestations of the principle apply within a particular technological context. Recognizing that technological neutrality, in either form,

---

38  See, for example, John Tehranian, "The New ©ensorship" (2015) 101 *Iowa Law Review* 245, online: http://ilr.law.uiowa.edu/files/ilr.law.uiowa.edu/files/ILR_101-1_Tehranian.pdf. One example therein is where a contract between doctor and patient refers to any review of the services of the doctor as a copyrighted work which is assigned to the doctor, thus allowing the doctor to demand its removal if it appears on a rating website.

39  2012 SCC 36 [*Bell*].

should apply in certain factual circumstances is only half of the challenge. The other half is how courts manage the factual differences between digital and extant technologies. Courts have developed three techniques to account for the differentness of digital facts, whether those divergences are of a kind mentioned in Section B, above in this chapter, or otherwise. These techniques are: (1) functional equivalency, (2) tiered meanings, and (3) negation of material differences. Functional equivalency is applied when courts deem that the differences between two classes of technology are immaterial, for example, that Internet streaming is functionally akin to television or radio performances for the purposes of section 3(1)(f) notwithstanding obvious differences. Courts will sometimes indirectly acknowledge that the differences are material but accommodate them within an existing rule by applying a different threshold to digital activities, that is, the two meanings of "to authorize" copyright infringement articulated in *CCH* and *CAIP*.[40] Relatedly, courts may be aware of material differences between the two classes of technologies but choose to ignore them; for example, in *Bell*,[41] the extent of dissemination of the work through the Internet, which had no analogue counterpart, did not negatively impact upon the fairness of the dealing.

### a) Non-discrimination

Courts have long taken the view that a copyright subsists not only in the medium in which the work is created but all existing and future media in which the work might be expressed. In other words, copyright does not discriminate against any technology — even those yet to come into being — so long as enough of the expression survives transfer into the new medium. The statutory basis cited for this principle is the section 3 right of copyright holders "... to produce or reproduce the work or any substantial part thereof *in any material form whatever* ...."

This language was in issue in *Robertson v Thomson Corp*[42] where the Court had to determine whether it was the individual article or collective-work newspaper copyright that was reproduced when archived newspaper content was transferred into new digital platforms such as CD-ROMs and online databases. Essentially, the Supreme Court adopted

---

40 See *CAIP*, above note 3; and *CCH*, above note 3.
41 Above note 39.
42 2006 SCC 43 [*Robertson*].

a functional equivalency approach to the issue, that is, assessing what in substance is presented to the reader who accesses the digital format. The Court also made its first articulation of what would later become the principle of technological neutrality:

> Media neutrality is reflected in s. 3(1) of the *Copyright Act* which describes a right to produce or reproduce a work "in any material form whatever". Media neutrality means that the Copyright Act *should continue to apply in different media, including more technologically advanced ones.*[43]

The first indication that media neutrality might apply beyond section 3 of the Act can be seen in the italicized words.

This broader ambit of the technological neutrality principle as non-discrimination was confirmed in two cases: *Rogers Communications Inc v Society of Composers, Authors and Music Publishers of Canada*[44] and *Bell*.[45] In *Rogers*, the issue was whether streamed music[46] via the Internet to individual users constituted a communication "to the public" under section 3(1)(f) of the Act. The appellant online music service providers cited *CCH*, in which the Court determined that a fax transmission of a single copy to a single person was not a communication to the public but that "a series of repeated fax transmissions of the same work to numerous different recipients" might be.[47] The appellants interpreted this *obiter* narrowly to mean that the right is engaged only when there are multiple transmissions originating *from the single act* of the sender as opposed to multiple pull transmissions by individual users (the latter being the typical model of content delivery over the Internet).

Justice Rothstein determined that the appellants' interpretation of section 3(1)(f) would lead to arbitrary results in that separate emails of a work to 100 recipients would *not* constitute infringement, but a single email to 100 addressees would.[48] The "true character of the communication activity," not its technicalities, must be considered to ensure that sub-

---

43   *Ibid* at para 49 [emphasis added].
44   2012 SCC 35 [*Rogers*].
45   Above note 39.
46   Unlike downloads which result in permanent copies, a stream "is a transmission of data that allows the user to listen to or view the content transmitted at the time of transmission, resulting only in a temporary copy of the file on the user's hard drive." *Rogers*, above note 44 at para 1.
47   Above note 3 at para 78.
48   *Rogers*, above note 44 at para 29.

stance trumps form and copyright protection develops on a principled basis.[49] The true character of streaming is that it is "targeted at an aggregation of individuals"[50] and thus "to the public," according to Rothstein J. Moreover, to accede to the appellants' interpretation would have had the effect of excluding all on-demand, or "pull," technologies from the ambit of section 3(1)(f). Here, Rothstein J notes that "the Act should be interpreted to extend to technologies that were not or could not have been contemplated at the time of its drafting."[51] Moreover, he reiterates dicta from *Robertson*:

> Media neutrality means that the *Copyright Act* should continue to apply in different media, including more technologically advanced ones .... [I]t exists to protect the rights of authors and others as technology evolves.[52]

Justice Rothstein thus applied the technological neutrality principle to the broadly worded language of section 3(1)(f).[53]

Furthermore, in *Bell*, technological neutrality was cited in the Court's fair dealing analysis. The case concerned whether music preview streams of thirty to ninety seconds for the purpose of identifying and purchasing music was "fair." In assessing the third factor for determining the fairness of the dealing—the "amount" taken—SOCAN argued that the *aggregate* number of previews by consumers should be the metric and given that, on average, there were ten previews for each song purchased, the dealing was unfair.[54] The Court disagreed, holding that it is only *individual* not aggregate use that is relevant for fair dealing analysis.[55] Moreover, the Court emphasized that focusing on aggregate use on the Internet as relevant to fair dealing could undermine the principle of technological neutrality:[56]

> [G]iven the ease and magnitude with which digital works are disseminated over the Internet, focusing on the "aggregate" amount of the

---

49 *Ibid* at para 30.
50 *Ibid* at para 33 (quoting the Copyright Board).
51 *Ibid* at para 39.
52 *Ibid*.
53 *Ibid*.
54 *Bell*, above note 39 at para 40.
55 *Ibid* at para 41.
56 *Ibid* at para 43.

dealing in cases involving digital works could well lead to disproportionate findings of unfairness when compared with non-digital works. If, as SOCAN urges, large-scale organized dealings are inherently unfair, most of what online service providers do with musical works would be treated as copyright infringement. This, it seems to me, potentially undermines the goal of technological neutrality, which seeks to have the *Copyright Act* applied in a way that operates consistently, regardless of the form of media involved, or its technological sophistication: *Robertson v. Thomson Corp.*, [2006] 2 S.C.R. 363, at para. 49.[57]

This application of technological neutrality to fair dealing implies that the principle applies to the whole Act, including user rights.

In all three of the above cases, technological neutrality as *non-discrimination* ensured that that copyright holder, as well as user, rights were appropriately extended into, as the case may have been, new mediums or methods of reproduction, dissemination, or research use. Moreover, in both *Robertson* and *Rogers*, functional equivalency was employed to equate the digital activity with subject matter known to be included under the rule in question.

### b) Non-interference

As a principle of non-interference, technological neutrality seeks to avoid imposing copyright liability on technologies and activities that, while theoretically capable of being included under the Act, only incidentally implicate copyright. Here, courts balance the potential rights of copyright owners against the interests of technological use and innovation. Moreover, insofar as such technologies facilitate the dissemination of works, one of the purposes of copyright, this further favours a non-infringement holding. There is established precedent in this regard in Supreme Court copyright jurisprudence, though the older caselaw does not explicitly identify technological neutrality by name.

In the two 2004 cases of *CCH* and *CAIP*, the Court considered the meaning of "authorizing" copyright infringement.[58] In *CCH*, the specific issue was whether installation of self-service photocopier machines in a

---

57  *Ibid.*
58  Section 3 of the Act provides, as a distinct right at the end of s 3, "… and to authorize any such acts," also known as the "authorization right."

library constituted an implicit "authorization" on the part of the library for patrons to commit copyright infringement. The Court held that

> [A] person does not authorize infringement by authorizing the mere use of equipment that could be used to infringe copyright. Courts should presume that a person who authorizes an activity does so only so far as it is in accordance with the law. The presumption may be rebutted if it is shown that a certain relationship of control existed between the alleged authorizer and the persons who committed the copyright infringement.[59]

In the context of Internet intermediary liability for illegal downloading in *CAIP*, the Court cited *CCH* in finding that Internet service providers do not "authorize" infringement by merely providing connectivity:

> ... but it is true here, as it was in the *CCH* case, that when massive amounts of non-copyrighted material are accessible to the end user, it is not possible to impute to the Internet Service Provider, based solely on the provision of Internet facilities, an authority to download copyrighted material as opposed to non-copyrighted material.[60]

The Court went on to speculate that knowledge of infringing acts by an Internet intermediary, coupled with a failure to act, might constitute authorization. The ratio of these cases is that the mere sale or provision of products or services that have substantial non-infringing uses will not, without more, trigger copyright infringement.

Another issue in *CAIP* was whether the practice of caching copies on servers came within the wording of the section 2.4(1)(b) safe harbour. That provision insulates from liability common carriers who merely provide the means of telecommunication "necessary for another person to so communicate the work." In reading down the language of "necessary" to mean that which maximizes the cost effectiveness and efficiency of the Internet (as opposed to its more ordinary meaning as "indispensable"), the Court was explicitly concerned about regulatory chill.[61] The Court reasoned that the practice of caching was an innovation that helped promote the dissemination of works (one goal of copyright law) without interfering with the legitimate entitlements of copyright

---

59   *CCH*, above note 3 at para 38.
60   *CAIP*, above note 3 at para 123.
61   *Ibid* at para 114.

owners.⁶² The interests of technological economy and efficiency trumped the making of mere technical copies that were imperceptible to an end user.

In *Entertainment Software*, the issue was whether an additional telecommunication right tariff should apply to Internet download purchases of video games for which a reproduction right fee had already been paid. The majority opinion characterized the section 3(1)(f) telecommunication right as a performance right which was not triggered by the downloading (or reproduction) of copies. The majority also affirmed that it would violate the principle of technological neutrality to treat a hard copy purchased in a store differently than a copy obtained via Internet download by imposing the extra tariff:⁶³

> The principle of technological neutrality requires that, absent evidence of Parliamentary intent to the contrary, we interpret the *Copyright Act* in a way that avoids imposing an additional layer of protections and fees based solely on the method of delivery of the work to the end user. To do otherwise would effectively impose a gratuitous cost for the use of more efficient, Internet-based technologies.⁶⁴

Again, an activity judged exogenous to copyright — the downloading of a work as a method of electronic commerce — was insulated from potential liability.

This string of cases, whether in name or in conceptual application, invokes a principle of technological neutrality as *non-interference* by (1) ensuring that appropriately high thresholds of active conduct (control or knowledge) are in place before the use of digital technologies will be hampered by copyright infringement concerns, (2) declaring that incidental non-usable copies made in the process of facilitating the efficient and economical transmission of Internet communications will not trigger copyright infringement, and (3) ensuring that the delivery of products by e-commerce does not attract copyright infringement. The principle of technological neutrality justified, and rationalized, the law in a way that balanced the legitimate rights of copyright holders against legitimate uses and innovations of technological development.

The recent case of *CBC* also fits within the categorization of technological neutrality as non-interference. However, the majority and

---

62  *Ibid* at para 115.
63  *Entertainment Software*, above note 11 at para 5.
64  *Ibid* at para 9 [emphasis omitted].

dissenting judgments understood and applied it in very different ways. The issue in that case was whether the CBC, which had obtained a licence to broadcast a work (the performance right) had to also pay a fee for the making of several incidental digital copies to facilitate the broadcast (the reproduction right).[65] Justice Abella, in dissent, clearly saw the connection between this case and the other non-interference cases. Technological neutrality, in her view, was comprised of two principles: (1) non-discrimination (which she called "media neutrality") and (2) functional equivalency. The latter, which focuses on what the technology is doing as opposed to how it is doing it, applied in this case, and aligns with technological neutrality as non-interference. According to her, the essential activity engaged in was broadcasting (the *what*), and the making of copies (the *how*) was merely to effect that purpose. The use of incidental copies here was no different than the characterization of cached copies in *CAIP* or the temporary copies transmitted to an end user's hard drive as part of the process of streaming content in *Rogers*.[66] Moreover, compensating for these copies is beyond the legitimate interests of rights holders and, on the negative side, would amount to differential and prejudicial treatment towards the use and development of copy-dependent technologies. Justice Abella's discussion of functional equivalency and essential character of the activity was a logical elaboration of the reasoning in *Entertainment Software* and *Rogers*, as well as a natural fulfillment of the principle of technological neutrality as applied to the facts of this case.

Justice Rothstein, for the majority, refused to invoke the principle of technological neutrality to override what he viewed as the plain text

---

65   Above note 16. Post production, a master of copy of a synchronized work is often uploaded onto a broadcaster's digital content management system. Further copies are made to effect certain functions in aid of a broadcast. As Rothstein J puts it, *ibid* at para 11:

> Broadcast-incidental copies may be made for several purposes. For example, a copy may be made to reformat the master copy to suit CBC's technical requirements, or to edit the copy for timing, language or closed captioning purposes. One or more additional copies may also be made to allow for screening of the program by various teams within CBC before broadcast.

Justice Abella also describes broadcast-incidental copies, referring to many of them as low-resolution copies: see para 137.

66   *Ibid* at paras 158 & 159.

of the Act.⁶⁷ He interpreted sections 30.08 and 30.09 as comprehensive exceptions to the issue of broadcast incidental copies: if the copies did not fit within these exceptions, then the intention of the legislature was for these to trigger infringement under the reproduction right.⁶⁸ As the copies were not held out by the CBC as fitting within either exception, they were therefore found to implicate the reproduction right. Justice Rothstein did, however, apply technological neutrality to the value to be placed on copies with the effect that users who assume the risks of using a new technology should pay less for incidental copies (thus not discouraging innovation). But it is apparent that that majority did not understand — or worse, ignored — the principle of technological neutrality as articulated in *Entertainment Software*. Justice Rothstein is wrong when he indicates that *Entertainment Software* did not "go so far as to allow [the principle of technological neutrality] to override express statutory terms."⁶⁹ Indeed, in *dissent* in *Entertainment Software*, he suggested the majority *did* override express statutory terms with the principle of technological neutrality.⁷⁰

Introducing technological neutrality into the realm of tariff setting veers the principle of non-interference in an entirely new direction. Much more concerning is the fact that the majority's treatment of incidental copies does not fit within the skein of technological neutrality rulings in previous cases which, unlike this case, have been generous in applying technological neutrality alongside the text of the Act. The emphasis on whether these copies fit within sections 30.08 and 30.09 appears to be misplaced for at least two reasons. First, as suggested earlier, those exceptions did not anticipate the kind or degree of incidental-broadcast copying that occurred in *CBC*. It is likely then that those exceptions are outdated. Second, the principle of technolog-

---

67  *Ibid* at paras 47 & 48.
68  *Ibid* at paras 50–53.
69  *Ibid* at para 47.
70  *Entertainment Software*, above note 11 at, for example, para 122: "A media neutral application of the Act, however does *not* imply that a court can depart from the ordinary meaning of the words of the Act to achieve a level of protection for copyright holders that the court considers is adequate" [emphasis in original]. See also para 49. Justice Rothstein appears to have done the same thing, referencing his own minority opinion in writing for the majority in *Canadian Artists' Representation v National Gallery of Canada*, 2014 SCC 42: see Normand Tamaro, *The 2015 Annotated Copyright Act* (Toronto: Carswell, 2014) at 453.

ical neutrality as non-interference, when invoked, informs the scope of rights under the Act. As *Rogers* and *CAIP* demonstrate, technological neutrality has limited the nature of the reproduction right even in cases where there was no textual basis for doing so.[71] To not similarly apply the principle in this case merely because there is a specific and outdated exception in play does not make sense.

The practical effect of the majority decision in this case is that there is now a seemingly artificial distinction to be made between different kinds of incidental copies: those that implicate copyright (broadcast incidental copies) and those that do not (e.g. transmission copies via the Internet). As discussed in the next chapter, future courts would do well to reconsider this issue using a purposive analysis of the reproduction right.

## E. NEUTRALIZING DIGITAL FACTS

The principle of technological neutrality ensures that the objectives of non-discrimination and non-interference are desirable in certain circumstances. However, there can be difficult challenges for courts as they attempt to accommodate digital facts vis-à-vis the legal question at issue. When courts apply a principle of technological neutrality, they do one of three things to accommodate digital facts. First, they may determine that there are no material differences between digital and non-digital technologies (functional equivalency). Second, they may acknowledge material differences but accommodate those differences by applying a different threshold for digital activities. Or third, they may effectively acknowledge material differences but choose to ignore them.

The very notion of differences in facts, or technologies, is central to analogical reasoning and serves as the basis for developing the common law and often statutory law as well. New technologies are never exactly the same as older ones. Courts may have determined in previous cases that certain activities are covered by a broadly conceived rule. For any new activity that comes along — digital or not — the question becomes whether in material respects (in ways that are relevant and significant

---

71   There was no specific exception for cached copying in *CAIP* at the time of the decision, nor is there any exception for transmission copies caused by streaming as in the *Rogers* case.

in relation to the purpose of the rule) the new activity is similar or not. If so, then the activity is included in the rule; if not, it is not. Again, it is a matter of judgment as often viable arguments can be made on both sides of the issue.

A particular legal issue may force a court to adopt one of two perspectives on the digital facts, in particular, the relevance of non-perceptible, technical copies. This question of perspective is best illustrated in the *Robertson* case.[72] In that case, the legal question was whose originality was *reproduced* through digitized copies: that of the newspaper (collective work) or the journalist (individual article). The Court had to choose a perspective about what it means to *reproduce* a work. According to a technical perspective (argued as the "input" perspective), if the collective work is entered as such in a digitized form, then it remains a collective work regardless of its screen display format to the end-user. The "output" perspective, on the other hand, asks whether what is displayed on the screen reproduces the originality of the newsprint collective work or the stand-alone article. The Court favoured, as it has in other cases, the functional end-user perspective. It is on the basis of the end-user's perspective that digital facts are assessed and judged to be relevant or not to a rule.

Functional equivalency is the process of analogizing between two technologies relative to a specific legal question that identifies a function. As implied in the above discussion on perspective, courts focus on *what* the technology is doing from an end-user perspective relative to the identified function, not *how* it is technically performing that function. Specifically, we look to the law to see what function is identified as relevant: for example, what is a "reproduction" or communication "to the public"? We then analogize between a known technology (that falls within the rule) and a new one (that we are not sure about) to see if they perform the same function, notwithstanding their obvious differences. Accordingly, as we have seen above, Internet streaming is functionally akin to television and radio performances, and downloading a copy of a work is equivalent to purchasing a hard copy in a store.

---

72    See above note 42. Perspective, or dimension, of the activity in question was also relevant in *CAIP*, above note 3, on the caching issue.

The situation is more complex when digital facts are materially different, yet the court determines that technological neutrality should apply. So, for example, when copyright doctrine sets a *control* test for authorizing copyright infringement, then providers of host servers are suddenly faced with the prospect of monitoring content of their customers for the presence of copyrighted works — a potentially cumbersome and expensive activity. In *CAIP*, however, the Court responded to this problem by applying a different, more lenient standard such that host service providers would not be liable unless they had *knowledge* of infringing activities occurring on their customer websites.

Alternatively, courts may choose simply to ignore the difference even if it is material. In the *Bell* court's fairness analysis, the degree to which a work is disseminated is an obviously important factor: the greater the dissemination, the less likely the activity will found to be "fair." However, since the Internet facilitates large-scale dissemination, it is impossible to not treat the digital facts differently under this analysis without some modification of its application. Accordingly, the court in *Bell* basically ignored this aspect of the facts in analyzing whether music sampling over the Internet was fair.

## F. THE FUTURE OF TECHNOLOGICAL NEUTRALITY

The future of the principle of technological neutrality as non-interference is in some doubt after the *CBC* decision. In the wake of *Entertainment Software*, *Rogers*, and *Bell*, the principle seemed robust and effective in rationalizing rights in the face of troublesome issues of digital copying and access. In particular, a true character and nature of the activity end-consumer perspective — adopted in both *Entertainment Software* and *Rogers* — suggested that the Court was receptive to the idea that incidental digital copying would not be caught under two rights. Equally promising was that the Court in *Bell*, as it had done many times before, insulated technological innovations from copyright infringement. On this latter point, there is nothing in *CBC* that diminishes the effect or application of technological neutrality as it applies to fair dealing or indeed other areas of the Act. The real question is how these seemingly irreconcilable authorities — *Entertainment Software* and *Rogers* on the one hand, and *CBC* on the other — will play out in future cases of digital copying. In the next chapter, I propose a purposive approach to the interpretation of the reproduction right which may be the only coherent way to address copying in the digital age.

CHAPTER 2

# Authored Works

## A. INTRODUCTION

In its broadest sense, the term "copyright" refers to two categories of creation, in addition to the bundle of rights attaching to each, as provided for under the *Copyright Act*. The two categories are (1) original literary, dramatic, musical, or artistic works of authorship, or "authored works," and (2) "other subject matter" as in sound recordings, performers' performances, and broadcasts. Each is given a particular bundle of rights under the Act. In this chapter, authored works, and the rights attaching thereto, will be discussed. "Other subject matter," or neighbouring rights, as they are sometimes called, is addressed in Chapter 3.

Section B of this chapter discusses the necessary conditions for obtaining a copyright in a work. Except for the Act's treatment of computer programs, there is much that is functionally equivalent between pre-digital and digital technologies vis-à-vis these requirements, thus making the accommodation of the law within long-standing legal doctrine relatively easy. Still, the digital context may, in certain circumstances, create complications for existing doctrine, for example, authorship using computer programs. The same may be said of moral rights, discussed in Section D: the doctrine, in most cases, is easily accommodated though it is possible to imagine unique scenarios for which there are no clear answers.

Section C discusses the important rights that are given under the Act to authored works: reproduction, telecommunication, distribution, and authorization. Digitization poses some interesting challenges for the interpretation of these rights. For example, should temporary non-perceptible copies, made in the process of digital production or transmission of works, be captured under the reproduction right? Is it possible that courts will, in some circumstances, deem the transfer of a digital work, ostensibly under a licensing arrangement, as the sale of the work, thus exhausting a copyright holder's control over the work?

## B. REQUIREMENTS FOR COPYRIGHT IN AUTHORED WORKS

There are five requirements to be met for copyright to subsist in a work of authorship. First, the work must be a literary, dramatic, musical, or artistic work as defined under the Act. Second, the work must be fixed in a tangible form. Third, the work must contain expression. Fourth, that expression must be original. Fifth, the originality of the work must be attributable to a person. It should also be borne in mind that works of foreign origin may be protected by Canadian copyright under certain circumstances, as well.[1]

### 1) Literary, Dramatic, Musical, or Artistic Work

For a creation to be protected under the *Copyright Act*, it must fit within one of the four general categories of works defined in section 2. The Act defines each of the four categories of works — literary, dramatic, musical, and artistic — broadly and non-exhaustively.[2] Thus, for example, artistic work "includes paintings, drawings, maps, charts, plans, photographs, engravings, sculptures, works of artistic craftsmanship, architectural works, and compilations of artistic works." Similarly, illustrative and broadly conceived definitions are offered for dramatic work ("includes . . . any piece of recitation") and literary work ("includes tables and computer programs"). These definitions suggest that copyright applies to informational and knowledge creations as much as it does to literary, dramatic, musical, or artistic works as understood in the conventional sense.

In many instances, copyright doctrine regarding works has been easily adapted to the digital context. For example, the rule that copyright

---

1   See s 5; see also Chapter 8.
2   In addition to defining each of these categorizations, the Act, in s 2, defines "every original literary, dramatic, musical and artistic work."

does not subsist in a game or sport as a dramatic work, for reasons of performance unpredictability,[3] has equal force for video games.[4] Similarly, a website or domain name would not be eligible for copyright protection unless, as with any title, it is both "original and distinctive."[5] Two issues deserve special mention. First, the digital format has made the creation of informational and multimedia content easy and ubiquitous, and thus the treatment of compilations as works will be discussed. Second, the inclusion of computer programs as literary works under the Act has presented particular challenges for copyright.

A "compilation" is defined as "(a) a work resulting from the selection or arrangement of literary, dramatic, musical or artistic works or parts thereof, or (b) a work resulting from the selection or arrangement of data." While Canadian copyright does not protect databases per se, compilations of data will enjoy copyright protection if the author shows skill and judgment (authorial originality) in her selection or arrangement in assembling and presenting the information.[6] Automated or mechanical compilations of data are thus excluded. As well, protection will extend only to the originality expressed in the selection and arrangement of the compilation and not to the underlying data (or works) on their own. The originality standard for collective works, such as newspapers, is the same as for compilations under the Act.[7]

---

3   *FWS Joint Sports Claimants v Canada (Copyright Board)* (1991), 36 CPR (3d) 483 (FCA).
4   See, for example, *Nova Productions Ltd v Mazooma Games Ltd and Others*, [2006] EWHC 24 at para 116 (Ch) [*Mazooma Games*]:

> Although [the video game in question] has a set of rules, the particular sequence of images displayed on the screen will depend in very large part on the manner in which it is played. The sequence of images will not be the same from one game to another, even if the game is played by the same individual. There is simply no sufficient unity within the game for it to be capable of performance.

> The graphics of the game, however, were protected as an artistic work. It is important to note that the author was the designer of the game, not the person playing the game: see para 106.

5   See definition of "work" in s 2 of the Act. The threshold of originality and distinctiveness is not insignificant: see *Francis, Day & Hunter Ltd v 20th Century Fox*, [1940] AC 112, where the title *The Man Who Broke the Bank at Monte Carlo* failed to garner copyright protection.
6   See *Robertson v Thomson Corp*, 2006 SCC 43 at para 37 [*Robertson SCC*].
7   Under the Act, "collective work means (a) an encyclopedia, dictionary, year book or similar work, (b) a newspaper, review, magazine or similar periodical, and (c) any work written in distinct parts by different authors, or in which works or parts of works of different authors are incorporated." *Robertson SCC*, *ibid*, adopted a selection

A related issue is the treatment of multimedia works comprised of some combination of literary, artistic, musical, and dramatic aspects: for example, a music video may consist of an amalgam of musical, artistic (graphic), and dramatic (choreography) works. It is not always easy to distinguish multimedia works from compilations or collective works, which also may be arrangements of works of different categories. This issue is resolved by identifying where the author has exercised her creativity. Generally, multimedia works arise where the different expressive dimensions are the contemporaneous expression of an author, whereas compilations typically involve a third party who assembles pre-existing works, or parts thereof, of different authors. The distinction is legally significant as the author of a compilation copyright has a limited claim over selection or arrangement in the creation whereas copyright in a multimedia work extends to all original expressive aspects of the work.[8]

The legal implications of fitting a work, be it multimedia or compilation, into a single categorization as literary, dramatic, musical, or artistic may be of some significance. For example, the Act may confer different rights to works of different categories. The Act takes a "dominant aspect" approach to multimedia compilations:

> A compilation containing two or more of the categories of literary, dramatic, musical or artistic works shall be deemed to be a compilation *of the category making up the most substantial part* of the compilation.[9]

It is not entirely clear if multimedia works of a single author would be assessed the same way though there seems little by way of an alternative approach. However, when judging infringement, it would seem wrong to protect only the expressive aspects of the dominant part of the multimedia work, for example, the choreography of a dance as a dramatic work but not graphic aspects of the performance as an artistic work. In this sense, it may be wise to characterize a multimedia work under a single heading only to the extent that it is necessary to do so.

---

or arrangement standard as the basis for originality in a collective work even though this language is absent in the definition. There does not appear to be any legal significance attached to characterizing a work as a collective work or compilation since the standard of originality is the same.

8   Infringement analysis should be assessed on all elements of originality in the compilation or multimedia work, as the case may be, and not to the exclusion of a particular dimension of it.

9   Section 2.2(1) [emphasis added].

The inclusion of computer programs as literary works under the Act has led to some challenging problems in copyright law. The term "computer program" means "a set of instructions or statements, expressed, fixed, embodied or stored in any manner, that is to be used directly or indirectly in a computer in order to bring about a specific result."[10] This definition encompasses a process that begins with code and ends with the performance of "a specific result." To the extent that the computer program performs "functional" results, these are not protected by copyright. But, in terms of characterizing a computer program as a work, are we to look at the code (the literary aspect), the display (the artistic aspect), or both? It is an important issue since very different code may be employed to create the same or similar display features.[11]

There are two possibilities, each with very different infringement implications. One possibility is that each of the code and display features exists as a separate work (dual works). It is also possible, in light of the broad definition of *computer program*, to characterize both code and display features as comprising a single multimedia work with both literary and artistic aspects (single work). Infringement analysis under a dual works interpretation would consider whether either the code or display features have been copied whereas, under a single work perspective, both code and display features would be considered as part of a whole. A defendant who develops a similar display of an existing program using different code would fare better under a single work approach.

Courts have not directly addressed this issue. In *Apple Computer Inc v Mackintosh Computers Ltd*, the Supreme Court of Canada affirmed that the assembly code of a computer program is protected as a literary work.[12] In *British Columbia Automobile Assn v Office and Professional Employees' International Union Local 378*, the display features (the look

---

10  This seems to accord with general understandings of a computer program as "a collection of code which instructs hardware, and possibly other software, to carry out some task": Jon Crowcroft, "Copyright, Piracy and Software" in Lionel Bently, Jennifer Davis, & Jane C Ginsburg, eds, *Copyright and Piracy: An Interdisciplinary Critique* (New York: Cambridge University Press, 2010) 209 at 210.

11  Jennifer Davis, "Of Plots, Puddings and Draught-Excluders: The Law as It Applies to the Infringement of Computer Programs" in Bently, Davis, & Ginsburg, *ibid*, 230 at 235, quoting Pumfrey J.

12  [1987] 1 FC 673 (CA), aff'd [1990] 2 SCR 209 [*Apple Computer*].

and layout) of web pages were characterized as an artistic work.[13] The relationship, if any, between code as a literary work and display features as an artistic work is not addressed in either decision. In *Delrina Corp (cob Carolian Systems) v Triolet Systems Inc*, the trial court characterized screen display as a reproduction *in any material form* of the source code.[14] Further, the trial judge held:

> Under the *Copyright Act* only the holder of the copyright in the work (instructions) so stored has the right to produce or reproduce that work. If someone else copies the screen display *so produced*, for use in another program, he infringes any copyright the owner of the work held in it.[15]

While not entirely clear, this passage seems to imply that a similar screen display based on different code may not constitute copyright infringement.

## 2) Fixation

A second requirement for copyright to subsist is that the work be fixed in a physical form of some permanence.[16] Thus, for example, an unrecorded theatrical improvisation will not receive copyright protection. Rather, the improvisation would need to be written down or recorded (even contemporaneously with its performance) for copyright to subsist. This requirement is an anomaly in copyright law as the language of the Act seems to contemplate the inclusion of works that may not be fixed. For example, while the definition of "dramatic work" in section 2 is explicit in requiring that a work be fixed, there is no such language found in the definition of "lecture." The implication might be that the omission is meaningful and that the fixation requirement is unnecessary for lectures or other works that are not explicit in specifying fixation.[17] Courts, however, have extended the fixation requirement to all works, even lectures.[18] This is not only legally anomalous but discriminatory in that original expressive works lacking fixation are denied

---

13 2001 BCSC 156 at paras 189 and 200: "The ... website was an original artistic work. It had certain colours, frames, margins, logos, apparent navigation tools and a particular arrangement of those items."
14 (1993), 47 CPR (3d) 1 (Ont Ct Gen Div) [*Delrina*].
15 *Ibid* at 28 [emphasis added].
16 *Théberge v Galerie d'Art du Petit Champlain inc*, 2002 SCC 34 [*Théberge*].
17 The appropriate statutory interpretation maxim here is *expressio unius*.
18 See *Gould Estate v Stoddart Publishing Co* (1996), 30 OR (3d) 520 (Gen Div).

copyright protection. It seems that the main purpose of the fixation requirement is that of proving the existence of the work, and perhaps its rightful author. In other words, without fixation, it might be difficult to prove that there was infringement of a lecture or that it belonged to the putative author. It is, however, unclear why a question of evidence as to whether a work exists, and by whom, should be elevated to the level of becoming a requirement for copyright protection.

The Act protects works created in either analogue or digital formats. It matters not, for copyright to subsist, that a musical composition is recorded in digital format, or that graphic art is created using digital tools on a digital platform, not on canvas, provided that it is the product of an individual's skill and judgment. In one sense, digitization has facilitated compliance with the fixation requirement. Software programs make the fixation of the works easy and abundant. Consider, for example, how easy it has become to photograph an image or to digitally record sound. Moreover, it has facilitated the saving and alteration of works to a readily accessible and retrievable format for authors. To the extent that there is some dispute about whether an author's work was indeed created or not, it may be possible to access such works from the memory of a computer or from web-page archives, such as the Wayback Machine, an archive created by the non-profit Internet Archive. But in another sense, digitization complicates the fixation requirement. In the pre-digital setting, fixation was premised more or less on the notion of a completed work. With digital creations, it is often possible to trace the evolution of a work — its many changes — making determinations of when a work is fixed (or perhaps more likely, how many works have been made) very difficult.

## 3) Expression

The next three requirements — expression, originality, and authorship — could be grouped under one general requirement, namely, that a fixed work must embody the author's original expressive content. For analytical clarity, however, each component will be addressed separately.

The requirement that the work consist of expression is usually described in terms of what copyright does not protect — ideas, facts, functionality, works in the public domain, and (in the dramatic and literary context) stock characters and *scènes-à-faire*. This critical substructure of content is available for all to use and not subject to monopoly protection. Thus, copyright will not protect the idea of a small, hairy, primitive space-alien creature (available for all to develop) but will extend it to the myriad expressive details in which a particular manifestation of this idea might take form as the result of an individual's creativity. Not surprisingly, courts often experience great difficulty in separating an idea from its expression. In rare instances, an idea can be expressed only in one way or in a very limited number of ways, for example, the bare description of a food recipe. In such cases, courts may conclude that the expression has merged with the idea and not extend copyright protection to the creation.[19]

The relevance of certain non-protectable elements may change in nature or emphasis depending on the work at issue. For dramatic works, for example, courts may need to consider whether certain expression is *scènes-à-faire* and therefore not protected, but to a musical work, this consideration would be irrelevant. There is a particularly unique analysis of non-protectable elements in the case of computer programs. The trial court in *Delrina* listed a range of non-protectable elements that must be distinguished from expressive content in a program. Functional operations and ideas that can be expressed only in a limited number of ways are not protected. A program's structure, sequencing, and organization, mathematical algorithms, and procedures for solving a problem are not protectable per se, though a particular expression of them might still qualify as a literary work. Finally, both the trial and appellate courts in *Delrina* seemed willing to draw on a generous conception of the public domain. For example, lines of source code, or ways of creating code, common throughout a software design community, are considered part of the public domain.[20]

Courts have not extended copyright protection to all forms of fixed expression, however. In *Gould Estate v Stoddart Publishing Co*, the court did not recognize copyright in casual expression or offhand remarks made during the course of a conversation (as opposed to a structured lecture).[21] In *Hager v ECW Press Ltd*, the court found that, in a more formal interview setting, the interviewer was entitled to the copyright of

---

19   *Delrina Corp (cob Carolian Systems) v Triolet Systems Inc* (2002), 58 OR (3d) 339 at para 52 (CA).
20   See, in particular, *ibid* at para 55.
21   Above note 18 at para 37, aff'd (1998), 30 OR (3d) 555 (CA).

the interviewee's expression on the basis of the originality in the questions asked.[22] The reasoning in these cases reveals a concern that public figures not use copyright as a way of preventing the dissemination of their comments and that interviewers are justly rewarded for their efforts in bringing such information to light.

The implication in the digital context is significant as many extemporaneous oral expressions of public individuals are recorded and uploaded to the Internet. We now know that, even if these expressions are original, they lie beyond the reach of copyright. While perhaps a sensible outcome from a public interest perspective, the exception is without basis in the Act. It is unclear to what extent the same rule would apply to conversations or comments of private individuals. There is, however, the practical reality that, if these are subject to copyright protection, the incidence of copyright infringement in an age of ubiquitous recording devices will spike sharply.

## 4) Originality

The Act requires that a work be "original," but it does not define the term. Originality pertains to two concepts: (1) that the work originates from the author (authorial originality) and (2) that the work shows a measure of creativity (creative originality). Authorial originality requires that the work not be a copied one: that it emanates from the author. When a work is not copied but nonetheless appears the same or substantially similar to a work under copyright, a defence of independent creation will shield the second author from a claim of copyright infringement.

Prior to 2004, the creative originality threshold was "skill, judgment and labour."[23] The labour component ensured that mere effort, as opposed to creativity, would be enough to satisfy the originality requirement. In *CCH Canadian Ltd v Law Society of Upper Canada*, the standard was recast as "skill and judgment." In rejecting both an industriousness (effort or labour) *and* creativity (as novel or unique) standard as the basis for originality, McLachlin CJC opted for a middle ground between these poles:

> What is required to attract copyright protection in the expression of an idea is an exercise in skill and judgment. By skill, I mean the use of one's

---

22   [1999] 2 FC 287 at paras 68 & 69.
23   See, for example, *Hager v ECW Press Ltd*, ibid.

knowledge, developed aptitude or practised ability in producing the work. By judgment, I mean the use of one's capacity for discernment or ability to form an opinion or evaluation by comparing different possible options in producing the work .... The exercise of skill and judgment required to produce the work must not be so trivial that it could be characterized as a purely mechanical exercise.[24]

The conjunctive requirements of skill and judgment, defined as such, arguably set the creativity bar quite high. Read in context, however, it seems that McLachlin CJC wished to raise the standard above mere labour or effort.[25] This interpretation is confirmed by the application of the standard to the facts in *CCH*. A topical index to a book, *Canada GST Cases*, which provided a list of cases with one-phrase descriptions under various subject headings, was enough for copyright to subsist. The Court, in that instance, inferred skill and judgment merely on the basis of the author deciding which cases were authorities on GST.[26] Indeed, without question this demands some skill (developed aptitude to read and understand legal cases) and judgment (deciding which cases were authorities). As this illustrates, a work does not require "big-C" creativity or need to reach a level of "high art"[27] to garner copyright protection, nor do courts engage in such aesthetic judgments.[28] Indeed, there is basis for believing that truly creative or groundbreaking works might even have problems in meeting copyright's originality standard.[29]

---

24  2004 SCC 13 at para 16 [*CCH*].
25  Perhaps on par with the "modicum of creativity" standard adopted by the US Supreme Court in *Feist Publications, Inc v Rural Telephone Service Company*, 111 S Ct 1282 (1991).
26  *CCH*, above note 24 at para 32. The Court noted that deciding which headings to include and where the cases fit, as well as reducing the cases to one-phrase summaries under those headings, also required skill and judgment.
27  See *University of London Press Ltd v University Tutorial Press Ltd*, [1916] 2 Ch 601.
28  The most famous dicta in this regard is that of Oliver Wendell Holmes J in *Bleistein v Donaldson Lithographing Co*, 188 US 239 at 251–52 (1903) [*Bleistein*]:

>   It would be a dangerous undertaking for persons trained only to the law to constitute themselves as final judges of the worth of pictorial illustrations, outside of the narrowest and most obvious limits. At the one extreme some works of genius would be sure to miss appreciation. Their very novelty would make them repulsive until the public had learned the new language in which the authors spoke. It may be more than doubted, for instance, whether the etchings of Goya or the paintings of Manet would have been sure of protection when seen for the first time.

29  See Cameron Hutchison, "Insights from Psychology for Copyright's Originality Doctrine" (2012) 52 *IDEA: The Intellectual Property Law Review* 101 [Hutchison], where

The real concern lies at the other end of the spectrum: how low will originality go? It is hard to reconcile even the broadest conception of skill and judgment with too low a standard. The standard is at least suggestive of some measure of technical competence. But is technical competence to be viewed from the perspective of the qualifications of the *person* creating the work, from the *process* by which the work is made, or from objectively studying the *product* for the hallmarks of skill and judgment?[30] Usually, courts make skill and judgment determinations primarily on the basis of assessing the skill and judgment of the *product* or creative outcome, perhaps with some context as to putative author and creative process. Thus, when computer code is basic, generic, and error prone, as certain modules were in *Harmony Consulting Ltd v GA Foss Transport Ltd*[31] then there is an absence of originality based on the attributes of the *product*.

Assessing skill and judgment of product outcomes comes with two cautions. First, assessments of technical competence reflected in a work are different from aesthetic judgments about the work. We may appreciate the technical competence of a piece of art, for example, without liking the piece. Second, all successful product outcomes, however, do not imply skill and judgment. A photograph of friends at a dinner table or of a famous landmark, without any apparent attempt to orchestrate a pose or enhance the setting or lighting, lacks the hallmarks of skill and judgment.[32] Courts will be looking for some attributes, however

---

social psychologists are cited in support of the proposition that judgments of creativity are historically and culturally situated. At any given time, judgment about what is appropriate and, therefore, acceptable work within a community is determined by domain gatekeepers. Truly creative or groundbreaking work is disruptive of traditions and thus may not be accepted as appropriate to domain gatekeepers. Justice Holmes makes a similar point in *Bleistein*.

30   Psychology sometimes views creativity through this framework; see Hutchison, *ibid*.
31   2011 FC 340.
32   See *Ateliers Tango argentin Inc c Festival d'Espagne & d'Amérique latine Inc*, [1997] RJQ 3030 at 3035–37 (CS) [translation from Normand Tamaro, *The 2015 Annotated Copyright Act* (Toronto: Carswell, 2014) at 199]. In fact, the photographs in that case were found to be subject to copyright protection due to the choice of setting and staging of subjects. In *obiter* the court stated, "one can hardly imagine that a simple snapshot of the Montreal Olympic stadium ... taken at random, without any research of setting, might benefit from [copyright] protection ...." See also *Century 21 Canada Limited Partnership v Rogers Communications Inc*, 2011 BCSC 1196 at para 187 [*Century 21*], where the court found originality in photographs for real-estate listings copyrightable on the basis of the choice of subject matter, the creation of the scene, and the angle of the other photographs.

minimal, in a photo or video as demonstrating skill and judgment. The upshot of this is that it is not a foregone conclusion that photos and videos are subject to copyright protection.

## 5) Authorship

The requirement of authorship means that original expression must emanate from a human being. In the non-digital context, this requirement was not particularly problematic as it meant (to use a famous example) that the paintings of elephants were not eligible for copyright. With advances in technology, an increasing number of would-be works are computer generated or computer assisted, and the copyright status of such works may be in question. A distinction should be made between these two forms. Computer-assisted works encompass activities such as using word-processing software to write a book. If skill and judgment are shown in the making of the work, the use of computer assistance is not a barrier to copyright protection. The critical factor is human originality, not the means through which that originality is expressed.

Computer-generated works are those created without human agency of any meaningful kind (except, of course, in the development of the software). The range of works not eligible would include "animated images created by movies studios for cartoons and special effects; computer software produced by generator software; crosswords produced by a computer using a random generator; weather maps generated with data obtained from weather balloons, satellites and weathering stations; share price lists produced from automatic data transmissions from stock markets; 3D landscapes and environments used for simulations; and synthetic music."[33] Nor would copyright protection extend to a work which results from a person who inputs "note parameters for a musical composition" which the software uses to create "an opus of several hours duration."[34] In such a case, the originality is computer generated, not human, and thus copyright does not subsist.

What about works that are created from the interaction between software code and a user? As in the analogue world, the issue may turn

---

33  Anne Fitzgerald & Tim Seidenspinner, "Copyright and Computer-Generated Materials — Is It Time to Reboot the Discussion about Authorship?" (2013) 3 *Victoria University Law and Justice Journal* 47 at 47.
34  *Ibid* at 52.

on the context in which the creation is made. For example, a player of a video game whose actions are responsible for eliciting a series of display frames is not an author since he has not contributed skill to the creation of an *artistic work* but merely in the performance of a game task.[35] In other contexts, the answer is more difficult. For example, the author of code may have a claim to user creations where there are a limited number of possibilities that are already set and predetermined in the code.[36] The issue is trickier when the work is the unique result of a user's artistic creation that is generated through pre-existing software, for example, the avatar creations of Second Life. To the extent a user creates a work from an expanded range of possibilities that are enabled by the software, that user may have a claim to authorship based on skill and judgment in creating the expression (and assuming that the creation is fixed).

A "work of joint authorship" in the Act is defined as "a work produced by the collaboration of two or more authors in which the contribution of one author is not distinct from the contribution of the other author or authors." The caselaw rightly points out that this definition involves two elements: contribution and collaboration. To be considered a joint author, one must make a "significant" — though not necessarily equal — contribution of expression, as opposed to ideas. The requirement of collaboration is met if the expressive contributions are with a view to "common design," that is, they are intended to be merged into a unitary whole, or single work. Thus, it is possible that joint authorship would arise where one author writes the lyrics and another writes the music, if the intention is to merge the contributions into a single song.[37]

The already difficult determination of joint authorship in copyright law is complicated by split authority in Canadian law. Lower courts have applied two different tests, both which require significant contribution of expression and a common design to create a single work. However, in *Neudorf v Nettwerk Productions*,[38] the BC Supreme Court added a third requirement which it imported from US copyright law: that each of the authors intends the other to be a joint author. There

---

35  See *Mazooma Games*, above note 4 at para 106.
36  We know from existing cases that eligibility would extend to the author of the computer program who creates the software that generates such works, both to code and original display features independently created by that code. In the Australian context, see *Sega Enterprises Ltd v Galaxy Electronics Pty Ltd*, [1996] FCA 761.
37  This would also accord with the definition of a musical work.
38  1999 CanLII 7014 (BCSC).

is no statutory basis for such a requirement in our Act.[39] More important, this third requirement causes unfairness to an important class of creators. It excludes those who do not consider (or are not aware of) issues of authorship in the creative process or if they do, cannot prove their own or their co-author's intention. There is also a practical fallacy to this third requirement: what if each views herself as the author and does not intend the other to be a joint author? Paradoxically, each would be both sole author and not author of the work at the same time.

As yet, there are no Canadian cases that consider joint authorship in the digital environment; however, wiki creations have important joint authorship implications. In the absence of open-source licences that divest would-be authors of their claims to authorship or ownership, wiki creations such as Wikipedia might have unmanageable joint authorship problems. As one author puts it, copyright rules are stretched to their limits since wikis are ongoing works-in-progress, involve large-scale and impersonal contribution, and operate according to norms antithetical to proprietary claims.[40]

## C. ECONOMIC RIGHTS

Section 3 of the Act outlines the specific rights granted to authored works. These rights serve as the legal basis for copyright infringement. According to the introductory wording of the section, these are the sole right to "produce or reproduce the work or any substantial part thereof in any material form whatever;" "to perform the work or any substantial part thereof in public;" and "if the work is unpublished, to publish the work or any substantial part thereof." The section continues by enumerating several more specific rights under sections 3(1)(a) to (j). Some of these are specific instances of the more general rights while others are distinct rights unconnected to the introductory wording, for example, the rental rights. Finally, the last words of section 3 — "and to authorize any such acts" — denote that the authorizing of any of the section 3 rights belongs to the copyright holder. This section of the book will

---

39  Moreover, the addition of this requirement in US law was motivated by a desire to exclude those who do not view themselves as authors — most famously, editors — from claiming authorship rights after a work becomes commercially successful.

40  Daniela Simone, "Copyright or Copyleft? Wikipedia as a Turning Point for Authorship" (2014) 25 *King's Law Journal* 102 at 103.

address the following as rights most germane to the digital context: reproduction and substantial takings; communication to the public by telecommunication; distribution and exhaustion; and authorization.

## 1) Reproduction and the Status of Non-consumptive Copies

The first right recited in section 3 is the sole right to "produce or reproduce the work or any substantial part thereof in any material form whatever." The majority of the Supreme Court in *Théberge* clarified that this, in essence, is the right to copy.[41] Although this includes making full copies of a work, the right is much broader than that. It extends to copying of a substantial part of the work in any medium and in any material form, discussed in Section C(2), below in this chapter. In this section, we will consider reproduction as the copying of an *entire* work with particular emphasis on whether this includes the making of incidental digital copies.[42]

The target of the reproduction right has always been to prevent the unauthorized copying of, for example, books and music by members of the purchasing public who would otherwise freely consume the content of these works. The purpose of the right to copy, in other words, is to protect against the unauthorized dissemination of an author's expressive creation. These copies, through which we experience the author's expressive creation, are consumptive. And, to be clear, digital expressive content — for example, an e-book — is as much a consumptive copy as analogue expressive content — for example, a paperback. The touchstone is access to content, not medium of delivery. Thus, the downloading of a digital file is an act of copying.[43] Moreover, the "burning" of a computer program into a silicon chip is copying as that chip is capable of performing the functions written in that code.[44]

---

41  Above note 16.
42  See also the discussion of the relationship between the reproduction right and purchaser rights in Section C(4), below in this chapter, in particular, notes 110 and 111, and accompanying text.
43  *Entertainment Software Association v Society of Composers, Authors and Music Publishers of Canada*, 2012 SCC 34 [*Entertainment Software*].
44  In *Apple Computer*, above note 12 at para 15, the issue was whether computer code, the subject of copyright protection, was infringed when it was burned into a silicon chip. The Supreme Court of Canada characterized the transformation into a chip as a reproduction of the assembly code.

Until very recently, the technology did not exist (and thus the issue never arose) in which copying for another purpose — for example, to facilitate communication of the work — was even remotely possible. Digital technologies changed all of that. They make copying ubiquitous for both consumptive and non-consumptive uses. The term *non-consumptive*, used in other jurisdictions, "captures uses which do not trade on the underlying creative or expressive purpose of the material" and includes caching, indexing by search engines, and data mining.[45] In fact, there is no reason to exclude under this definition other kinds of copies, such as RAM copies or broadcast incidental copies to name a few, which also do not trade on the underlying *expressive* content of a work. Indeed, we might expect the list to grow as digital technological innovation progresses.

For analytical purposes, it might be useful to divide non-consumptive use copies into three categories. First, there are *transmission* copies that serve to facilitate communication on the Internet. For example, the downloading of a work perceptible to an end-user on her home computer may involve the making of several copies in the process. These include cached copies stored on servers, copies made for buffering, and copies made in the RAM of the home computer. These copies are usually deleted shortly after they have performed their function and are not per se perceptible to an end-user.

A second class of non-perceptible copies consists of *digitization* copies that underlie particular end-user access. An example is the imperceptible digitized copying *into the database* that occurred in *Robertson v Thomson Corp*.[46] Another example would be *computational* copies, or those works that are digitized on a massive scale but never presented to an end-user as works; rather, the digitized copies exist solely to perform computational functions. For example, word searches of the HathiTrust digital repository retrieve the name of the work, page number, and number of times the search term appears on that page.[47] The work

---

45  Australian Law Reform Commission, *Copyright and the Digital Economy*, Discussion Paper 79 (Sydney, AU: Australian Law Reform Commission, 2013) at 8, citing the language of Ian Hargreaves, *Digital Opportunity: A Review of Intellectual Property and Growth* (London: Intellectual Property Office, 2011) at 5.23 [Hargreaves Report].

46  Above note 6. In that case, digital copies qua digital copies were legally meaningless. The only copying that was relevant to the reproduction right was how a work was displayed to an end-user.

47  *Authors Guild, Inc v HathiTrust*, 755 F3d 87 at 91 (2d Cir 2014) [*HathiTrust*].

*qua* work is never displayed in any way and thus is imperceptible to the end-user.

A third class is that of digital *production* copies: copies made to facilitate digital production processes incidental to a consumptive purpose, or a purpose which *does* trade in the expressive content of a work. These are the kinds of copies that were in issue in *Canadian Broadcasting Corp v SODRAC 2003 Inc*[48] though the specific class discussed in that case were broadcast incidental copies.[49] Unlike other non-consumptive copies, these copies are perceptible in that technicians and production personnel access them for content during the production or pre-broadcast process. However, this use is non-consumptive in that access is minimal and the expressive content is not consumed but merely altered for technical purposes. By the same token, an archived copy (sometimes discussed within this category) would qualify as a copy of the work as expressive content is created and maintained for an intended end-user access.[50]

In the analysis that follows, a distinction is made between consumptive copies (that an end-user is able to access to consume the content of the work) and non-consumptive copies, as discussed above. It will be argued that only the former kind of copying should be legally significant and that non-consumptive copies, as a class, are not eligible for copyright protection.

The Supreme Court of Canada's treatment of non-consumptive copying has been inconsistent.[51] In *Rogers Communications Inc v Society of Composers, Authors and Music Publishers of Canada*[52] and *Entertainment*

---

48  2015 SCC 57 [*CBC*].
49  See Chapter 1.
50  Not all copying fits neatly into these categories. For example, buffering (or copying) of streamed content for playback may be viewed as either consumptive or non-consumptive, or both. Since it adds value to an expressive use, it would not be incorrect to categorize it as consumptive. See Cameron Hutchison, "Understanding Copy Right" (under submission for publication; on file with author).
51  Lower courts, on the other hand, have reflexively assumed that transmission copying is infringement. In *Century 21*, above note 32 at para 204, the court held that copying property descriptions from the plaintiff's website for storage on the defendant's server was enough to constitute copyright infringement. Similarly, while the court in *Red Label Vacations Inc (redtag.ca) v 411 Travel Buys Limited (411travelbuys.ca)*, 2015 FC 18 at para 101, found that the metatags, or coding statements, in issue lacked originality, it, nonetheless, affirmed that original metatags would be eligible for copyright protection. In both of these lower court cases, the copies in issue were not and never would be perceptible to an end-user.
52  2012 SCC 35 [*Rogers*].

*Software*,[53] the Court was of the view that streaming content, which involves the making of copies on the receiving computer, did not implicate the reproduction right. In *Society of Composers, Authors and Music Publishers of Canada v Canadian Assn of Internet Providers*,[54] the Court read the ambiguous wording of the common-carrier exception (the word "necessary") in a way that insulated caching from copyright infringement. Yet, in *CBC*,[55] the Court found that broadcast incidental copies that did not fit within exceptions in the Act were copies.

This discrepancy in the treatment of non-consumptive copying can mostly be attributed to the Court's purposive interpretation of the Act in *Rogers* and *Entertainment Software* and the plain meaning approach adopted in *CBC*. As discussed in Chapter 1, the Court in *Entertainment Software* and *Rogers* rationalized the reproduction and telecommunication rights based on a purposive understanding of those rights, namely, telecommunication as performance (streaming) and reproduction as durable copies (downloading). Notably, the Court did not exempt the streaming copies from infringement on the basis of an exception in the Act (which did not exist). Similarly, interpreting "necessary" in the common-carrier exception to mean that which enhances Internet economy and efficiency so as to exclude caching from copyright implications is a purposive, not a plain, understanding of the language (i.e. "necessary" as that which is indispensable).[56] However, the majority in *CBC* failed to adopt a purposive understanding of the reproduction right; instead, it implied that a copy is a copy unless there is an explicit exception in the Act.

The Court departed from the purposive tradition in *CBC* by placing too much emphasis on stale exceptions in the Act. Those exceptions, outlined in sections 30.08 and 30.09, were a specific reaction to the pre-digital single-copy-for-broadcast copying that took place in *Bishop v Stevens*.[57] The kinds of digital technologies that would emerge, and the kind and extent of the copying that these new technologies would require, could not have been foreseen when the amendments to sec-

---

53  Above note 43.
54  2004 SCC 45 [*CAIP*].
55  Above note 48.
56  *CAIP*, above note 54 at para 91: "the word 'necessary' in s 2.4(1)(*b*) is satisfied if the means are reasonably useful and proper to achieve the benefits of enhanced economy and efficiency."
57  [1990] 2 SCR 467 [*Bishop*].

tions 30.08 and 30.09 were passed in 1997. The exceptions, therefore, are arguably not comprehensive in scope and do not necessarily convey a legislative intention that acts of non-consumptive copying fall under the reproduction right. More important, the mere existence of these exceptions, if they are to address *Bishop*-type copying, reveals nothing about the intended scope of the reproduction right any more than the absence of a clear exception had a bearing on the interpretation of the right to copy in *CAIP* or *Rogers*.

The exceptions under the Act do not comprehensively define the contours of the reproduction right. Rather, they function to offer greater certainty as to what does not constitute infringement. Moreover, there is nothing in the Act which conveys a legislative intent for the treatment of non-consumptive copies as a class.[58] Nor is it unreasonable to expect the legislature to amend the Act to include non-consumptive copying under the reproduction right if that is truly what is intended. For example, an unsuccessful proposal for inclusion under the *WIPO Copyright Treaty*[59] defined copying as "direct and indirect reproduction of . . . works, either permanent or temporary, in any manner or form."[60] Since such

---

58  There are, however, new exceptions in the Act, such as s 30.07, which address certain kinds or instances of non-consumptive copying.
59  Can TS 2014 No 20.
60  Eric H Smith, "The Reproduction Right and Temporary Copies: The International Framework, the U.S. Approach and Practical Implications" (Paper delivered at the SOFTIC Symposium 2001, Tokyo, 20–21 November 2001) at 4–5. The agreed statement eventually adopted was ambiguous with respect to the status of non-consumptive copies: "The reproduction right, as set out in Article 9 of the *Berne Convention*, and the exceptions permitted thereunder, fully apply in the digital environment, in particular to the use of works in digital form. *It is understood that the storage of a protected work in digital form in an electronic medium constitutes a reproduction* within the meaning of Article 9 of the *Berne Convention*" [emphasis added]. The italicized language — and, in particular, the meaning of "storage" — is ambiguous. Does this imply the possibility of ultimate retrieval of the work in perceptible form, as the ordinary usage of the word "storage" might imply, or is temporary storage enough? See *Cambridge Dictionaries Online*, "storage: the act of putting things in a special place *for use in the future*" [emphasis added]. See also Zohar Efroni, *Access-Right: The Future of Digital Copyright Law* (Oxford: Oxford University Press, 2011) at 224: "storage in the context of digital data often describes information that is *kept*, in contrast to information that automatically evaporates after a moment." Pamela Samuelson observes that "[t]he most honest thing that can be said about temporary copying of works in computer memory is that there is no international consensus on the topic": Pamela Samuelson, "The US Digital Agenda at WIPO" (1996) 37 *Virginia Journal of International Law* 369 at 392.

a legislative amendment including non-consumptive copies under the reproduction right in the Act has not been made, we might infer that such copies are not intended to be captured by the right to copy.

Given that there is no discernible legislative intent concerning the treatment of non-consumptive copies and that judicial interpretation has exempted some of these copies from infringement but not others, it is time to reassess the fundamentals of the right to copy. A purposive interpretation promises to rationalize the right to copy much like it did for the telecommunication right in *Entertainment Software*.[61] In that case, the fundamental question asked was this: What was that right designed to protect? When the answer was that it was a species of a performance right, the Court was able to find an analogy between TV and radio, on the one hand, and Internet streaming, on the other. Similarly, what is the purpose behind the right to copy? And is non-consumptive copying analogically similar to consumptive copying? Historically, the right to copy served to preserve authorial incentive and reward by protecting against the free distribution of a work's consumable content of expression (consumptive copies). As one commentator puts it, "copyright has never been understood as a right to prevent copying as such — that is, the mere act of copying *in abstracto*. Early copyright statutes make clear that copying is wrong on the grounds that it is the preliminary — and, in some cases, the necessary — condition for disseminating the author's creation to the public."[62] Non-consumptive copying is not analogically the same as consumptive copying since the purpose for the copying is for reasons unconnected to its consumption as expressive content.

Moreover, we protect against the free dissemination of content of an author's work to preserve the incentive to create. But in the US court case of *HathiTrust*, where entire works were digitized to facilitate compre-

---

61 Above note 43.
62 Maurizio Borghi & Stavroula Karapapa, *Copyright and Mass Digitization: A Cross-Jurisdictional Perspective* (Oxford: Oxford University Press, 2013) at 52. See also William F Patry, *How to Fix Copyright* (New York: Oxford University Press, 2011) at 41: the mere act of copying in the *verb* sense does not always implicate the purpose of copying, which is the *noun* sense; and Jessica Litman, "Fetishizing Copies" *University of Michigan Public Law Research Paper No 422* (Ann Arbor, MI: University of Michigan, 2014), online: Social Science Research Network http://ssrn.com/abstract=2506867. Or see Hargreaves Report, above note 45 at 5.3: the law should not block new technologies that rely on copying "simply because those technologies were not imagined when the law was formed."

hensive full-text searches, the court stated flatly: "There is no evidence that the Authors write for the purpose of enabling text searches of their books. Consequently, the full-text search function does not 'supersede the objects [or purposes] of the original creation.'"[63] If authors do not create for the incentive of profiting from digital uses, then there seems little basis to stifle the development of new technological uses that facilitate dissemination of works (yet another purpose of copyright).

This purposive analysis, moreover, is not at all affected by the question of whether an incidental copy has value extraneous to the expressive content of the work. Consider the following from the Copyright Board decision that led to the appeal in *CBC*:

> The adoption of copy-dependent technologies allows broadcasters to remain competitive and to protect their core business even when it does not generate direct profits. These technologies are necessary for Astral and CBC to remain relevant so that services continue to be seen by the public. *These are clear benefits arising from copy-dependant technologies. Since these technologies involve the use of additional copies, some of the benefits associated with the technologies must be reflected in the remuneration that flows from these incidental, additional copies.*[64]

In other words, the Copyright Board compensates authors for value attributed to copying *independent of the content of that work*. Essentially, the majority opinion in *CBC* agreed with this.[65] But this is the same as extending copyright to value created by using a book as a door stopper and not for its written expression. Or to make an analogy with patent law, this is much like granting a patent for new use for an old product *not to the person who discovers the new use* but to the person who originally disclosed the known product or process for a different purpose. Where copying creates value extraneous to its expressive content, there is no reason grounded in the purpose of copyright law for an author to profit from this at the expense of technology users and developers.[66]

---

63   *HathiTrust*, above note 47 at 97.
64   *Copyright Act*, ss 70.2 and 70.15 (Re), [2012] CBD No 11 at para 81 [emphasis added].
65   Indeed, this fallacy is continued in the majority judgment which applied technological neutrality to the valuation of copies, in particular, assessing value based on risk and investment in the use of copy-dependent digital technologies.
66   Hargreaves Report, above note 45, agrees at 5.20: "Copyright law was never intended to be an instrument for regulating the development of consumer technology.

Modern digital technologies may require the use of dozens of non-consumptive copies to create better and more efficient outcomes. Given these continuing technological developments, there is every reason to calibrate the balancing of interests in favour of supporting technological innovation over the relatively weak claims of authorial incentive in non-consumptive copies. When copyright adds a cost, and possible disincentive, for the development of new technologies or new non-expressive uses of the work, and authors do not create for the incentive of profiting from non-consumptive uses, then there is no reason for non-consumptive copies to attract copyright protection. A purposive approach to the reproduction right should raise concerns about extending copyright protection to non-consumptive copies, as these in no way correlate to the intended object of copyright protection.

## 2) Substantial Taking

As part of the reproduction right, a copyright holder enjoys the exclusive right to copy "a substantial part" of a work "in any material form." So, either copying less than the entirety of a work or copying it in a medium or form that is different than the original mode of expression may still constitute copyright infringement. Digital technologies facilitate the borrowing of works into the creation of new works, whether in the same or different media. When it is alleged that one author has copied from another in creating his work, it is usually on the basis that he borrowed elements from the first author's work. The question becomes whether the taking was substantial. Formally, a plaintiff must prove (1) copying of, or access to, the work (since independent creation of the same or similar work is a complete defence to copyright infringement); and (2) appropriation of the work, that is, all or a substantial part of the work has been taken.

While not always an easy determination, the methodology of satisfying the first requirement is not controversial. If a defendant admits to copying the plaintiff's work or there is otherwise direct evidence of access to the work, then copying will be established. In other cases, where access to the work is denied by the defendant, copying may still be inferred from circumstantial or indirect evidence. Since the issue is wheth-

---

But where it can block or permit developments or applications of technology that is precisely what it becomes."

er copying has occurred, courts do not limit the evidence to expressive elements but will also consider whether ideas and other non-protectable elements have been borrowed. Moreover, courts will generally consider expert evidence for proof of copying. In light of the easy access to works on the Internet, it should be interesting to see whether these inferences are more readily made in the digital environment.

Once access has been established, the second part of substantial similarity analysis is to consider whether there is wrongful appropriation of the plaintiff's copyrighted work. Courts have uniformly stated that substantial similarity analysis involves a consideration not just of how much is taken from the plaintiff's work (the quantitative inquiry) but also the nature of what is taken (the qualitative element). Indeed, it will often be the case that a small quantitative portion of a work is borrowed relative to the whole; nonetheless, that portion may consist of the most aesthetically pleasing part of the work, perhaps the thirty-second chorus ringtone of a five-minute song. Prior to *Cinar Corporation v Robinson*,[67] courts had adopted varying approaches to making the qualitative assessment. These approaches may be grouped into two different categories. The "holistic" approach assesses a qualitative aspect in light of the work as a whole, without factoring out unprotectable elements of the work, including ideas, facts, stock devices, and *scènes-à-faire*. The "dissection" approach separates protectable expression from unprotectable elements in both works, then determines whether there has been a substantial taking of the former.

In *Cinar*, the Supreme Court made its first pronouncement on substantial similarity analysis. In that case, Robinson conceived a children's television series called *Robinson Curiosité*, so named for the main character who interacts with other characters living on a tropical island. He created a set of characters both graphically and by written description, wrote scripts, prepared storyboards, and eventually registered his copyright in this creation. He approached various entities (including the defendant corporation) about the series, but no production deal was ever reached. In 1995, the first episode of a children's series titled *Robinson Sucroë*, produced by the defendant corporation, was broadcast in Quebec. The plaintiff alleged many similarities in that production as compared with his work, which formed the basis of this copyright infringement

---

67   2013 SCC 73 [*Cinar*].

action. The main legal issues in the case were (1) the proper analysis to be applied to substantial similarity as appropriation and (2) the role of expert evidence in making this assessment.

On the first issue, the Supreme Court of Canada decision endorsed the holistic approach. It held that substantial similarity is to be qualitatively assessed by looking at the two works as wholes and not in isolated parts.[68] To abstract a work into component parts, in the Court's opinion, would undermine an accurate assessment of the "cumulative effect" of the features copied.[69] This reasoning appears to reflect a fear that reducing a work into component parts, as proposed by the dissection approach, risks overlooking what might otherwise be considered a qualitative taking of the work when viewed as a whole.[70]

There are several problems with the holistic approach and the way in which it was articulated and applied in this case. First, the refusal to identify those elements not subject to copyright protection undermines a key balancing mechanism within copyright doctrine: the idea/expression dichotomy. A substantial taking may now include unprotectable elements — in whole or in part — that heretofore were available for all to use. Second, even if we accept that the whole of the work may well be more than the sum of its parts, the whole is not incapable of explication and analysis.[71] A final criticism of this aspect of the case is

---

68  *Ibid* at para 35.
69  *Ibid* at para 36.
70  This reasoning resembles a strand of US caselaw that supports a "total concept and feel" approach to substantial similarity where, in the absence of any literal copying, the taking of the "gestalt of creative elements" is enough to constitute infringement. Robert C Osterberg & Eric C Osterberg, *Substantial Similarity in Copyright Law* (New York: Practising Law Institute, 2003) (loose-leaf updated to June 2013) at 2-29. *TMTV, Corp v Mass Productions, Inc*, 645 F3d 464 at 470 (1st Cir 2011): "Infringement can occur where — without copying a single line — the later author borrows wholesale the entire backdrop characters, inter-relationships, genre, and plot design of an earlier work." In more concrete terms, see, for example, Jarrod M Mohler, "Toward a Better Understanding of Substantial Similarity in Copyright Infringement Cases" (2000) 68 *University of Cincinnati Law Review* 971 at 988:

> [T]he problem with dissection is that one could dissect anything down to unoriginal parts, without noticing the expressiveness of the ensemble. For example, if one dissected a song into component parts, such as the chord progression, the notes played, and the instrumentation, almost no popular song could be classified as "original." Yet, the parts put together make up an entirely original song.

71  For example, the expression borrowed in this case included the individual complex character descriptions (component parts), as well as the fact that so many of the

that, in analyzing substantial similarity, the Court did not actually apply the holistic approach it purported to adopt. Consider this passage in a different part of the judgment addressing the issue of whether the defendant borrowed ideas or expression:

> The trial judge clearly grounded his finding of copying of a substantial part *not in the idea behind Curiosity, but in the way Robinson expressed that idea* .... He concluded that the overall architecture of Robinson's submission for a television show was copied. He found that the graphic appearance and several aspects of the personality of Curiosity's protagonist were copied; the personalities of the secondary characters that gravitate around Curiosity's protagonist were copied; and the graphic appearance of the makeshift village that these characters inhabit was also copied in part .... *These findings are not confined to reproduction of an abstract idea; they focus on the detailed manner in which Robinson's ideas were expressed.*[72]

Does this imply "reverse" dissection wherein stage 1 is a holistic assessment and stage 2 is filtering out ideas from expression? Where the Court may have tried to offer clarity on the proper test to apply, it might have sowed an uncertainty that will undoubtedly be explored by lower courts.

Although the Court endorsed holistic assessment (at least in theory if not in practice), it is important to note that it did not outright reject the dissection approach:

> I do not exclude the possibility that [the dissection] approach might be useful in deciding whether a substantial part of some works, for example computer programs, has been copied. But many types of works do not lend themselves to a reductive analysis.[73]

This ruling implies an endorsement of the approach to analyzing infringement of computer programs as outlined in *Delrina*.[74] Still, the basis upon which such works are more amenable to a dissection approach is not clear. Are computer programs considered more appropriate for this approach because they have more easily identifiable public domain

---

    characters, and their relationships to one another, *in the aggregate* were similar (the whole). This "whole" is amenable to description.
72  *Cinar*, above note 67 at para 43 [emphasis added].
73  *Ibid* at para 35.
74  Above note 14. See notes 19 and 20, and accompanying text.

components, or because there is no whole that is greater than the sum of its parts? The Court offers no rationale to guide future courts to further define this exception.

The *Cinar* court also addressed two other issues in substantial similarity analysis as appropriation. First, it affirmed that the borrowing from the plaintiff's work, not the extent to which the borrowing contributes to the defendant's work, is the proper inquiry.[75] Although this approach accords with basic copyright principles, it can also lead to unfairness in specific cases as I have discussed elsewhere.[76] Second, where a work is a complex multi-dimensional creation, such as a fictional novel or a movie or television series, wrongful appropriation may be found in the underlying elements that are not obvious to the "ordinary observer." This represents a break from established copyright analysis of substantial similarity which has tended to focus on the superficial similarities, as apparent to an ordinary observer, between works.

With the inclusion of latent or structural aspects as part of the qualitative analysis, there are now two options open to courts. First, this expands the horizon of substantial similarity analysis which, in tandem with a holistic analysis, might increase the prospect of infringement, thus significantly bolstering copyright holder rights. Alternatively, courts may elevate the threshold of substantial similarity such that superficial qualitative takings under the old approach will seem non-infringing when the work is considered in its totality, including its structural aspects.

The *Cinar* court also ruled on the admissibility of expert evidence to aid in the determination of whether there was a qualitative taking. The Supreme Court held that expert evidence will be admitted if it is relevant, necessary, and does not involve an exclusionary rule; it also requires that the expert be properly qualified.[77] The appellants argued that expert evidence is not necessary since the test for substantial similarity is to be judged from the perspective of "the lay person in the intended audience."[78] While this perspective is "useful," the Court maintained that

---

75  *Cinar*, above note 67 at para 39. For a commentary of this part of the judgment, see Hutchison, above note 29.
76  See *ibid*.
77  *Cinar*, above note 67 at para 49.
78  *Ibid* at para 50.

the question always remains whether a substantial part of the plaintiff's work was copied. The question should be answered from the perspective of a person whose senses and knowledge allow him or her to fully assess and appreciate all relevant aspects — patent and latent — of the work at issue. In some cases, it may be necessary to go beyond the perspective of a lay person in the intended audience for the work, and to call upon an expert to place the trial judge in the shoes of "someone reasonably versed in the relevant art or technology."[79]

The Supreme Court then justified the necessity of expert evidence with reference to three points. First, the intended audience of both works is young children. Second, the media and stage of development of the two works are different. Finally, the works at issue have both patent and latent similarities. In other words, less obvious, or latent, similarities — atmosphere, dynamics, motifs, and structure — are not apparent to the lay observer and justify expert evidence.[80] Since it will be the exceptional case where at least some of these factors — intended audience as a subset of the population, works expressed in different mediums or at different stages of development, or works involved being layered and complex — are not present, it may become common for courts to admit expert evidence for substantial similarity analysis.

Digital formats and platforms may also raise questions about which of two or more competing copyrights are being "substantially" reproduced. In *Robertson v Thomson Corp* a freelance journalist sold articles to the *Globe and Mail* without licence or assignment in respect of the electronic rights.[81] The *Globe* subsequently published the articles in its print and online daily editions of the newspaper. The legal controversy arose when the *Globe* also included the article in other digital formats such as CD-ROMs and online Internet databases for which it charged fee for service. The legal issue became whether conversion and reproduction of the article (together with other news of the day) into these digital and electronic formats was a reproduction of the freelance author's work, on

---

79  *Ibid* at para 51.
80  *Ibid* at para 55.
81  One article was an excerpt from a book the author had written for which her publisher had authorized "one time usage" in exchange for a fee. The other article was purchased by oral contract. Electronic rights were not addressed in either contract: *Robertson v Thomson Corp* (2001), 15 CPR (4th) 147 at paras 17 & 18 (Ont SCJ) [*Robertson* SCJ].

the one hand, or the newspaper as a collective work, on the other.[82] The former characterization would expose the *Globe* to copyright infringement while the latter would merely be an exercise of its legal rights in the collective work.

One perspective is to view the digital uploading of each day's paper edition into the electronic archive as the act of reproducing the collective work.[83] In other words, the skill and judgment of the collective work is maintained in the digitized form of the newspaper as it is inputted into the electronic archive. Although the article is retrieved from this digitized version and appears as a stand-alone piece, this is merely a convenience of the technology (the search function), not something that affects the characterization of the work. The competing "output" perspective is that determining which work is reproduced — the individual article or the collective work as a whole — turns on which is displayed to the reader through the digital technologies.

The majority Supreme Court judgment adopted the output perspective, holding that "[w]e cannot avoid comparing the original collective work with the finished collective work when determining whether there has been a reproduction."[84] Thus, where enough of the context of the newspaper can be displayed to the user, then it is the collective work that is qualitatively being reproduced.[85] A CD-ROM that presents daily newspapers that can be viewed separately and displays other articles from one day's edition in a column to the side of a particular article preserves enough of the collective work context.

---

82 A copyright subsists in a newspaper as a collective work when originality (skill and judgment) is exercised in the selection or arrangement of the work: s 2 of the *Copyright Act*; *Robertson* SCC, above note 6 at para 37.

83 According to this "input" perspective, the article itself is the same as the one that appears in the newsprint version and identifies the *Globe* as its source, including the date of publication, the page number, and the headline. The article is "mechanically derived from a digitalized version of the deconstructed given edition of the newspaper." *Robertson* SCJ, above note 81 at para 113.

84 *Robertson* SCC, above note 6 at para 46.

85 When most of the context of an individual article is removed — for example, only the name of the paper, the date, and the page number are displayed with the article — then the collective work is not maintained.

## 3) Telecommunication

As the Court clarified in *Entertainment Software*, the right to "communicate to the public by telecommunication" is a species of the performance right:

> In our view, this historical connection between communication and performance still exists today. With respect, the Board ignored this connection when it concluded that transmitting a download of a musical work over the Internet could amount to a "communication".... Although a download and a stream are both "transmissions" in technical terms (they both use "data packet technology"), they are not both "communications" for the purposes of the *Copyright Act*. This is clear from the Board's definition of a stream as "a transmission of data that allows the user to listen or view the content at the time of transmission and that is not meant to be reproduced".... Unlike a download, the experience of a stream is much more akin to a broadcast or performance.[86]

As this passage suggests, this right is not, as previous Supreme Court and appellate court jurisprudence suggested, connected in any way with the reproduction right.[87] As such, one who downloads a file without consent of the copyright holder violates the reproduction right, not the telecommunication right. Rather, as a performance right, section 3(1)(f) applies to those who broadcast works over TV or radio, or, in the Internet context, who stream content.

Notwithstanding the holdings in *Entertainment Software* and *Rogers*, which seemed to make a clear distinction between the reproduction right (as download) and the telecommunication right (as streaming or other non-permanent displays of content), there remain grey-area cases. For example, assume that buffering for the purpose of facilitating the playback of content to a viewer, as in the *Sirius* case, attracts copyright.[88] Should it be considered a reproduction (technical copies are made) or telecommunication (because it occurs in the streaming process)? Given the main purpose of the activity — streaming — it would more properly be categorized under the telecommunication right. More important is

---

86  Above note 43 at paras 27 & 28.
87  See *CAIP*, above note 54 at para 45; and the *Canadian Wireless Telecommunications Assn v Society of Composers, Authors and Music Publishers of Canada*, 2008 FCA 6 [*CWTA*] which interpreted downloads as falling under the reproduction right.
88  *Sirius Canada v CMRRA/SODRAC*, 2010 FCA 348 at para 14 [*Sirius*].

that a grey-area activity not be characterized as both, as this would lead to the kind of double-dipping of rights that the Court in *Entertainment Software* sought to avoid.

What does "to the public" mean under section 3(1)(f)? Does it include content that is streamed on-demand in individual private settings? Does it include content that is not necessarily accessible to the public as a whole? Much like television and radio broadcasting, the fact that a streamed transmission over the Internet may occur in a private setting does not defeat what otherwise would be characterized as "to the public." The court in *Rogers* also clarified that a series of individual communications elicited on-demand by viewers is still "to the public." As the court stated:

> Where such a series of point-to-point communications of the same work to an aggregation of individuals is found to exist, it matters little for the purposes of copyright protection whether the members of the public receive the communication in the same or in different places, at the same or at different times or at their own of the sender's initiative.[89]

Finally, as prior caselaw has established, "the public" does not necessarily mean all Canadians. The court in *Rogers* seemed to imply that a "significant segment of the public" is enough.[90] Thus, subscription-based services, which require payment for access to content, would still be considered "to the public."[91]

It is clear that persons who view copyrighted content through streaming (as opposed to downloading files) are not liable for infringement even where proper authorization has not been obtained. The person who uploads the content onto the web for streamed access, on the other hand, is liable. Not only was this the holding in *Rogers*, but the *Copyright Modernization Act* added the following statutory provision:

> For the purposes of this Act, communication of a work or other subject-matter to the public by telecommunication includes making it available to the public by telecommunication in a way that allows a member of the public to have access to it from a place and at a time individually chosen by that member of the public.[92]

---

89   *Rogers*, above note 52 at para 52.
90   Adopting the language of Sharlow J in *CWTA*, above note 87. In *CWTA*, ringtones available to cellphone subscribers were considered "communication to the public."
91   See, for example, *CWTA*, above note 87.
92   Section 2.4(1.1) of the Act.

Since this making available right is part of the telecommunication right, uploading files for others to download (and not for streaming) does not come within its purview. Rather, such an activity implicates the reproduction right.[93] After *Entertainment Software* and *Rogers*, it seems clear that the telecommunication right has been interpreted under section 3(1)(f) in a way that eclipses the making available right. However, as we will see in the discussion of neighbouring rights, this does not mean the two rights are coterminous. The making available right is essentially a right exclusive to the Internet and thus would not apply to radio or TV since these push technologies do not allow individual on-demand access. Under neighbouring rights provisions, making available, as a pull Internet right, and telecommunication, as representing push media, can be distinct rights.

### 4) Distribution and Exhaustion

Exhaustion rules pertain to both (1) the right of the owner of a copyright to distribute (sell) his work in a market and (2) the right of a purchaser to freely use and dispose of a duly purchased copy of a work. Section 3(1)(j) grants a right of distribution to owners of *tangible* but not *intangible* (or digital) objects in the Canadian market:

> in the case of a work that is in the form of a tangible object, to sell or otherwise transfer ownership of the tangible object, as long as that ownership has never previously been transferred in or outside Canada with the authorization of the copyright owner ....

This codifies a rule of national exhaustion; in other words, the holder of the copyright in Canada has the exclusive right to import into, and sell the work in, Canada. Canadian copyright owners thereby have an advantage because they do not have to compete with the importation of cheaper versions of the work legally made abroad. As Rothstein J put it in *Euro-Excellence Inc v Kraft Canada Inc* in the context of the hypothetical infringement rule, "[w]ithout [a basis for preventing parallel imports], the foreign copyright holder who could manufacture the

---

93 It remains to be seen whether courts will include this activity under the reproduction right. See Chapter 8. Also, intermediaries, such as BitTorrent sites, which facilitate file-sharing, may be caught under other provisions of the Act. See Chapter 7.

work more cheaply abroad, could flood the Canadian market with the work, thereby rendering the Canadian copyright worthless."[94]

According to the legislative summary, section 3(1)(j) implements the "right of distribution" under article 6 of the *WIPO Copyright Treaty*. Consistent with that treaty obligation, the right applies only to *tangible* objects (or put another way, to physical copies, not digital copies).[95] The implication is that intangible digital downloads are not subject to the distribution right; in other words, the Canadian copyright owner has no right of first sale in Canada.

Moreover, the language of section 27(2), the so-called hypothetical infringement rule, was not changed by the *Copyright Modernization Act*.[96] To state it simply, the hypothetical infringement rule requires that works imported and sold in Canada must have the consent of the Canadian copyright holder to be non-infringing. This section, referring as it does to the "import" of copies and copies "made" in Canada, connotes tangible, not digital products.[97] Considering all of these inferences together — the reference to tangible objects only in section 3(1)(j), and the unchanged wording of the hypothetical infringement rule connoting physical products — it seems that there is no legislative intent to give the Canadian owner of a copyright a right of first sale in the Canadian market in connection with digital goods.

Therefore, digital downloads that are purchased in Canada from foreign copyright owners abroad should be non-infringing. The implications of this are significant. Physical copies for sale in Canada will be

---

94   2007 SCC 37 at para 21 [*Euro-Excellence*].
95   Library of Parliament, *Legislative Summary: Bill C-11: An Act to Amend the Copyright Act*, Publication No 41-1-C11-E (Ottawa: Library of Parliament, 2012) at 5: The *Legislative Summary* confirms that "tangible object" applies to "tangible goods, such as copies of CDs." The Agreed Statement to art 6 of the *WIPO Copyright Treaty*, above note 59, indicates that the language "original and copies" refers only to fixed copies that can be put into circulation as tangible objects.
96   SC 2012, c 20.
97   Similar concerns are apparent in the wording of s 27.1 of the Act, which prevents parallel imports of books (to protect exclusive distributors in Canada) under certain defined circumstances. The definition of *book* as meaning "in printed form" as well as the recurring reference to "import" is strongly suggestive of physical copies. See definition of "book," s 2. Even more clearly, s 5 of the *Book Importation Regulations*, SOR/99-324, as amended SOR/2008-169, ss 1, 2, 3(1), 2(Fr), (3), 4(Fr), refers to "ship the books" and books "in stock" as well as books in a requested "format," which is defined in terms of binding and paper quality.

exposed to downward price pressure vis-à-vis digital download offerings of foreign provenance that require zero production costs.[98] Although of obvious benefit to consumers, this diminishes or eliminates gains for Canadian distributors of copyrighted products and likely lessens the overall return to the first copyright holder who is unable to benefit from differential pricing in segregated markets.[99]

A second dimension of the exhaustion doctrine is that once the copyright holder sells or transfers ownership in a copy, her rights in the copy are "exhausted," that is, she can no longer control the use or disposition of that copy. In *Théberge*, Binnie J effectively endorsed the principle of exhaustion by upholding the purchaser's right to make legitimate uses of her copies. In that case, a purchaser of poster copies was found not to have infringed copyright by transforming paper posters to canvas-backed posters without, in that process, making additional copies.

The Act is silent on the issue of exhaustion rights for consumers, leading to the inference that digital copies should be treated the same as physical copies in this respect. Caselaw in other jurisdictions (also with established rules of exhaustion), however, has not extended exhaustion to digital products.[100] The main policy concern against digital

---

98 Digital transmissions are zero-cost and do not require the inputs that physical copies do, for example, transportation costs and raw materials such as paper and ink. See Petar Cimentarov, "The Exhaustion of Copyright in the Digital Environment: Are the Rules Suitable to Deal with Digitally Transmitted Goods? A Comparative Approach between the USA and the EU" (Master's Thesis, University of Ghent, 2010–11) at 24.

99 This, in turn, could lessen the incentive to create. It should be mentioned that price discrimination in segregated markets can benefit global welfare as the copyright holder is able to offer her product to poorer countries at reduced costs without concern for trade leakage back into developed country markets (where the price is higher).

100 US *Copyright Act*, 17 USC §§ 101–810, s 109 (first sale doctrine), which allows the owner of a copy to sell or transfer that copy, refers only to "copy." Article 4 and recital 28 of the EC, *Commission Directive 2001/29/EC of the European Parliament and of the Council of 22 May 2001 on the harmonisation of certain aspects of copyright and related rights in the information society*, [2001] OJ, L 167/10 [EC *Directive*], closely mirrors the content of Canadian legislation by referring to tangible objects in connection with the distribution right. German legislation implementing the EC *Directive* was interpreted in such a way as to deny digital exhaustion in connection with the resale of audio book downloads: Oberlandesgericht Hamm 22 U 60/13 (15.05.2014) (translated and summarized by Johannes GroBedekettler). In *Capitol Records v ReDigi*, US Dist Ct Southern Dist of NY, 12 Civ 95 (RJS), the court refused to apply the first sale doctrine to digital resales of music files. However, in that case, the outcome was premised on the fact that the copies needed to effect resale were not "lawfully made" as required for first sale to apply under s 109.

exhaustion is that there is no viable means to ensure that an original purchaser who resells a copy in a secondary market (thereby making a new copy) deletes the original copy purchased. In other words, there is a fear that a digital exhaustion rule will lead to rampant and largely undetectable unauthorized copying to an extent that will undermine the value of the copyright. There is also concern about the unfavourable comparison between physical copies that deteriorate (ultimately leading to the purchase of new copies) and digital copies that never diminish in quality. Moreover, with perfect non-degradable copies, the reseller would compete in the same market as the copyright owner, thus leading to "pure price competition."[101]

Proponents of a digital exhaustion rule counter that it is not fair (or technologically neutral) to give the resale right to physical copies but not to digital ones for which value has been paid. Moreover, a non-exhaustion rule for digital products tilts the balance of interests between copyright holder and purchaser too far in favour of the former.[102] In a series of papers on the topic in connection with the US first publication rule doctrine, Perzanowski and Schultz strongly advocate for digital exhaustion. In their view, there are numerous advantages to digital exhaustion, including increased dissemination of works through lower initial prices and a vibrant secondary market, increased competition between digital platforms when content is not restricted by licensing arrangements, incentive to participate in the legal acquisition of copyright goods, and consumer-driven innovations and legitimate uses with fully owned copies.[103] One theme here is that the alternative to digital exhaustion is a "post copy world" of tethered content through restrictive licensing arrangements.[104]

Exhaustion is premised on the idea of initial sale or transfer of ownership. If content providers license non-exclusive use of their

---

101 Andreas Wiebe, "The Economic Perspective: Exhaustion in the Digital Age" in Lionel Bently, Uma Suthersanen, & Paul Torremans, eds, *Global Copyright: Three Hundred Years since the Statute of Anne, from 1709 to Cyberspace* (Cheltenham, UK: Edward Elgar, 2010) at 324.
102 Tomasz Targosz, "Exhaustion in Digital Products and the 'Accidental' Impact on the Balance of Interests in Copyright Law" in Bently, Suthersanen, & Torremans, *ibid* at 349.
103 Aaron Perzanowski & Jason Schultz, "Legislating Digital Exhaustion" (2015) 29 *Berkeley Technology Law Journal* 1535 at 1537-38.
104 *Ibid* at 1539-41.

products — rather than outright sale — then exhaustion can never be triggered. The copyright holder will not have alienated their interest in the copy, but will retain control through licensing terms. The reality is that many digital products are already "tethered" through licensing arrangements. As Perzanowski and Schultz document, Amazon's Kindle and MP3 stores, as well as Apple's iTunes Store, restrict the consumer who purchases a book or music file from, *inter alia*, reselling the copy.[105]

One might think that courts would defer to market characterizations of whether a digital product is transferred or merely licensed for use. But in some jurisdictions, courts have intervened to characterize the substance of the transaction as a sale notwithstanding licensing provisions designed to contract out of exhaustion.[106] Perzanowski and Schultz propose the following factor analysis to determine whether a sale has occurred: "(1) the duration of the consumer possession or access; (2) whether the payment structure is one-time or ongoing; and (3) the characterization of the transaction communicated to the consumer, including whether it is referred to as a sale or purchase."[107] Such steps will be necessary if courts wish to preserve an effective exhaustion doctrine in the digital context.

There are very strong dicta in the Supreme Court case of *Théberge* in support of purchaser rights. In that case, the Court reasoned that copyright should not unduly "create practical obstacles to proper utilization"[108] nor create "elusive distinctions"[109] about the kinds of uses that can be made of purchased products. A Canadian court faced with the issue of digital exhaustion will have to account for this strong reasoning in favour of consumer rights.

There is yet another dimension to the digital exhaustion issue. Where market or judicially imposed transfers of digital products do occur, there is the question of the extent of a purchaser's rights. As Binnie J commented in *Théberge*:

---

105 *Ibid* at 1543.
106 See Targosz, above note 102 at n 4 and accompanying text: the German Federal Supreme Court ruled that a copyright holder's rights in a product are exhausted once "it has been put on the market" regardless of what the licensing conditions might say.
107 Perzanowski & Schultz, above note 103 at 1554.
108 *Théberge*, above note 16 at para 32.
109 *Ibid* at para 40.

I do not foreclose the possibility that a change of substrate could, as part of a more extensive set of changes, amount to reproduction in a new form (perhaps, for example, if the respondent's work were incorporated by the ink transfer method into some other artist's original work) but the present case does not rise to that level.[110]

The implication here is that, even though no additional copy is made, new expressive content resulting from (for example) the mashing of two works implicates the right of the copyright holder to reproduce the work in a new expressive form.[111] However, it is a question of degree as to what constitutes a cosmetic change, within the purchaser's rights, as opposed to a new original expression that implicates the economic rights of the copyright holder. There are many relatively easy ways to alter digital copies, and so this issue may become prominent should exhaustion apply to digital products. For example, there now exist apps that promise to delete bad language from e-books.[112] While such a modification seems clearly in the domain of purchaser rights, more radical modifications, such as the juxtaposing of excerpts from two or more books, could cross the line into owner rights.

## 5) Authorization

A separate and distinct right is to "authorize" any of the copyright holder rights mentioned in section 3. The right is particularly relevant to various types of intermediaries that may facilitate acts of infringement. In the digital context, these intermediaries may be makers of technological devices, or those who provide Internet services or host websites that permit infringing activities. Special provisions of the Act have been adopted to address certain types of intermediary activities (these are the subject of Chapter 7). Notwithstanding those special provisions, the authorization right stands on its own and is, as with all section 3 rights, of general application and exclusive to the copyright holder.

---

110 *Ibid* at para 41.
111 In terms of a statutory basis for this right, the Court seems to imply that this would constitute reproduction "in any material form whatever" as per s 3.
112 For example, Clean Reader.

In both the 2004 cases of *CCH* and *CAIP*, the Court considered the meaning of "authorizing" copyright infringement.[113] In *CCH*, the specific issue was whether self-service photocopier machines located in the Great Library constituted an implicit "authorization" on the part of the library for patrons to commit copyright infringement. The Court held that

> "[a]uthorize" means to "sanction, approve, countenance". Countenance in the context of authorizing copyright infringement must be understood in its strongest dictionary meaning, namely, "[g]ive approval to; sanction, permit; favour, encourage." Authorization is a question of fact that depends on the circumstances of each particular case and can be inferred from acts that are less than direct and positive, including a sufficient degree of indifference. However, a person does not authorize infringement by authorizing the mere use of equipment that could be used to infringe copyright. Courts should presume that a person who authorizes an activity does so only so far as it is in accordance with the law. The presumption may be rebutted if it is shown that a certain relationship of control existed between the alleged authorizer and the persons who committed the copyright infringement.[114]

There are two key points in this passage. First, authorization *may* arise where there is a "sufficient degree of indifference" in terms of facilitating an infringement by a third party. Second, there is a presumption against authorization based on the provision of technology, but this may be rebutted by a relationship of control.

On this second point and in the context of Internet intermediary liability for illegal downloading by customers in the *CAIP* case, the Court cited the *CCH* case in finding that Internet service providers do not "authorize" infringement by merely providing connectivity:

> ... but it is true here, as it was in *CCH* case, that when massive amounts of non-copyrighted material are accessible to the end user, it is not possible to impute to the Internet Service Provider, based solely on the provision of Internet facilities, an authority to download copyrighted material as opposed to non-copyrighted material.[115]

---

113   Section 3 of the Act provides, as a distinct right at its end, "... and to authorize any such acts," also known as the "authorization right."
114   *CCH*, above note 24 at para 38 [internal citations omitted].
115   *CAIP*, above note 54 at para 123.

The essence of this holding is that the mere sale or provision of products or services that have substantial non-infringing uses will not, without more, invite copyright infringement.[116] But whereas a relationship of *control* was the basis for authorization in the analogue library environment, *knowledge* of the intermediary Internet service provider was the test in the Internet context.[117] As discussed in Chapter 1, this difference in formulation of the test was intended to accommodate the differences between digital and analogue technologies in order to achieve technological neutrality, so as not to unduly burden Internet service providers with copyright liability.

As *CCH* instructs, the presumption that technology will be used for a legal purpose may be rebutted. *Sirius Canada Inc v CMRRA/SODRAC Inc* provided the Federal Court of Appeal with an opportunity to test the strength of this presumption. At issue was the provision of a radio receiver by Sirius to its subscribers that buffered forty-four to sixty minutes of programming to facilitate pause or playback features for viewers. The Federal Court of Appeal accepted the Copyright Board's characterization of buffering for this purpose as copying.[118] The Copyright Board found, as fact, that Sirius had the ability to program their receivers to prevent this copying. The Federal Court of Appeal determined that the presumption against authorizing infringement was rebutted by the relationship of control that the satellite radio station had with its subscribers:

> Because the copying is automatic, the only control that can be exercised over copying initiated by the subscriber rests with the satellite

---

116 See also *Sony Corp of America v Universal City Studios*, 464 US 417 (1984), which considered whether the sale of videocassette recorders, which had infringing and non-infringing uses, constituted contributory infringement under US copyright law. At 442:

> The staple article of commerce doctrine must strike a balance between a copyright holder's legitimate demand for effective — not merely symbolic — protection of the statutory monopoly, and the rights of others freely to engage in substantially unrelated areas of commerce. Accordingly, the sale of copying equipment, like the sale of other articles of commerce, does not constitute contributory infringement if the product is widely used for legitimate, unobjectionable purposes. Indeed, it need merely be capable of substantial noninfringing uses.

117 See, for example, *CAIP*, above note 54 at para 124: "copyright liability may well attach if the activities of the Internet Service Provider cease to be content neutral, e.g. if it has notice that a content provider has posted infringing material on its system and fails to take remedial action."

118 *Sirius*, above note 88.

radio service providers. They alone know what is being broadcast and when, and what broadcast content is subject to copyright. They alone have chosen to supply their subscribers with receivers that preclude them from exercising any choice as to what is copied in the extended buffer once the receiver is turned on....[119]

The fact that the defendant in this case was the *provider* of both the technology (the receiver) and the copyrighted content is a critical factor that distinguished it from content-neutral libraries or Internet service providers.

What is the status of hyperlinking to copyrighted material in relation to the authorization right? One issue is whether a person who provides hyperlinks on their web page (say, a blog) which automatically connects a reader to another web page (say, a copyrighted newspaper article) is liable for authorizing infringement. In *Nils Svensson and Others v Retriever Sverige AB*,[120] the European Court of Justice considered this very issue. The court first considered the underlying right, being the "making available to the public" right. Since the original article, as it appeared on the plaintiff's web page, was open to all to view, the court determined that the right to make the work available to the public had not been infringed. This was because the hyperlinking did not make the work available to a "new public" but part of the larger public that were "potential recipients of the initial communication." The court also noted that the result would have been different if the hyperlink connected the work to a new public, for example, if the plaintiff's website was restricted or subscriber based.

*Svensson* illustrates quite well that one can not authorize infringement if the underlying right (in that case, the making available right) is not infringed. How might a Canadian court view hyperlinking to content behind a paywall in terms of infringing the authorization right? Surely, there is a relationship of control between an infringer and the content to which she decides to hyperlink. Moreover, a knowledge requirement seems inappropriate on such facts since the reason for that rule in *CAIP* had to do with the prodigious amount of content to be

---

119 *Ibid* at para 28.
120 (13 February 2014), C-466/12 (Court of Justice of the European Union (Fourth Chamber)) [*Svensson*].

monitored by an intermediary in absence of such a standard. For these reasons, hyperlinking to infringing content may infringe the authorization right.

There is support for a different interpretation based on the Supreme Court's decision in *Crookes v Newton*.[121] In the context of whether hyperlinking constitutes re-publication of defamatory material (admittedly a different question than authorizing infringement), quite different perspectives were expressed by different members of the Court. The majority view was that hyperlinking was no more than referencing information; it does not involve any element of control over the creation or change to the defamatory material. Perhaps most revealing was the following reasoning in that judgment:

> The Internet cannot, in short, provide access to information without hyperlinks. Limiting their usefulness by subjecting them to the traditional publication rule would have the effect of seriously restricting the flow of information and, as a result, freedom of expression.[122]

A minority concurring opinion, authored by the Chief Justice, viewed the majority's holding as too broad. In her view, publication would occur if the defendant endorsed the defamatory material (a general reference to the website was not enough). Both of these judgments are encouraging for those who would seek to shield passive hyperlinking from copyright liability.

## D. MORAL RIGHTS

The Act establishes a separate regime of moral rights that specifically protect certain enduring interests that an author has in her work. These rights are not transferable to others though they may be waived, in whole or in part, by the author.[123] They consist of a right of paternity, a right of association, and a right of integrity.

The right of paternity requires that a work be attributed to an author (whether by name or pseudonym) where it is reasonable in the

---

121  2011 SCC 47.
122  *Ibid* at para 36.
123  Section 14.1(2). A waiver in whole or in part of moral rights attaches to the work for subsequent licensees unless there is an indication to the contrary: s 14(4).

circumstances to do so.[124] This right seeks to protect the goodwill and reputation that attaches to a work to the benefit of an author even after copyright in the work has been sold.[125] There are many situations where compliance with this rule is eminently reasonable, for example, ensuring that the name of the artist is referenced underneath a digital image of an artwork. However, there may be situations where attribution would be unreasonable, and thus the requirement would be dispensed with. It would be cumbersome, for example, for a radio disc jockey to mention the song writers of every song broadcast. Similar concerns might apply to works created through large-scale collaboration over the Internet, for example, software programs.

The right of integrity seeks to protect a work from being used or modified in a way that injures the author's honour or reputation. There are two ways in which the author's reputation may be harmed. In the first instance, the work is "used in association with a product, service, cause or institution."[126] This might occur where a song is used for a political rally or cause that is antithetical to the known views of the author, and presumably much of his fan base as well. Second, an author may experience detriment to honour or reputation through the distortion or even modification of his work. In *Snow v Eaton Centre Ltd*, the court held that the draping of the plaintiff's flock of geese sculpture with ribbons during the Christmas season constituted a moral rights violation.[127] The court found prejudice to honour and reputation based on the subjective feelings of the author as well as the opinions of "a number of other well respected artists and people knowledgeable in the field." Expert opinion or possibly evidence of public reaction[128] will therefore be needed to support harm to honour or reputation as subjectively experienced by the author. An interesting question, for which there is no authority in

---

124  Section 14.1(1). It also provides for the right to be anonymous. These rights are connected to acts done under s 3.
125  See *Enrietti-Zoppo v Colla*, [2007] OJ No 5183 (Sm Cl Ct), where removal of the author's name was found actionable under the right of integrity, as it constituted a modification that prejudiced her reputation by not providing the plaintiff with the opportunity to promote herself. See also *Boudreau v Lin* (1997), 150 DLR (4th) 324 (Ont Ct Gen Div).
126  Section 28.2(1).
127  (1982), 70 CPR (2d) 105 (Ont HCJ).
128  See *Prise de Parole Inc c Guerin* (1995), 66 CPR (3d) 257 at para 26 (FCTD) [emphasis added]: "also requires an objective evaluation of the prejudice based on *public* or expert opinion."

Canadian law, is whether a fair dealing of work, for example, its use for parody, may give rise to an infringement of the integrity right, to the extent that the parody lessens the author's reputation.

The contours of the integrity right in the digital environment remain largely unexplored and reflect this tension between fair dealing and moral rights. In a remix culture, where amateurs can modify digital works with relative ease, the incidence of work modification is sure to increase. There are competing goals here. In one sense, expressive uses of works through remix are to be encouraged; on the other hand, in addition to the author's honour and reputation, there is a concern that original works will not be preserved or recognized — either because of repeated modification or widespread dissemination of modified versions.[129] There is also the issue of how digitization affects the quality of reproduction of works. In *Kelly v Aribba Soft Corp*,[130] the reproduction of low-quality thumbnails was essential to the search engine's argument that the use was fair (since it did not compete with the original), but that same issue gives rise to a right of integrity issue: is that lower-quality image a threat to the author's honour and reputation?

★ ★ ★ ★ ★

Despite numerous court decisions and a substantial amendment to the Act, fundamental issues about copyright in the digital age are unresolved. The most obvious of these, discussed above, are the status of incidental copying relative to the reproduction right and digital exhaustion doctrine. The uncertainty in the law is not exclusively tied to digital issues, nor is it always tied to legal silence. As an example of the former, the relationship between economic and moral rights in copyright has never been addressed in the law. The malleability, and large-scale distribution, of works in the digital age may bring this issue to a head.

---

129  See Borghi & Karapapa, above note 62 at 120–21.
130  336 F3d 811 (9th Cir 2003).

CHAPTER 3

# Neighbouring Rights and Collective Management

## A. INTRODUCTION

A separate scheme of copyrights is in place under the *Copyright Act* for subject matter other than works of authorship: performers' performances, sound recordings, and broadcasts. These rights, which are discussed in Section B, will be referred to as "neighbouring rights," as they are in the United States. These rights do not arise through an act of authorship or by satisfying the originality standard or even by necessarily being expressive. Instead, they subsist by meeting definitional criteria. Many of these rights are the same as the rights given to works of authorship. The regime of neighbouring rights is rather complicated, and summaries of these provisions remain dense paraphrases of the various provisions. In this chapter an effort is made to describe the law in accessible language and to highlight the practical significance of main provisions.

Section C discusses the legal regime of collective management that administers copyright and neighbouring rights on behalf of their owners. Collective management is aimed at lowering transaction costs, such as search, negotiation, and enforcement, for copyright holders as well as users. For example, just think of how difficult it might be for a radio station to find rightholders and negotiate with them the licences for the musical works, sound recordings, and performers' performances that are connected with their broadcasts. It would similarly be difficult for copyright holders to collect the royalties due to them on a per-transaction basis. The idea behind collective management is that a single entity representing a catalogue of certain kinds of copyrighted material sets and collects fees on behalf of the copyright owners.

The two topics of this chapter — neighbouring rights and collective management — are tied together since many of the former are administered by entities or regimes of the latter. In particular, collective management societies serve as the primary means by which neighbouring rights are realized in a practical sense. For this reason, the two topics are presented together. However, collective management can apply to authored work copyrights, as well. In fact, some of the biggest and most powerful collective management societies, such as SOCAN (Society of Composers, Authors and Music Publishers of Canada), administer such rights.

## B. NEIGHBOURING RIGHTS

### 1) Performers' Performances

From the outset, it is important to distinguish between two different kinds of performance in copyright law: *performance as a right*, and *performers' performances as subject matter*. The first kind is the *right* to perform in public and the right to communicate to the public by telecommunication; it is part of the bundle of rights given to an authored work or neighbouring right. The second kind, performers' performances, is the *subject* of protection as a neighbouring right which, akin to a work of authorship, is accorded its own bundle of rights. Here, we are discussing the second kind, performers' performances as subject matter.

A performer, for example, a backup musician or a mime artist, has a copyright in her performance of certain works under section 15 of the *Copyright Act*. A *performance* is defined under the Act broadly to mean "any acoustic or visual representation of a work, performer's performance, sound recording or communication signal . . . ." A *performer's performance* is defined as a performance of an artistic, dramatic, or musical work whether or not that work is previously fixed, or recorded, or its copyright term has expired. The definition also specifically includes a "recitation or reading of a literary work" and an "improvisation of a dramatic work, musical or literary work whether or not the improvised work is based on a pre-existing work." The basic effect of these definitions is that the copyright applies to the sound or visual *performance* that is, in most cases, based on a *work*. Thus, the host of a poker game show does not have a copyright in his performance since the underlying subject matter — a game — is not protected as a work.[1] On the other hand, a session musician who plays a piano composition *would* have a performer's copyright since the underlying work *is* protected.

There are three regimes of rights accorded to performers' performances under the Act and that reflect Canada's treaty commitments: a World Intellectual Property Organization (WIPO) treaty, the *International Convention for the Protection of Performers, Producers of Phonograms and Broadcasting Organizations*, which is known as the *Rome Convention*; the World Trade Organization's *Agreement on Trade-Related Aspects of Intellectual Property*, or *TRIPS Agreement*; and the *WIPO Performances and Phonograms Treaty*, or *WPPT*.[2] These three regimes are set out in the following sections of the Canadian *Copyright Act*: section 15 (*Rome Convention*), section 15(1.1) (*WPPT*), and section 26 (*TRIPS Agreement*). Each regime applies to a performance that occurs in Canada or in a respective treaty country. In fact, that is the only basis for application of section 26 (*TRIPS Agreement*). In both the *Rome Convention* and the *WPPT*, two additional bases for application are indicated: a transmission of the communication signal broadcasting the performance occurs in Canada or a respective treaty country; or the maker of the sound recording in which the performance is fixed is a national (or equivalent) of Canada or a respective treaty country, or that is where the sound recording is first published.[3] Each regime grants similar rights to performers' performances

---

1    See *Tokatlidis v MxN Media Corp*, [2009] OJ No 6030 (SCJ). The reason given in this case was that the host's commentary or performance could not be characterized as an artistic, dramatic, musical, or literary work. This interpretation of what constitutes a performer's performance appears incorrect based on a plain reading of s 15 of the Act.

2    *International Convention for the Protection of Performers, Producers of Phonograms and Broadcasting Organisations*, Can TS 1998 No 21 [*Rome Convention*]; *Agreement on Trade-Related Aspects of Intellectual Property Rights, Including Trade in Counterfeit Goods*, (1994) IIC 209 [*TRIPS Agreement*]; *WIPO Performances and Phonograms Treaty*, Can TS 2014 No 21 [*WPPT*].

3    Since the WTO's *TRIPS Agreement* has 161 member states, including the United States and European Union, s 26 will apply to most performances in the world. The *Rome Convention* has the next highest number of member states at ninety-two, but does *not* include the United States. The *WPPT* includes the United States but has only fifty members.

but with some important variations. In general terms, these rights pertain to a performer's live performance, to fixation of that performance, and to making copies of that fixed performance. The rights extend to the entire performance or "a substantial part thereof."

All three regimes confer the right of the performer to communicate her unfixed *live performance* to the public by telecommunication. Essentially, the performer has a right to broadcast the live performance by radio or TV or to stream by way of the Internet. All regimes also provide for a right to "fix," or record, the performance onto a tangible medium. This right is more expansive for the *Rome Convention* and the *WPPT* in that the right extends to fixation *in any material form* whereas, for the *TRIPS Agreement*, it is a right to fix the performance into a sound recording only. The *Rome Convention* and *WPPT* regimes are obviously more beneficial to performers since fixation rights could extend to any number of formats or mediums, including visual displays of the musical performance.

The regimes diverge significantly on the reproduction rights of fixed performances. The *TRIPS Agreement* effectively grants performers reproduction rights to sound recordings to their performances but only when fixation occurs *without* their consent. The *Rome Convention* offers reproduction rights not just to sound recordings but to any fixation of the performance that is made without the performer's consent or where reproduction is for a purpose *other than* that for which fixation was authorized by the performer. The general idea behind these provisions is to limit compensation to performers in the form of either a fixation right or a reproduction right but not usually both. The *WPPT* is more generous to performers in that it gives them both rights; however, it is limited to sound recordings only. Unlike the other regimes, the *WPPT* also gives a making available right (on-demand Internet streams, but not TV or radio) and a distribution right to sound recordings of performers' performances.

Each regime, therefore, offers performers different advantages. The main advantage of the *Rome Convention* is that performers have an extensive set of media rights (not just sound recordings) in their performances. But since the United States is not a treaty member, performances in that country may not be included. However, if sound recordings are the only or main enduring product after the performance, then the *WPPT* offers a more expansive set of rights, including reproduction, making available, and distribution. Although only fifty countries are members

CHAPTER 3: NEIGHBOURING RIGHTS AND COLLECTIVE MANAGEMENT

of this regime, it does include the United States. The only advantage to applying section 26 (*TRIPS Agreement*) from a performer's perspective is if the performance occurs in a country other than a *Rome Convention* or *WPPT* member country. In other words, the *TRIPS Agreement* does not offer any substantive legal advantage over the other two regimes.

Many of the rights granted under sections 15, 15(1.1), and 26 of the Act will be the subject matter of negotiations between performers and various media producers. Typically, performer rights will be assigned or licensed to these producers in exchange for royalties or some other form of compensation. Section 16 of the *Copyright Act* is explicit in preserving contractual rights of performers in connection with certain section 15 (*Rome Convention*) rights. Section 17 may help shield inexperienced filmmakers who do not secure the proper copyright clearances by contract from hired actors. This matter arose in US copyright law in the ongoing case of an actress asserting her copyright in the film *The Innocence of Muslims*. Section 17 provides that a performer cannot assert her performance rights where she has "authorized the embodiment of [her] performance in a cinematographic work." The use of the word "authorized" provides ample room for movie makers to claim a waiver of copyright by an actor through word or conduct and not in writing. There is a loophole, however, in that the bar applies only to section 15, not performer rights under sections 15(1.1) and 26.

Finally, the 2012 *Copyright Modernization Act* extends moral rights protections to performers' performances. It did so by adding "performer's performance" to the right of integrity and right of association contained in section 28.2 of the Act. As such, moral rights caselaw in connection with authored works, discussed in chapter 2, should apply *mutatis mutandis* to all performers' performances. A more specific provision is set out for *WPPT* performances in section 17.1. In addition to section 28.2 protections, this grants a right of association to a "live aural performance or a performance fixed in sound recording."

## 2) Sound Recordings

Sound recordings are entitled to monopoly protections under the *Copyright Act*. *Sound recording* is defined broadly to mean a "recording, fixed in any material form, consisting of sounds, whether or not of a performance of a work." Although the right is normally advanced in connection with music, the definition is not that restrictive. The definition also excludes "any soundtrack of a cinematographic work *where it accompanies the cinematographic work.*" The wording shown as italicized was cited recently by the Supreme Court in its holding that music that is sold separately from a movie it is associated with is still a sound recording.[4]

Sound recording rights inure to the benefit of the *maker* of the sound recording. The maker is the person who undertakes "the arrangements necessary for the first fixation of the sounds." Those arrangements include financial and technical aspects as well as the entering into contracts with the performers.[5] As the court in *Pinto v Bronfman Jewish Education Centre* clarified, the maker is not necessarily the person who makes the essential arrangements for producing the sound recording but instead is "the individual or corporation that bore the financial risk of doing so, such as a record company."[6] Often, the maker will be the record company, though where a musician makes her own recordings, this right will obviously be hers.

The regime of rights accorded to sound recordings is less complicated than for performers' performances. As with the latter, protection under the *Copyright Act* is given to sound recordings whose makers are Canadian or certain foreign nationals (or equivalents) or where first publication occurs in Canada or in a treaty country. Section 18(1) applies to virtually all sound recordings, since the maker need only be a national (or equivalent) of Canada or of any of the countries covered by the three treaties — *Rome Convention, TRIPS Agreement,* the *WPPT* — or alternatively, first publication occurs in Canada or in one of the treaty countries. The right to reproduce the sound recording "in any material form" is the most lucrative of the section 18 bundle of rights since it includes copies made of the sound recordings per se and their synchronization into visual media, such as videos. Section 18 rights also include the rights to first publication of the sound recording, to rent out the sound recording, and to authorize any of the acts mentioned in the provision.

Where the maker of a sound recording is a Canadian or *WPPT* member national (or equivalent) or first publication occurs in Canada or in a *WPPT* member country, the maker is also entitled to making available

---

4  Re:Sound v Motion Picture Theatre Associations of Canada, 2012 SCC 38 at para 6 [emphasis added].
5  Section 2.11.
6  2013 FC 945 at para 144.

and distribution rights. The making available right is essentially a right exclusive to on-demand streaming services on the Internet. The performing rights related to sound recordings (and performers' performances) through push technologies, such as radio and TV, are captured under a "right of equitable remuneration," discussed next.

## 3) Equitable Remuneration

The regime of rights for sound recordings and performers' performances offers a limited performing right, in particular, a making available right under the *WPPT* regime. Noticeably absent from these provisions is the right to communicate sound recordings and performers' performances to the public by telecommunication or the general right of performance in public. These are dealt with through a right of equitable remuneration, which applies to all published sound recordings whose maker is a national (or equivalent) of Canada or of one of the countries under the *Rome Convention*, *TRIPS Agreement*, or the *WPPT*, or if fixation of the sound recording happens in one of these places.

The beneficiaries of this right are both makers of sound recordings and performers. It is a very lucrative right particularly since it applies to all push technology broadcasts of a work, most commonly radio and TV. Since the sections explicitly exclude the making available right, equitable remuneration does not apply to on-demand delivery models over the Internet. The nature of the equitable remuneration right is unique. Anyone who publicly performs sound recordings is obliged to pay a tariff to the collective management society that administers the rights.[7] According to caselaw, equitable remuneration is not an exclusive right and holders cannot bring an infringement action against a person who performs the sound recording without authorization.[8] Their only recourse is through the society responsible for collecting any applicable tariff.

---

[7] Except where it is a sound recording of a literary or dramatic work in which case it is payable directly to either the maker of the sound recording or the performer: s 19.2.

[8] *Re:Sound v Fitness Industry Council of Canada*, 2014 FCA 48 at para 10; *Astral Media Radio Inc v Society of Composers, Authors and Music Publishers of Canada*, 2010 FCA 16 at para 20.

## 4) Broadcasts

Section 21 of the Act protects "communication signals" of a "broadcaster." Both of these terms are defined in section 2. A broadcaster is a body that operates a "broadcasting undertaking" in accordance with the laws of the country in which it carries on, and which broadcasts a communication signal. It does not include "a body whose primary activity in relation to communication signals is their retransmission." *Broadcasting undertaking* is not defined in the Act although it is central to the regulatory regime of the *Broadcasting Act*. According to Professor Howell, the categories of broadcasting undertaking under that Act "reflect the media of radio, television, and cable distribution — historically the ambit of broadcasting for all practical purposes."[9] However, Professor Howell also notes that certain new media, such as YouTube, would meet the definitional requirements of broadcasting undertaking.[10] If we import this analysis of "broadcasting undertaking" into the *Copyright Act*, then YouTube transmissions (and a host of other Internet content distribution entities) would be protected as copyrighted broadcasts. This is all the more so since *communication signal* is broadly defined as "radio waves transmitted through space without any artificial guide, for reception by the public."[11]

The scope of protection under the Act is broad in that it is afforded to broadcasters located in, or communication signals emanating from, Canada or *Rome Convention* or *TRIPS Agreement* member countries. The rights enjoyed by broadcasters in their communication signals are fixation, reproduction (if fixation is made without consent), simultaneous retransmission to the public by another broadcaster, performance in a public place on payment of an entrance fee (in the case of a TV signal), and authorization. In the recent case *American Broadcasting Cos v Aereo, Inc*,[12] the US Supreme Court found copyright infringement where an Internet service allowed subscribers to stream programs simultaneously with the TV broadcast. Under Canadian law, this would run afoul of the simultaneous retransmission right under section 21 if the subscription service could be classified as a broadcaster (see discussion above). The

---

9   Robert Howell, *Canadian Telecommunications Law* (Toronto: Irwin Law, 2011) at 98.
10  *Ibid*.
11  According to Howell, *ibid* at 233, this would not include encrypted signals since these are not "to the public."
12  573 US ___ (2014).

CHAPTER 3: NEIGHBOURING RIGHTS AND COLLECTIVE MANAGEMENT

right to rebroadcast a communication signal, that is, to communicate to the public by telecommunication, is curiously absent from the list of rights. This may be because rebroadcast implies fixation, a right that is granted to broadcasts.

## C. COLLECTIVE MANAGEMENT OF COPYRIGHT

Collective management regimes are premised on owners of works or neighbouring rights licensing or assigning relevant copyrights to a collective society for it to administer. A collective society seeks out licensing fees (usually through the setting of tariffs through the Copyright Board) and subsequently collects these fees from users of a catalogue of works. The money is then funnelled back to copyright owners less an administrative fee. As suggested in the Introduction, this can be an efficient method by which copyright owners get paid and users are able to obtain copyright clearances. There are four regimes of collective management under the Act: (1) musical performing rights, (2) the general regime, (3) private copying, and (4) retransmission and certain uses by educational institutions.[13]

The musical performing rights regime is limited to a subset of works and neighbouring rights subject matter: musical works, dramatico-musical works, performers' performances of such works, and sound recordings embodying such works. The rights administered are the right to performance in public and the right to communicate a work to the public by telecommunication.[14] These implicate the right to equitable remuneration to the extent that such performances relate to performers' performances and sound recordings (sections 19 and 20).

This regime requires collective societies to propose tariffs that are ultimately to be set by the Copyright Board, thus supplanting any room for negotiation of fees directly with users of repertoire works. Where the collective society fails to propose a tariff for which a work is performed, no action for infringement can be brought against the user.[15] In other words, "without the tariff, there is, practically speaking, no right

---

13   Daniel Gervais, "Collective Management of Copyright and Neighboring Rights in Canada: An International Perspective" (2002) 1 *Canadian Journal of Law and Technology* 21.
14   For the telecommunication right, the s 31(2) right is excluded from this regime: s 67(b).
15   Section 67.1(4).

to compensation."[16] It is also the case that a user who pays or offers to pay the royalties of a tariff is insulated against any action for infringement.[17] The biggest and most famous of the musical performing rights collective societies is SOCAN (Society of Composers, Authors and Music Publishers), which administers rights for composers and publishers of musical works.

A voluntary regime of collective administration of copyright is available for works, performers' performances, sound recordings, and broadcast signals in respect of rights under sections 3, 15, 18, and 21. Unlike performing rights societies, these collectives are free to pursue licensing deals with individual users. In fact, "in the general regime, such agreements trump the tariff."[18] Tariffs may be submitted to the Copyright Board for approval either for a class of uses or to fix, or set, royalties in individual cases. Users who pay or offer to pay royalties that are set by the Copyright Board are immune to infringement proceedings.

In 1997, a unique regime was set up under Part VII of the Act to compensate owners of musical works (both composers and publishers), as well as makers of, and performers in sound recordings for the private copying by consumers of sound recordings. The general aim of the regime is to place a levy on blank media that are ordinarily used for such copying of sound recordings, for example, cassette tapes and CDs. The levy is to be paid by the manufacturer and importers of these blank recording mediums with that cost presumably being passed on to the consumer. Despite the technologically neutral wording of the regime, the Federal Court of Appeal refused to extend the private copy levy to MP3 players.[19] The regime was thus effectively frozen in time. In any event, the language of the provision bears little relevance to current methods of consuming music.[20] Further, the *Copyright Modernization Act*

---

16   *Entertainment Software Association v Society of Composers, Authors and Music Publishers*, 2010 FCA 221 at para 18.
17   Section 68.2(2).
18   *Re Reproduction of Sound Recordings*, 2008 CarswellNat 516 at para 11 (Copyright Board); and s 70.191.
19   See *Canadian Private Copying Collective v Canadian Storage Media Alliance*, 2014 FCA 424. For a criticism of the interpretation of the law in this case, see Cameron Hutchison, "Interpreting Copyright Law and Internet Facts" (2010) 8 *Canadian Journal of Law and Technology* 195.
20   This is true for two reasons: (1) to the extent that people consume music as copies, they do so through multimedia devices (not MP3 players, which only play music), and thus it would not be possible to call digital memory in such devices "ordinarily

permits the making of private copies in digital formats while explicitly excluding this exception from the private copying regime of Part VII.[21]

A special regime of collective administration is established for two specific rights: (1) the making of copies for broadcasts by educational institutions that are not destroyed under the terms of section 29.7(2) and (2) retransmissions of distant signals under section 31(2)(d). To collect under either right, the appropriate collective society is required to file a tariff for certification before the Copyright Board.

*****

There is an absence of caselaw interpreting the neighbouring rights provisions, and thus the preceding is largely an analysis of the statutory text. Many of the neighbouring rights are administered by collective societies which, in turn, apply to the Copyright Board to set tariffs connected to these rights. While much copyright jurisprudence is generated by appeals of Copyright Board interpretations of the *Copyright Act*, this has not been the case for neighbouring rights in particular.

---

used" for making sound recording copies; (2) the regime does not apply to telecommunication and making available rights (only reproductions) and thus would not apply to music streaming.

21    Sections 29.22(2) & (3).

**TABLE 3.1** RIGHTS SPREADSHEET

NOTE: For the purposes of Table 3.1, "WTO" refers to the *Trips Agreement*, and "Rome" refers to the *Rome Convention*. As is established earlier in the chapter, WPPT refers to the *WIPO Performances and Phonograms Treaty*. "SOCAN" is the Society of Composers, Authors and Music Publishers of Canada.

| | Communication of live performance | Fixation | Copying | Copying into new form | Performance | Telecommunication | Making available | Rental | Retransmission |
|---|---|---|---|---|---|---|---|---|---|
| Works | ✓ | | ✓ | ✓ | ✓ | ✓ | ✓ | • Yes for sound recordings<br>• computer programs | |
| Performance Rights | | • ROME and WPPT, all;<br>• WTO, sound recording only | • ROME, all;<br>WPPT and WTO, sound recording only | ✓ (ROME only) | | | • sound recordings, WPPT only | • ROME and WPPT, sound recording only | |
| Sound Recording | | | ✓ | ✓ | | | ✓ (WPPT only) | ✓ | |
| Equitable Remuneration | | | | | ✓ | ✓ | | | |
| Broadcast Signals | | ✓ | ✓ | | ✓ | | | | ✓ |

# CHAPTER 3: NEIGHBOURING RIGHTS AND COLLECTIVE MANAGEMENT

**TABLE 3.2** COLLECTIVE SOCIETIES SUMMARY

| Collective society | Who does the collective represent? | Which works does it represent? | Which specific copyrights does it administer? |
|---|---|---|---|
| Access Copyright | Writers, visual artists, and publishers | Works published in books, magazines, journals, and newspapers | Reproduction rights, performing rights |
| ACTRA Performers' Rights Society | Recording artists | Musical works | Reproduction rights, performing rights, broadcast rights |
| Audio Ciné Films | Canadian, American, and foreign feature film producers | Films | Performing rights |
| Border Broadcasters' Inc. (BBI) | US border broadcasters (a mix of network affliated and independent stations) | Television programs | Broadcast rights |
| Canadian Artists' Representation Copyright Collective | Visual and media artists | Visual arts (photographs, paintings, etc.) | Reproduction rights |
| Canadian Broadcasters Rights Agency | Commercial and independent radio and television stations and private affiliates of CBC and SRC | Radio and television programming | Broadcast rights |
| Canadian Federation of Musicians (CFM) | Professional musicians in Canada | Musical works | Reproduction rights |
| Canadian Musical Reproduction Rights Agency | Over 6,000 Canadian and US publishers who own and administer approx. 75% of Canada's music | Musical works | Reproduction rights |

[97]

| Collective society | Who does the collective represent? | Which works does it represent? | Which specific copyrights does it administer? |
|---|---|---|---|
| Canadian Private Copying Collective | Songwriters, recording artists, music publishers, and record companies | Musical works | Reproduction rights |
| Canadian Retransmission Collective | Canadian and foreign producers and broadcasters | Television programs and music videos | Broadcast rights |
| Canadian Retransmission Right Association (CRRA) | CBC, ABC, NBC, CBS, and Télé-Québec | Radio and television programming | Broadcast rights |
| Canadian Screenwriters Collection Society | Film and television writers | Audiovisual works | Reproduction rights, broadcast rights |
| Christian Copyright Licensing Inc. | Churches and copyright owners | Songs and worship services | Reproduction rights |
| Christian Video Licensing International | Churches and other religious institutions | Copyrighted motion pictures and other audiovisual programs | Performing rights |
| CONNECT Music Licensing | All the major record companies, many independent labels, as well as artists and producers | Sound recordings and music videos | Reproduction rights, broadcast rights |
| COPIBEC | Quebec and Canadian publishers and authors | Newspapers, periodicals, and books | Reproduction rights |
| Copyright Collective of Canada (CCC) | Copyright owners (producers and distributors) of the US motion picture and TV industry | Motion pictures and television programming | Broadcast rights |

# CHAPTER 3: NEIGHBOURING RIGHTS AND COLLECTIVE MANAGEMENT

| Collective society | Who does the collective represent? | Which works does it represent? | Which specific copyrights does it administer? |
|---|---|---|---|
| Criterion Pictures | Many of Hollywood's Major Motion Picture Studios | Films | Performing rights |
| Direct Response Television Collective (DRTVC) | Producers, owners, and distributors of direct response TV programming (infomercials) | Television programming (infomercials) | Broadcast rights |
| Directors Rights Collective of Canada | Film and television directors | Films and television programs | Reproduction rights, performing rights, broadcast rights |
| FWS Joint Sports Claimants (FWS) | NHL, CFL, NBA, and NFL and their member teams | Broadcasts of games | Broadcast rights |
| Major League Baseball Collective of Canada (MLB) | MLB and its member teams | Broadcasts of major league baseball games | Broadcast rights |
| Musicians' Rights Organization Canada | Musicians | Sound recordings | Reproduction rights, performing rights, broadcast rights |
| Playwrights Guild of Canada | Professional playwrights | Stage works | Performing rights, reproduction rights |
| Producers Audiovisual Collective of Canada | Producers and rights holders | Audiovisual works | Reproduction rights, performing rights, broadcast rights |
| Re:Sound Music Licensing Company | Recording artists and record companies | Sound recordings | Reproduction rights, performing rights, broadcast rights |
| SOCAN | Canadian and foreign composers, creators, and publishers | Musical works | Performing rights |

| Collective society | Who does the collective represent? | Which works does it represent? | Which specific copyrights does it administer? |
| --- | --- | --- | --- |
| Société civile des auteurs multimédias (SCAM) | Multimedia authors | Audiovisual documentaries, radio and literary works | Broadcast rights, reproduction rights |
| Société de gestion des droits des artistes-musiciens | Canadian and foreign musicians | Sound recordings | Reproduction rights, performing rights, broadcast rights |
| Société des auteurs et compositeurs dramatiques | Playwrights, screenwriters, composers, producers, choreographers, directors, and other creators | Stage works, audiovisual works, photographic, and radio works | Reproduction rights, performing rights, broadcast rights |
| Société québécoise des auteurs dramatiques | Quebec, Canadian, and foreign playwrights | Stage works | Performing rights |
| SODRAC | Canadian authors, composers and music publisher; also creators in over 90 countries | Musical works, artistic works | Reproduction rights, performing rights |
| SOPROQ | Quebec makers of video and sound recordings | Sound and video recordings | Reproduction rights, performing rights, broadcast rights |
| Union des artistes (UDA) | Actors, singers, entertainers, and dancers | Musical works, sound recordings, and other audio-visual works | Performing rights, reproduction rights, broadcast rights |

**TABLE 3.3** COPYRIGHTS AND COLLECTIVE SOCIETIES

| | Works | Performance Rights | Sound Recording | Equitable Remuneration | Broadcast Signals |
|---|---|---|---|---|---|
| **Communication of live performance** | | • ACTRA<br>• MROC | • CONNECT (musical) | • MROC, Re: Sound (music)<br>• PACC | |
| **Fixation** | • CARCC (visual arts) | • ACTRA (musical) | | • CARCC (visual arts) | |
| **Copying** | • Access Copyright, COPIBEC (literary)<br>• Re:Sound, SODRAC, CMRRA, CPCC (music)<br>• CARCC (visual arts)<br>• CSCS, PACC, SOPROQ (audiovisual) | • ACTRA, MROC, UDA (musical) | • CONNECT (musical)<br>• DRCC (films) | • MROC, SODRAC (musical)<br>• SOPROQ | |
| **Performance** | • SOCAN. CFM (musical)<br>• Audio Ciné, CVLI (films)<br>• Re:Sound (music)<br>• SOQAD (plays) | • PACC<br>• ACTRA (musical) | • SOGEDAM<br>• CONNECT | • ACTRA, Re: Sound (musical)<br>• PGC (literary);<br>UDA (performers) | |
| **Telecommunication** | • SOCAN, CFM, CMRRA (musical)<br>• Access Copyright (literary)<br>• Criterion, CVLI (films) | • ACTRA (musical) | • CONNECT | • DRCC<br>• MROC | |
| **Making available** | • Access Copyright, PGC (literary)<br>• CARCC (visual arts)<br>• CVLI (films) | • ACTRA (musical) | | | |

|  | Works | Performance Rights | Sound Recording | Equitable Remuneration | Broadcast Signals |
|---|---|---|---|---|---|
| Rental | • CSCS, PACC (videos) | • ACTRA (musical) | | | |
| Retransmission | • BBI, CBRA, CRC, CRRA, CCC, DRTVC, FWS, MLB, SCAM, SACD | • ACTRA (musical) | • SCAM | • SCAM | • CBRA, FWS |

CHAPTER 4

# Ownership, Licensing, Registration, and Infringement

## A. INTRODUCTION

This chapter addresses the following practical questions about copyright ownership and matters related to it: Who is entitled to ownership of a copyright? In what circumstances is it advantageous to register a copyright interest? How may a copyright interest be licensed or sold to others? To what extent can provisions in the *Copyright Act* be varied by contract? And what is the nature of copyright infringement action? Two further questions of particular relevance to the digital environment will also be discussed: the nature and legality of open-source licensing, and the rules pertaining to uncovering the identity of purported infringers on the Internet.

## B. OWNERSHIP

The *Copyright Act* designates certain individuals or entities as first owners of a copyright. In the case of neighbouring rights, the first owner is the *performer* in the performance, the *maker* of the sound recording, or the *broadcaster* of a communication signal.[1] In the case of works, the first

---

1   Act, s 24. See discussion of "maker" of the sound recording, as well as "broadcaster," in Chapter 3.

owner of the copyright is the *author* (or authors).[2] One major exception to this rule for works is stipulated in section 13(3):

> Where the author of a work was in the employment of some other person under a contract of service or apprenticeship and the work was made in the course of his employment by that person, the person by whom the author was employed shall, in the absence of any agreement to the contrary, be the first owner of the copyright, but where the work is an article or other contribution to a newspaper, magazine or similar periodical, there shall, in the absence of any agreement to the contrary, be deemed to be reserved to the author a right to restrain the publication of the work, otherwise than as part of a newspaper, magazine or similar periodical.

There are two propositions in this rule. First, there is a negative right of restraint given to an employee journalist over the re-publication of her article without permission. Second, an employer, under certain circumstances, may own the copyright of their employee author.

For an employer to gain ownership of an employee author's copyright, three conditions must be met: (1) there is an employment contract, (2) the work is made in the course of employment, and (3) there is no agreement suggesting otherwise. The first requirement may be met even though the employment contract is unwritten.[3] Problems may arise where the author claims to be an independent operator performing a contract for service rather than an employee. The characterization of employee versus independent operator arises in several legal contexts, including vicarious liability in tort. In that context, the Supreme Court held that such determinations are made after a highly contextualized inquiry though generally courts should look to factors such as degree of control, financial risk, and ownership of equipment to determine the existence of an employment relationship.[4] Second, the work must be

---

2 Section 13(1). See discussion of authorship in Chapter 2.
3 *Century 21 Canada Limited Partnership v Rogers Communications Inc*, 2011 BCSC 1196 [*Century 21*].
4 *671122 Ontario Ltd v Sagaz Industries Canada Inc*, 2001 SCC 59 at para 47:
> The central question is whether the person who has been engaged to perform the services is performing them as a person in business on his own account. In making this determination, the level of control the employer has over the worker's activities will always be a factor. However, other factors to consider include whether the worker provides his or her own equipment, whether the worker hires

created "in the course of employment." Again, this is a factual inquiry. A work that is created both during work hours and during one's own time would be co-owned by both the employee and the employer.[5]

Finally, even if these two conditions are satisfied, there may be an agreement to the contrary which would override employer ownership. Such an agreement need not be contractual nor does it need to be in writing.[6]

## C. LICENSING

### 1) Assignments, Exclusive Licences, and Non-exclusive Licences

An owner may transfer her copyrights, either in whole or in part, by way of assignment or exclusive licence (discussed below). Alternatively, a copyright holder who retains all of his rights may give permission to use a work by way of a non-exclusive licence. The term "non-exclusive" underscores the retention of exclusive ownership interest in the copyright. Non-exclusive licences are typically limited in nature and may be explicit or implied by conduct or circumstances.[7] As an example of the latter, the author (first owner) of a blog entry posted on his website that has a print icon may be said to be implicitly giving permission to readers to print off a copy of the article for personal use. Usually, such implied uses are limited in nature as suggested by the context. There is nothing in the above example that would suggest the copyright holder is authorizing the republication of the blog entry in a newspaper. A similar example is offered in the case of *Labrecque (O Sauna) c Trudel (Centre Bellaza, senc)*, where a Quebec court found infringement when the defendant posted the plaintiff's photograph on its website, which it had obtained on the Internet through a Google Images search.[8] In other words, posting of an image on the Internet is not to be construed as implicitly authorizing someone to re-publish that image on their website.

---

      his or her own helpers, the degree of financial risk taken by the worker, the degree of responsibility for investment and management held by the worker, and the worker's opportunity for profit in the performance of his or her tasks.

5    Normand Tamaro, *The 2015 Annotated Copyright Act* (Toronto: Carswell, 2014) at 433.
6    *Ibid* at 434–35.
7    See, for example, *Tremblay v Orio Canada Inc*, 2013 FC 109 at para 53 [*Tremblay*].
8    2014 QCCQ 2595 [obtained in French from CanLII and translated using Google Translate].

Of course, non-exclusive licences may be explicit. The terms of service of many user-generated content websites provide for a rather expansive set of non-exclusive uses. Facebook, for example, has the following:

> For content that is covered by intellectual property rights, like photos and videos (IP content), you specifically give us the following permission, subject to your privacy and application settings: you grant us a non-exclusive, transferable, sub-licensable, royalty-free, worldwide license to use any IP content that you post on or in connection with Facebook (IP License) .... [9]

Basically, these terms allow the website to use content in any way without compensating uploaders, including a right to sublicense the content to a third party. In financial terms, this means that the website may sell off your content for money with no obligation to share the proceeds with you. Non-exclusive licences, therefore, can amount to much more than a mere permission to use on a limited basis and, in some circumstances, may become quite valuable to the licensee.

Much more valuable to both parties to a transaction are exclusive licences and assignments since the buyer receives exclusivity in exploiting what it considers to be a valuable copyright, and the seller receives valuable consideration — usually money. The *Copyright Act* is permissive in the ways in which rights may be dealt:

> The owner of the copyright in any work may assign the right, either wholly or partially, and either generally or *subject to limitations relating to territory, medium or sector of the market or other limitations relating to the scope of the assignment, and either for the whole term of the copyright or for any other part thereof*, and may grant any interest in the right by licence, but no assignment or grant is valid unless it is in writing signed by the owner of the right in respect of which the assignment or grant is made, or by the owner's duly authorized agent.[10]

The italicized language is indicative of the myriad ways in which copyright in a work is divisible and may be transferred to third parties. Section 13(7) clarifies that a grant of an interest includes an exclusive

---

9  Facebook.com Terms of Service at para 1. Similar language is found in the terms of service for YouTube.ca, twitter.com, Instagram.com, and pinterest.com, among others.
10  Section 13.4 [emphasis added].

licence. Note that these transfers of exclusivity require a document "in writing signed by the owner of the right." The court in *Tremblay v Orio Canada Inc* confirmed that a valid transfer requires both a written document and a signature by the owner of the relevant copyright interest.[11] As happened in that case, the failure to meet one of these conditions, while fatal to the transfer, may still be enough to establish a non-exclusive licence.

In one sense, the legal distinction between an assignment, on the one hand, and an exclusive licence, on the other, is straightforward. An assignment is an outright transfer of a copyright interest to the assignee such that the assignor is completely divested of any present or future ownership interest in what has been transferred. An exclusive licence, by contrast, is a grant of exclusivity to exploit a copyright for a period of time without the licensor relinquishing ultimate ownership.[12] Using a simple comparison, it is not unlike the ownership implications associated with purchasing versus renting a motor vehicle.

In another sense, there is some confusion concerning certain legal implications connected to characterization as either an assignment or exclusive licence. The controversy specifically concerns whether or not, during the term of an exclusive licence, a licensor is allowed to exploit the licensed interest and stems from the inelegant resolution of *Euro-Excellence Inc v Kraft Canada Inc*.[13] In that decision, a highly fractured court rendered three separate opinions to resolve a legal issue concerning parallel imports of chocolate bars bearing copyrighted logos. Justice Rothstein, in a dissenting opinion on this issue, held that an exclusive licence permits a licensee to sue third parties for copyright infringement of the licensed copyright interest but not the owner licensor. In other words, for Rothstein J, the exclusive licence is not really exclusive since the owner licensor retains a right to use the copyrighted interest for itself.

Two other opinions, which together constituted a majority of the Court on this issue, ruled that an exclusive licence can be enforced against an owner licensor as copyright infringement. In other words, the owner licensor has no right to exploit the copyrighted interest

---

11  *Tremblay*, above note 7 at para 47.
12  See, for example, *Century 21*, above note 3 at para 174.
13  2007 SCC 37 at para 28 [*Euro-Excellence*]. For Rothstein J, an exclusive licensee might still have a claim in contract against the owner licensor but not in copyright.

during the term of the exclusive licence and, if she does, would be liable for copyright infringement. In *Canadian Artists' Representation v National Gallery of Canada*[14] Rothstein J, in writing for the entire Court, referenced his minority opinion in *Euro-Excellence* in support of the proposition that a grant of interest must be in writing under section 13(4). That this casual reference would mark a change in the law on such an important and controversial issue seems beyond belief at the level of the Supreme Court of Canada. It must therefore still be the case that an owner licensor does *not* retain any residual interest in a transferred copyright to an exclusive licensee.

When courts need to characterize an agreement as an assignment, exclusive licence, or non-exclusive licence, they consider the "substance of the transaction" rather than merely the superficial language employed to describe the agreement.[15] In *Century 21*, for example, the court found that an agreement that permitted certain uses was non-exclusive even though the term "non-exclusive" was not used in the contract.[16] With respect to contracts granting an interest on exclusive terms, courts presumably would be looking to determine whether the agreement expires or otherwise allows for a reversion of the copyright interest to the owner, for example, a revocable or irrevocable interest, to determine whether it is an exclusive licence or an assignment. Although little may turn on this from a copyright perspective, the characterization of whether a copyright is owned or merely licensed can be critical in areas such as bankruptcy law where, for example, it would be relevant to determine the value of a copyright interest as an asset.

## 2) Contract Law Issues

Copyright interests are frequently assigned and licensed by way of contract. Principles of contract law are therefore of central importance to the formation, validity, and interpretation of such agreements. A discussion of contract principles as it relates to intellectual property licensing is a book unto itself. Here, I intend to address the nature of the

---

14  2014 SCC 42.
15  *Century 21*, above note 3 at para 173, quoting from John S McKeown, *Fox on Canadian Law of Copyright and Industrial Designs*, 3d ed (Scarborough, ON: Carswell, 2000) at 380.
16  *Century 21*, above note 3 at para 175.

## CHAPTER 4: OWNERSHIP, LICENSING, REGISTRATION, AND INFRINGEMENT

fundamental relationship between contract and copyright, as well as a prominent contracting issue that arises in the digital context: terms of use agreements used by websites.

As section 13(4) of the *Copyright Act* suggests, parties to a contract are generally free to agree on terms and conditions connected with the licensing or transfer of a copyright interest. Foresight and skill in drafting clear licensing terms may avoid contentious issues about the scope of a licence. For example, in the kind of fact situation found in *Théberge v Galerie d'Art du Petit Champlain inc*,[17] if the owner restricts the licence to the making of copies to paper-backed posters only, then he may sue for breach of contract (assuming privity) if the defendant transforms them into canvas-backed copies.

Of course, it can be difficult to foresee all possibilities to which a work may be used or exploited under a licence, or the kinds of interpretive arguments a contracting party may advance in litigation. For example, in *Canadian Broadcasting Corp v SODRAC 2003 Inc*, the CBC argued that its synchronization licence with the reproduction rights society included the implied right to make incidental copies for the purpose of broadcasting. The majority opinion of the Supreme Court rejected that argument.[18] Still, it is wise for the parties to be as clear as possible in specifying the authorized uses to which a work is to be made to avoid any possible claims that a licence has been granted in connection with new activities arising from advances in technology.[19] Otherwise, a contract that, for example, transfers "performing rights" of a work may embrace all established or emerging methods of Internet delivery.

An unclear area of the law is the extent to which a party may "contract out" of the provisions of the Act. For example, could parties make a contract dispensing with the co-requirements of writing and signature for valid grants of copyright interests as required by section 13(4)? There is no Canadian authority on this fundamental issue. Presumably, courts would uphold seemingly peremptory provisions in the Act, for example, the prohibition against the assignment of an author's moral

---

17 2002 SCC 34.
18 2015 SCC 57 at para 58.
19 Broadly worded transfers that do not restrict known uses of a work may be interpreted in favour of licensees. See David Vaver, *Copyright Law* (Toronto: Irwin Law, 2000) at 229–30.

rights.[20] Beyond this, it becomes difficult to make principled distinctions between provisions of the Act that can or cannot be contracted out from. In the United States, the American Law Institute has taken the position that "courts should respect freedom of contract and generally enforce provisions affecting intellectual property rights unless they conflict with a mandatory rule of intellectual property law. For example, parties cannot contract around the rule that an oral transfer of copyright ownership is unenforceable."[21] It is not clear, however, why the formalities of contract formation in the copyright context are mandatory rules whereas other provisions in the Act — including the respective rights of the parties — might not be.

Contracts between publishers, on the one hand, and libraries and educational institutions, on the other, frequently contain provisions that effectively prevent these licensees and their clientele from exercising their fair dealing rights. The extent of the practice is such that both the Australian Law Reform Commission and the Hargreaves Report (in the United Kingdom) recommend that their respective copyright legislation be amended to prevent the contracting out of user exceptions.[22] The main argument for this reform is compelling: private ordering should not be allowed to upset the careful balancing of interests achieved through the legislated regime of rights reflected in copyright legislation.[23] This argument has particular force in Canada where the judicial rhetoric of balance, and of user rights, is often framed in inviolate terms. A more technical legal argument could also be made, namely, that such unusual terms need to be specifically brought to the attention of the contracting party who is to be bound by such terms.[24] The argument in favour of contracting out is based in freedom of contract as well as on inferences of statutory interpretation (statutes can be explicit in

---

20  Section 14.1(2).
21  Roberta A Hillman & Maureen O'Rourke, "Principles of the Law of Software Contracts: Some Highlights" (2010) 84 *Tulane Law Review* 1519 at 1526–527.
22  Australian Law Review Commission, *Copyright and the Digital Economy*, ALRC Report 122 (Sydney, AU: ALRC, 2013) at 17.3 [ALRC]; Ian Hargreaves, *Digital Opportunity: A Review of Intellectual Property and Growth* (London: Intellectual Property Office, 2011) at 5.40 [Hargreaves Report].
23  As such, contracting out of fair dealing rights is against public policy, and contract law will not recognize it: see ALRC, above note 22 at 17.37ff.
24  See *Chitty on Contracts*, below note 28 and accompanying text.

## CHAPTER 4: OWNERSHIP, LICENSING, REGISTRATION, AND INFRINGEMENT

proscribing the contracting out of their provisions so when it does not happen, then it must be allowed).[25]

Terms of service agreements are a feature of most websites. The intention behind these agreements is to create enforceable legal duties and obligations on users of the website. As the terms of service examples referenced above in connection with social media or content provider sites suggest, copyright licensing is a common feature in these agreements. Depending on the type of site, these terms of service usually bind users to allowing their uploaded content to be used by the website under an expansive non-exclusive licence or they restrict people from using website content in various ways — or both. But how binding are such licences? And does it matter whether the terms of licence are "browse wrap" (merely available on the website) or "click wrap" (requiring a click on an "I agree" icon)?

In *Century 21*, the court affirmed the legality of the browse wrap practices of most websites, at least insofar as reasonable terms are concerned. In that case, the defendant used automated robots to extract data from the plaintiff's website in contravention of the terms of service. The defendant argued that since the terms of service were not click wrap, it could not be legally bound to the contract. The court concluded:

> The act of browsing past the initial page of the website or searching the site is conduct indicating agreement with the Terms of Use if those terms are provided with sufficient notice, are available for review prior to acceptance, and clearly state that proceeding further is acceptance of the terms.[26]

On the facts in *Century 21*, the court found that the defendant had actual notice of the terms of use. However, the above quotation seems to suggest that absence of notice may not vitiate formation of the contract if the stated requirements are otherwise met. Moreover, the fact that access to, as well as copying on, the website was conducted through

---

25 See Rebecca Giblin & Kimberlee Weatherall, "At the Intersection of Public Service and the Market: Libraries and the Future of Lending" (2015) 26 *Australian Intellectual Property Journal* 4 at 23–24. In the context of contracting out of statutory exceptions through licensing agreements, they note that the legality of such arrangements is uncertain in Australian law. They also note that private ordering may upset the statutory balance of copyright law, but it may be the case that, where legislation does not explicitly prevent contracting out, it is generally allowed.

26 Above note 3 at para 119.

the use of automated robots did not negate contract formation. The court did, however, limit its ruling to the facts of this case insofar as the terms here were standard and reasonable.[27]

The question remains as to the legal status of unusual or unreasonable terms of use, such as, for example, the assignment of copyright to the website. Would click wrap licences bring these within the realm of enforceable terms of use? There is no authority on this issue in Canada. According to Chitty, if a particular condition in a contract is onerous or unusual, there is an obligation on the tendering party (the website) "to show that it has been brought fairly and reasonably to the other's attention."[28] Whether clicking "I agree" next to such highlighted terms in a contract would meet this requirement remains to be seen.

### 3) Open-Source Licences

Open-source licences use the proprietary tools of copyright law to promote the sharing, and collaboration in making, of content, usually software. The basic concept is simple but ingenious. Under an open-source licence, I may grant to others the right to use, modify, and distribute my software program but only on the condition that any future distribution to others, whether the content is modified or not, is conveyed on the same terms. The openness of the licence — for others to freely use, modify, and distribute to still others — is built into and perpetuated through each downstream distribution. The most commonly referenced open-source licence is the GNU General Public License, or GPL. Now in its third version, the General Public License is a detailed document. It permits downstream users of a program to run, copy, and distribute unmodified copies (with appropriate notices so that downstream users are aware of the licence). When distributing modified versions of the program, the conveyor must "license the entire work, as a whole, under this License to anyone who comes into possession of a copy. This license will thereof apply . . . to the whole of the work, and all its parts . . . ."[29] As well, "each time you convey a covered work, the

---

27  *Ibid* at para 120.
28  Hugh Beale, ed, *Chitty on Contracts*, vol 1: *General Principles*, 31st ed (London: Thomson Reuters/Sweet & Maxwell, 2012) 12-015 at 915.
29  GPL, version 3, s 5.

recipient automatically receives a license from the original licensors to run, modify, and propagate that work, subject to this License."[30]

As the General Public License suggests, downstream conveyances of the program remain free in the sense that no one can assert copyright in their contribution except in accordance with the licence.[31] This model has been adapted to various other contexts, including the creative arts. The Creative Commons licence is used by artists to upload content according to various licensing arrangements. As the website indicates, it offers "a pool of content that can be copied, distributed, edited, remixed and built upon . . . all within the boundaries of copyright law."[32] The website offers a range of licences for licensors (artists) to choose from. The most permissive licence allows others to distribute and alter the work, even for commercial purposes, so long as attribution of the original is given to the artist. The most restrictive allows others to download and distribute the work with attribution, so long as the work is not altered or used commercially. The licence follows the General Public License by having the artist licensor grant a non-exclusive licence to perform permitted activities. Thereafter, "every recipient of the Licensed Material automatically receives an offer from the Licensor to exercise the Licensed Rights under the terms and conditions of this Public License."[33] The licence also prevents any licensor from adding conditions that are incompatible with the licence.

The legality of open-source licences was on trial in the landmark US case of *Jacobsen v Katzer*.[34] In that case, the plaintiff alleged that the defendant used portions of the open-sourced code in the latter's proprietary software without complying with attribution and copyright notice requirements that were contained in the licence. These notice requirements are essential to open-source licences as they notify downstream users that the content is open source. Before addressing the legal issues, the court noted the widespread and beneficial uses of open source in both the arts and sciences. The essential legal argument put forward by the defendants was that the licence waived any right

---

30   *Ibid*, s 10.
31   It is permissible, however, to charge a fee to those receiving copies of the program you are distributing: see GPL, version 3, s 4.
32   Creative Commons, "About the Licenses."
33   See Creative Commons License, s 2.5, online: https://creativecommons.org/licenses/by-nc-nd/4.0/legalcode.
34   535 F3d 1373 (Fed Cir 2008).

to pursue a copyright infringement action and that the breach of the terms of the licence was actionable only in contract. In contract law language, this was a breach of the covenant (obligations created and enforceable under contract), not a precondition to the granting of the non-exclusive licence.

The court held that the terms of the licence were conditions and that the breach by the defendants put their activities outside the scope of the licence, thus resulting in infringement. The court was influenced by the language of the licensing terms (the disputed terms were prefaced by "provided that" and were identified as "conditions"). However, the court seemed as much motivated by the benefits of upholding the basic premise of open-source licensing: "Copyright holders who engage in open source licensing have the right to control the modification and distribution of copyright materials."[35] The importance of the decision lies in the recognition that open-source licences will be treated as other licences and that breaches of their terms can be actionable and enforceable under copyright law.[36]

## D. COPYRIGHT REGISTRATION

Registration is not required for a work or neighbouring right to receive protections under the *Copyright Act*. This is also true for exclusive licences and assignments: these do not need to be registered in order to ensure their validity or legal effect. Registration of a work or a transfer of an interest with the Registrar of Copyright does, however, offer certain evidentiary and legal benefits.

Section 53(2) provides that a copyright registration is "evidence that the copyright subsists and that the person registered is the owner of the copyright." This supersedes the presumption in section 34.1 that an author, performer, maker, or broadcaster is the first owner of a work.[37] Similar evidentiary provisions are in place for a registered assignment or exclusive licence.[38] Despite these provisions, registration proves little.

---

35 *Ibid* at 1381.
36 See Brian Fitzgerald & Rami Olwan, "The Legality of Free and Open Source Software Licences: The Case of *Jacobsen v. Katzer*" in Mark Perry & Brian Fitzgerald, eds, *Knowledge Policy for the Twenty-First Century: A Legal Perspective* (Toronto: Irwin Law, 2011) 115 at 125.
37 Tamaro, above note 5 at 957.
38 Sections 53(2.1) & 53(2.2).

## CHAPTER 4: OWNERSHIP, LICENSING, REGISTRATION, AND INFRINGEMENT

Unlike trademarks or patents, there is no review process to ensure the legitimacy or accuracy of what is being registered. For this reason, these provisions are advantageous to a registrant if there is a complete absence of evidence about, for example, ownership of a copyright. At the same time, courts do not place much, if any, weight on these provisions where "extrinsic" evidence is to the contrary.[39]

Registration can have more legally meaningful advantages under the Act. First, assignees or licensees should register valuable transfers to protect against the possibility of the copyright owner double-dealing to other assignees or licensees. Section 57(3) provides that unless a prior assignment or licence is registered before a subsequent assignment or licence that *is* registered, the prior "shall be judged void against any subsequent ... for valuable consideration without notice." In other words, a later registered assignment or licence of the same interest by a copyright owner may trump an earlier unregistered one.

Registration can also help to protect a copyright owner's full range of infringement remedies under the Act. Section 39 limits infringement remedies to an injunction if the defendant can show that she was neither aware nor had reasonable grounds for suspecting that a work or neighbouring right was under copyright. Section 39(2) clarifies that if a work is registered, then this provision does not apply and thus all remedies are available to the copyright holder. There are, of course, methods, other than registration, for ensuring that a defendant cannot claim ignorance that a work is under copyright. For example, a copyright symbol together with a date affixed to copies of a work should suffice as enough notice that a copyright in the work subsists.

The absence of the registration copyright requirement for copyright undermines an obvious mechanism of public notice about not only the subsistence of copyright in a work but also the identity of its holder. This has led to the problem of "orphan works" — works that are under copyright but in which would-be users cannot locate the owner for the purpose of obtaining a licence. In such scenarios, users (and owners) of a copyright are both worse off. A user is faced with either not using the desired work or risking infringement. An owner is deprived of control over the use of the work and potential licensing revenue. There have been many solutions put forward to fixing this problem, including

---

39   *Winkler v Roy*, 2002 FCT 950.

proposals to require registration of a work a certain number of years after the work is created. For now, the Act offers a cumbersome process by which the Copyright Board may issue a statutory licence where the owner of a copyright cannot be located. Section 77 allows the Board to issue a licence for a work or neighbouring right, on terms and conditions it sees fit, upon "being satisfied that the applicant has made reasonable efforts to locate the owner of the copyright and that the owner cannot be located."

## E. INFRINGEMENT

"Primary infringement" is an infringement of copyright which occurs when someone does an act within the scope of a right afforded to a copyholder and does it without the copyholder's consent.[40] The absence of intent to infringe is not relevant. An assignee or exclusive licensee of a copyright interest can bring an action for infringement of their granted rights if the assignment or licence so permits.[41] However, efforts to transfer an interest, along with a right of action, after the alleged infringing acts and for no apparent purpose other than to give a plaintiff standing, will not be recognized by the courts.[42] Each infringing act constitutes a separate incident of infringement and extends to both economic and moral rights under the Act.[43] As discussed above, certain presumptions pertaining to subsistence of a copyright and ownership are in place.[44] While a copyright owner must prove the act of infringement, the defendant must prove that consent was given.[45] At minimum, consent means that permission (including implied licence) was given for the use of the work; thus, oral permission or conduct implying consent should suffice.

Although an innocent infringer may be liable for primary infringement, *secondary* infringement requires some knowledge, on the part of the defendant, that she is committing an infringing act. Such acts pertain to intermediary distributors of the work who import, distribute,

---

40   Section 27.
41   Section 13(6).
42   See *Harmony Consulting Ltd v GA Foss Transport Ltd*, 2011 FC 340 at para 218.
43   Tamaro, above note 5 at 544; ss 27 and 28.1.
44   Sections 34.1 and 53(2).
45   Tamaro, above note 5 at 543.

## CHAPTER 4: OWNERSHIP, LICENSING, REGISTRATION, AND INFRINGEMENT

or sell the infringing copies. As the Supreme Court has set out: "three elements must be proven to establish secondary infringement: (1) a primary infringement; (2) the secondary infringer should have known that he or she was dealing with a product of infringement; and (3) the secondary infringer sold, distributed or exposed for sale the infringing goods."[46] The *Copyright Modernization Act* added a new secondary infringement provision for lessons and the exportation of infringing copies.[47] An action for infringement, whether primary or secondary, has a three-year limitation period from the time that the plaintiff "knew, or could reasonably have been expected to know, of the act or omission at the time it occurred . . . ."[48]

Where infringement is proven, copyright holders are entitled to a full range of remedies, including injunction, damages, accounts, and delivering up,[49] subject to section 39, as discussed above. The Act permits a plaintiff to elect "statutory damages" rather than damages and profits.[50] The *Copyright Modernization Act* heeded to calls that statutory damages should be awarded on a reduced basis when infringement is for non-commercial purposes. In such cases, the range of damages is set at between $100 and $5,000 for all infringements done for non-commercial purposes.[51] Even this amount may be reduced substantially if the defendant can show that she was not, nor had any reasonable grounds for believing she was, infringing copyright.[52] In exercising discretion to award statutory damages of any kind, the court is permitted to consider the following factors: (1) the good or bad faith of the defendant; (2) the conduct of the parties; (3) the need for deterrence of other infringements of the copyright in question; and (4) for non-commercial acts, the need for proportionality, as well as hardship on the defendant, impact on the plaintiff, and the private or public nature of the infringement.[53] The non-commercial purpose statutory damages regime lessens the chill that otherwise might be experienced by users of content unsure of the legality of their actions.

---

46  *Euro-Excellence*, above note 13 at para 19.
47  See ss 29(2.2) and 29(2.11), respectively.
48  Section 43.1.
49  Sections 34(1) &(2).
50  Section 38.1.
51  Section 38.1(b), as contrasted to the range of $500–$20,000 for commercial uses.
52  Section 38.1(2).
53  Section 38.1(5).

## 1) Identifying Infringers on the Internet

Uncovering the true identity of Internet infringers of copyright content is notoriously difficult. For example, the identity of a subscriber to a peer-to-peer network may be discoverable only through an Internet service provider that can correlate an Internet protocol address with a subscriber (or possibly through the peer-to-peer intermediary subscription information). Intermediaries cannot release this information[54] to copyright owners nor can they be compelled to do so through normal discovery procedures since they are not party to the infringement action. In such cases, plaintiffs are unable to identify would-be defendants against whom to bring a copyright action. This inability has led to a number of John Doe cases where plaintiffs have asked courts to compel Internet service providers to disclose the identities behind Internet protocol addresses associated with the commission of copyright infringements. Plaintiffs, in such cases, have sought equitable bills of discovery, or *Norwich* orders.

In *BMG Canada Inc v John Doe*, record companies brought an action against Internet service providers to disclose the identities behind twenty-nine Internet protocol addresses that had each downloaded more than 1000 songs through peer-to-peer networks. The Federal Court of Appeal (FCA) adopted a five-fold test for compelling disclosure:[55]

1. The applicant must establish a bona fide claim against the proposed defendant;[56]
2. The person from whom discovery is sought must be in some way involved in the matter under dispute, he must be more than an innocent bystander;
3. The person from whom discovery is sought must be the only practical source of information available to the applicants;
4. The person from whom discovery is sought must be reasonably compensated for his expenses arising out of compliance with the discovery order in addition to his legal costs;

---

54 Privacy legislation prevents commercial entities from sharing personal information about their clients to others.
55 2005 FCA 193 at para 15 [*BMG FCA*]. The court considered both the applicable rules of court (statutory law) and the equitable remedy known as a "bill of discovery," also known as a *Norwich* order. In fact, the court conflated these two sources of law into one test.
56 *Ibid* at para 32: This first criterion is a modification of the trial judgment.

CHAPTER 4: OWNERSHIP, LICENSING, REGISTRATION, AND INFRINGEMENT

5. The public interests in favour of disclosure must outweigh the legitimate privacy concerns.[57]

The first criterion modified the trial judgment which required that a *prima facie* "case" be made out by the plaintiff. The standard was lowered to "claim" since it would be too demanding to require actual proof of the case to be made without knowing the details of the acts giving rise to the claim of infringement. Instead, "bona fide claim" merely requires that a court be satisfied that the plaintiffs "really do intend to bring an action for infringement of copyright based upon the information they obtain, and that there is no other improper purpose for seeking the identity of these persons."[58]

Second, an Internet service provider that connects the purported defendants to the Internet to facilitate alleged acts of infringement must be "involved in the matter under dispute," not a mere bystander.[59] Third, evidence in support of an equitable bill of discovery should clarify whether there are practical alternative means of obtaining the information, for example, peer-to-peer network subscriber information.[60] The Federal Court of Appeal seemed to raise this bar somewhat when it stated, "[t]here should be clear evidence to the effect that the information cannot be obtained from another source such as the operators of the named [peer-to-peer] websites . . . ."[61]

Finally, both trial and appellate courts in this case were particularly concerned about the balance between the public interest in disclosure and the privacy concerns of Internet users. Courts at both levels identified the sanctity and importance of privacy rights, on the one hand, and the public interest component of undermining authorial incentive to create through acts of infringement on the other, as the relevant interests. In weighing these interests, a court must be vigilant to ensure that there is little risk of inaccurate identification being obtained or the release of information irrelevant to the action. In fact, the trial court found that the request in this case was stale such that there was an increased risk of inaccurate information that could violate someone's

---

57  *BMG Canada v John Doe*, 2004 FC 488 at para 13 [*BMG FC*]. The latter four criteria were adopted by the FCA and are reproduced verbatim.
58  *BMG FCA*, above note 55 at para 34.
59  *BMG FC*, above note 57 at para 30.
60  *Ibid* at para 31.
61  *BMG FCA*, above note 55 at para 35.

privacy; the privacy interest therefore trumped the public interest in copyright.[62]

In the more recent case of *Voltage Picture LLC v John Doe*,[63] the Federal Court had reason to expand upon the law in this area. In that case, the plaintiff was alleged to be a "copyright troll" variously described in that case as a plaintiff "who file[s] multitudes of lawsuits solely to extort quick settlements"[64] and who "seeks to intimidate individuals into easy settlements by way of demand letters and threats of litigation."[65] As these descriptions imply, the business model of the troll is the large-scale dissemination of letters alleging infringement and demanding exorbitant amounts in the hope that a certain portion of the recipients will pay out to avoid litigation. The troll preys on the ignorance (of the law) and fear (of being sued) of its victim. The plaintiff in *Voltage* was seeking the names and addresses of 2,000 ISP subscribers through a *Norwich* order. For reasons of basic fairness *and* to protect scarce judicial resources, courts in various jurisdictions — and now Canada — have imposed conditions on *Norwich* orders in such cases.

In *Voltage*, the court outlined an extensive, but non-exhaustive, list of considerations in addition to the tests applied from *BMG*. These considerations include safeguards that a court may decide to be put in place in a *Norwich* order "where evidence suggests that an improper motive may be lurking in the actions of a copyright holder plaintiff."[66] As listed at paragraph 134, these include the following:

a) The moving party must demonstrate a *bona fide* case;
b) Putting safeguards in place so that alleged infringers receiving any "demand" letter from a party obtaining an order under Rule 238 or a *Norwich* Order not be intimidated into making a payment without the benefit of understanding their legal rights and obligations;
c) When issuing a *Norwich* Order the Court may retain the authority to ensure that it is not abused by the party obtaining it and can impose terms on how its provisions are carried out;

---

62  BMG FCA, *ibid* at paras 43–45. See also BMG FC, above note 57 at para 42.
63  2014 FC 161 [*Voltage*].
64  *Ibid* at Preamble.
65  *Ibid* at para 6.
66  *Ibid* at para 133. Moreover, if there is compelling evidence of an improper motive, the court may deny the motion entirely.

## CHAPTER 4: OWNERSHIP, LICENSING, REGISTRATION, AND INFRINGEMENT

d) The party enforcing the *Norwich* Order should pay the legal costs and disbursements of the innocent third-party;

e) Specific warnings regarding the obtaining of legal advice or the like should be included in any correspondence to individuals who are identified by the *Norwich* Order;

f) Limiting the information provided by the third party by releasing only the name and residential address but not telephone numbers and e-mail addresses;

g) Ensuring there is a mechanism for the Court to monitor the implementation of the *Norwich* Order;

h) Ensuring that the information that is released remains confidential and not be disclosed to the public and be used only in connection with the action;

I) Requiring the party obtaining the order to provide a copy of any proposed "demand" letter to all parties on the motion and to the Court prior to such letter being sent to the alleged infringers;

j) The Court should reserve the right to order amendments to the demand letter in the event it contains inappropriate statements;

k) Letters sent to individuals whose names are revealed pursuant to Court order must make clear that the fact that an order for disclosure has been made does not mean that the court has considered the merits of the allegations of infringement against the recipient and made any finding of liability;

l) Any demand letter should stipulate that the person receiving the letter may not be the person who was responsible for the infringing acts;

m) A copy of the Court order, or the entire decision should be included with any letter sent to an alleged infringer; and,

n) The Court should ensure that the remedy granted is proportional.

Given the high level of supervision implied in these possible conditions, courts are further directed to have these orders administered by a case management judge, and to ensure that any demand letter sent is approved by the court.[67]

★ ★ ★ ★ ★

---

67 *Ibid* at paras 137 & 138.

The relatively staid subject matter of copyright ownership and its incidents has been infused with some interesting developments over the past twenty years. Internet anonymity has created the need for adapting non-party discovery rules for the purposes of uncovering the identity of purported infringers. In this context, the interest of preserving copyright incentive wrestles with the privacy interest of ISP clients and of preserving the integrity of the court system against abuse. Another fascinating development has been the proliferation of the open-source licence model, grounded in proprietary copyright principles, to promote collaboration and cooperation in the making and sharing of content.

CHAPTER 5

# Technological Protection Measures and Rights Management Information

## A. INTRODUCTION

This chapter considers two kinds of measures whose intended purpose is to ensure the effective control and management of copyrights in the digital sphere: technological protection measures (TPM) and rights management information (RMI). The obligation to implement these measures appears in the two "Internet" treaties of the World Intellectual Property Organization (WIPO): the *WIPO Copyright Treaty* (*WCT*) and the *WIPO Performances and Phonograms Treaty* (*WPPT*),[1] and thus the measures are already implemented in many national copyright systems. Technological protection measures — more colloquially referred to as "digital locks" — are the means by which copyright holders can control the copying or use of work. Their appearance in copyright law is nothing if not controversial as these locks raise justifiable fears of obliterating user rights in copyright. The protection of rights management information is decidedly less controversial as these provisions merely ensure that users of works are notified of the author, owner, and terms of use pertaining to a work. Both TPM and RMI regimes raise a number of interesting and important interpretive issues.

---

1   *WIPO Copyright Treaty*, Can TS 2014 No 20 [*WCT*]; *WIPO Performances and Phonograms Treaty*, Can TS 2014 No 21 [*WPPT*].

## B. TECHNOLOGICAL PROTECTION MEASURES: SECTION 41

Section 41 of the *Copyright Act* has many pivotal interpretive issues that determine the scope afforded to anti-circumvention measures. In seeking to understand them, important guidance is to be gained by considering the international legal context of the measures and, in particular, the interpretation by US courts of the *Digital Millennium Copyright Act*.[2] This Act sheds light not only on the interpretation of specific provisions but also on the purpose behind these measures.

The heart of this chapter is an analysis of key language in section 41 pertaining to the offence of anti-circumvention, the targets of these measures, the remedies, and exceptions.

### 1) The International Legal Context

A 1994 US Green Paper rationalized the implementation of anti-circumvention measures on the following grounds: (1) there is a need to counteract the ease of committing infringement on the Internet and to help address the difficulty in detecting such activity, (2) technological protection measures are susceptible to circumvention, (3) intermediary liability for anti-circumvention activities under indirect infringement provisions is ineffective, and (4) greater dissemination of works (since copyright holders would be confident to put works online) and reduced prices (since the price of works legitimately purchased would not have to be offset by massive losses through online piracy) would promote the public interest.[3] In 1998, anti-circumvention measures were passed into law under the US *DMCA*. US caselaw has reiterated some of these factors as the policy goals underlying anti-circumvention provisions. In *Universal Studios v Corley*, the US Court of Appeals for the Second Circuit stated:

> Fearful that the ease with which pirates could copy and distribute a copyrightable work in digital form was overwhelming the capacity of conventional copyright enforcement to find and enjoin unlawfully

---

2  Pub L No 105-304, 112 Stat 2860 (1998) (codified in scattered sections of 17 USC) [*DMCA*].

3  Zohar Efroni, *Access-Right: The Future of Digital Copyright Law* (New York: Oxford University Press, 2011) at 293. Number (3) is the concern that the sale of technology that can be used for both infringing and non-infringing purposes does not attract liability. This principle is also found in Canadian law under the "authorization" jurisprudence: see Chapter 2.

copied material, Congress sought to combat piracy in its earlier stages, before the work was even copied.[4]

At the international level, anti-circumvention provisions were adopted into the WIPO "Internet" treaties: the *WCT* and the *WPPT*. Article 11 of the *WCT* reads as follows:

> Contracting Parties shall provide adequate legal protection and effective legal remedies against the circumvention of effective technological measures that are used by authors in connection with the exercise of their rights under this Treaty or the Berne Convention and that restrict acts, in respect of their works, which are not authorized by the authors concerned or permitted by law.[5]

This broadly worded provision is a minimum standard that individual states are required to implement into national law. Much leeway is allowed for tailoring anti-circumvention measures to the needs of national legal regimes. And, of course, states are free to adopt stronger anti-circumvention standards if they wish. However, article 11 is either vague or ambiguous on two key interpretive issues that have arisen in US, European, and now Canadian copyright law. These issues are (1) the scope of "effective" technological measures to be targeted and (2) whether anti-circumvention measures apply to accessing a work when that access does not result in an act of infringement.

The US and European Union experiences with anti-circumvention measures offer a helpful context to Canadian lawyers and judges struggling to understand the scheme of section 41. Specific comparisons with these legal regimes will be made when the language of section 41 is analyzed below. The basic structure of US and European laws is similar to section 41 although there are important substantive differences too.[6] All of these regimes distinguish between circumventing a technological protection measure to *gain access* to a work (access control) and circumventing a technological protection measure to *infringe copyright* (copy control). These regimes target both persons who engage in circumvention and the makers and intermediaries that facilitate

---

4   Efroni, *ibid* at 348, cites *Universal Studios v Corley*, 273 F3d 429 at 435 (2d Cir 2001).
5   A corresponding provision for neighbouring rights is set out in the *WPPT*.
6   DMCA, above note 2, 17 USC § 1201; EC, *Directive 2001/29/EC of the European Parliament and of the Council of 22 May 2001 on the harmonisation of certain aspects of copyright and related rights in the information society*, [2001] OJ, L 167/10, art 6.

distribution of such methods and products. Provision is also made in all regimes for certain exceptions to the rules, for example, encryption research and national security. Unlike section 41 of the Canadian Act, however, the US and European rules affirm that the anti-circumvention rules are without prejudice to exceptions under copyright law.

## 2) Purpose

Anti-circumvention measures may be justified on most of the grounds stated in the US Green Paper, discussed above. No one disputes that digitization and the Internet have created a piracy problem on an unprecedented scale for which traditional methods of detection and enforcement are inadequate. Nor could anyone convincingly argue that many technological protection measures are not susceptible to circumvention. Furthermore, as has been demonstrated in *Society of Composers, Authors and Music Publishers of Canada v Canadian Assn of Internet Providers*,[7] general intermediary liability rules ("right to authorize such acts") are inadequate to the task of reining in the distribution of TPM circumvention devices and products. Technological neutrality presumes that circumventing technology will be used for non-infringing purposes in the absence of evidence of infringement in individual cases. The fourth proposition, which pertains to the incentive to disseminate works and the prospect of reduced prices, is at best contestable. Twenty years after the US Green Paper, the Internet is an indispensable method of content distribution, and new business models have led to vastly reduced prices for content delivery. It seems likely that these developments had little to do with the successful implementation of anti-circumvention measures.[8]

Many scholars and policy-makers have complained — and for good reason — that while anti-circumvention measures may have legitimate purposes, they also have the potential to upset the balance of rights between authors and users of copyrighted material. The purpose of Ca-

---

7   2004 SCC 45 [*CAIP*].
8   If anything, it seems that the failure of anti-circumvention measures to achieve their objectives has led to a willingness of copyright owners to sell their content at reduced prices. Moreover, reduced prices for connectivity to content through broadband delivery and telecommunications policies have made the Internet a primary method of content distribution.

nadian copyright law is to incentivize the creation of works and reward authors for their efforts, as well as to encourage the dissemination and legitimate downstream uses of those rights. Anti-circumvention laws uphold authorial incentive and reward by targeting piracy activities that are corrosive to these objectives, but they also have the potential to do so at great sacrifice to user rights under the Act. If, for example, users cannot circumvent technological protection measures for the purpose of fair dealing or make legitimate private copies under the Act, then the system is no longer balanced but tilted towards author rights. It is difficult to reconcile these reinforced author rights with strong judicial statements about the value of user rights: see, for example, McLachlin CJC in *CCH Canadian Ltd v Law Society of Upper Canada*.[9]

### 3) "Effective" Technological Protection Measures

According to section 41, "technological protection measure"

> [m]eans any effective technology, device or component that, in the ordinary course of its operation,
> (a) controls access to a work, to a performer's performance fixed in a sound recording or to a sound recording and whose use is authorized by the copyright owner; or
> (b) restricts the doing — with respect to a work, to a performer's performance fixed in a sound recording or to a sound recording — of any act referred to in section 3, 15 or 18 and any act for which remuneration is payable under section 19.

This language is broad. Subject to determining what is meant by "effective" (discussed below), "any technology, device or component" that ordinarily functions to control access or restrict infringement qualifies. It is critical to bear in mind that the technological protection measure must be directed to one of these goals: either controlling access or restricting infringement. In *Agfa Monotype v Adobe Systems*,[10] the defendant was accused of circumventing a technological protection measure when it designed Adobe Acrobat 5.0 to access the plaintiff's copyrighted fonts. But since the alleged technological protection measure — that is,

---

9   2004 SCC 13 [*CCH*].
10  404 F Supp 2d 1030 (ND Ill 2005).

the embedding bits — were not protected by encryption, scrambling, or authentication of any kind, the plaintiff was unsuccessful in its *DMCA* circumvention action. The embedding bits, while technological protection measures of a kind, were not directed towards either controlling access to or restricting infringement of the copyrighted fonts.

It is also possible that a measure may be intended to achieve an access or infringement protection goal but fails in doing so. In the US case of *Lexmark International v Static Control Components*,[11] a manufacturer of replacement print cartridges was accused of circumventing the plaintiff's technological protection measure that permitted only authorized print cartridges from working on its machines. The problem for the plaintiff in this case was that there was more than one way to obtain the information needed to ensure compatibility between cartridge and machine: the technological protection measure (an authentication sequence) and the software code (available and accessible to anyone who purchased the printer). As there was a non-TPM method of gaining access, the court reasoned that the technological protection measure did not "control access."[12] The court also indicated that, for the same reason, the measure was not "effective."[13]

The descriptor "effective" can be traced back to the language of the WIPO "Internet" treaties. However, there is no definition or agreed-upon statement in those instruments as to what the term "effective" is to imply about the nature of the technological protection measure. The issue has important implications for the scope of application of section 41. The *Oxford Dictionary* defines "effective" as "successful in producing a desired result." While the ordinary meaning of language is not always coterminous with dictionary meanings, this may be an instance where that is the case. The connection between "effective" and intended outcome is apparent in *Directive 2001/29/EC of the European Parliament and of the Council of 22 May 2001 on the harmonisation of certain aspects of copyright and related rights in the information society* which defines the term as "application of an access control or protection process . . . *which achieves the protection objective.*"[14] While Canada chose not to define the term "effective" in this way, a connection between the measure and

---

11 387 F3d 522 (6th Cir 2004) [*Lexmark International*].
12 *Ibid* at 547.
13 *Ibid*.
14 Above note 6, art 6(3) [emphasis added].

## CHAPTER 5: TECHNOLOGICAL PROTECTION MEASURES AND RIGHTS MANAGEMENT INFORMATION

the objective sought may be implied in the choice to use the phrase "technological *protection* measure," not "technological measure," as it appears in the WIPO "Internet" treaties and US and European law. In other words, the word "protection" is directed towards achieving a particular result: the prevention of access or copying. Moreover, "[t]he specific acts or results over which rights-holders wish to exercise control are inferable from the features with which the technological protection system is equipped."[15] Understood in this way, technological protection measures that are defective or that malfunction or that achieve an unintended, or unprotected, purpose are not eligible.

The term "effective" also connotes a substantial level of competence in achieving the objective.[16] A measure which allows one to skirt copy protection by "holding down the shift key on a Windows PC,"[17] for example, does not competently achieve the objective. But how strong or technically robust does the measure have to be? Although a measure does not need to be impenetrable to be "effective" (this would hollow-out the need for anti-circumvention measures), the measure should require some technical skill of information technology to overcome.[18] Determining the exact threshold in individual cases will sometimes be difficult. We might imagine that a copy protection measure that requires someone to develop software code to circumvent would clearly be effective. However, would disabling a cookies function on a website to avoid a paywall constitute an effective technological protection measure? In such cases, court rulings may be influenced by the possibility of liability for accidental circumvention or the availability and feasibility of other, more effective, technological protection measures.

The term "effective" may also connote that the measure does not unduly affect other legal rights or interests. In other words, while "effective"

---

15   Efroni, above note 3 at 303.
16   Consider in this regard the definition of "effective" and the reference to "successful." This view is held by Michel M Walter & Silke von Lewinski, eds, *European Copyright Law: A Commentary* (Oxford: Oxford University Press, 2010) at 1067. Efroni, above note 3 at 304.
17   Electronic Frontier Foundation, *Unintended Consequences: 16 Years under the DMCA* (September 2014) at 5, online: www.eff.org/files/2014/09/16/unintendedconsequences2014.pdf [EFF].
18   Efroni, above note 3 at 304, refers to a standard of "special assistance" to an average user of average skills. Walter & Von Lewinski, above note 16 at 1067, refer to a "technical skills" standard.

means that the measure should competently accomplish its intended result, it should not be detrimental to a user's legitimate interests outside of copyright. A technological protection measure that installs a virus or malicious software on a computer to prevent access or restrict infringement might be effective in achieving its goal but highly inappropriate to the task at hand. A less extreme case is the person who disables cookies or uses a virtual private network (VPN) to protect his privacy but, in doing so, circumvents a technological protection measure, for example, accessing content in another jurisdiction that is geoblocked where he lives. Again, while the measure is effective to its goal, it may be too invasive of other legitimate interests to be effective in the sense of being appropriate to the task.

## 4) Circumvention

Section 41 provides these definitions of "circumvent":

> (a) in respect of a technological protection measure within the meaning of paragraph (a) of the definition "technological protection measure", to descramble a scrambled work or decrypt an encrypted work or to otherwise avoid, bypass, remove, deactivate or impair the technological protection measure, unless it is done with the authority of the copyright owner; and
>
> (b) in respect of a technological protection measure within the meaning of paragraph (b) of the definition "technological protection measure", to avoid, bypass, remove, deactivate or impair the technological protection measure.

Two definitions are offered here: (1) circumvention of the access control right as defined in section 41(a), and (2) circumvention of the copy control right as defined in section 41(b). The definitions are the same except that the access control right adds "to descramble a scrambled work or decrypt an encrypted work" to the list of prohibited activities. The definition of "circumvent" is broadly conceived and is intended to capture many of the ways in which a technological protection measure might be overcome.

The US experience with a similarly worded provision reveals, however, that there are ambiguities in how this language might be applied in specific cases. In *IMS Inquiry Management Systems, Ltd v Berkshire*

*Information Services, Inc*,[19] the defendant was accused of circumventing a technological measure by using a third-party password to access content. While the court agreed that password protection is a technological measure, it did not consider the use of a third-party password to constitute circumventing password protection as a technological measure. In the words of the court, although the defendant did not have permission to access the content, it did not "[avoid or bypass] the deployed technological measure in the measure's gatekeeping capacity."[20] While a plausible interpretation of the text, this holding seems to undermine the purpose behind anti-circumvention measures. If a password can be used by one unauthorized user, then it can be used by many, in which case, the technological protection measure (assuming it is "effective") is severely compromised. In this regard, it is interesting to note that, in an Ontario Small Claims Court action, which did not offer probative analysis of section 41, TPM infringement was found on very similar facts.[21]

## 5) Is There an Access Control Right?

By far the largest controversy that has arisen from the implementation of anti-circumvention legislation around the world is the question of whether such law provides a right of access to copyrighted content. Under section 3 of the Act, there is no right of a copyright holder that prevents someone from merely accessing a work, for example, viewing content over the Internet. The relevant provision in this regard is section 41.1(1)(a):

> No person shall
> (a) circumvent a technological protection measure within the meaning of paragraph (a) of the definition "technological protection measure" in section 41 ....

The paragraph (a) definition of "technological protection measure" is one that "controls access to a work ... whose use is authorized by the copyright owner." The question is whether this provision is to be interpreted literally such that it prohibits access of any kind to a work so protected.

---

19  307 F Supp 2d 521 (SDNY 2004).
20  Ibid.
21  *Blacklock's v Canadian Vintners Association*, 2015 CanLII 65885 (ON SCSM).

Faced with very similar language ("controls access to a work"), US courts have adopted two very different interpretations. Some courts have interpreted the provision literally to mean protection against access for any purpose, provided the underlying work is copyrighted. In other words, the copyright owner has the right to control access to the work even if such access does not lead to copyright infringement.[22] A second purposive interpretation holds that a right of access can be infringed only if the accessing results in infringement of the underlying copyright. In other words, there cannot be violation of the access right unless there is also infringement of the copyright in the work.

US caselaw has, in general, moved towards a purposive approach. In the case of *Chamberlain Group v Skyline Technologies*,[23] the defendant was accused of circumventing a technological measure for a garage door opener, the underlying code being the work protected. The plaintiff did not allege infringement of copyright. The outcome of the case turned on whether the access right must be accompanied by an act of infringement. In upholding a nexus between access and infringement, the court ascertained that it was the legislature's intention to maintain a balance between competing interests underlying copyright.[24] This was also reflected in the wording of the *DMCA*: "[n]othing in this section shall affect rights, remedies, limitations, or defenses to copyright infringement, including fair use . . . ."[25]

A nexus requirement for the access right would better serve the purposes of Canadian copyright law. There can be no doubt that the creation of an access right unanchored in any act of copyright infringement jeopardizes, if not eliminates, legitimate uses of a work found elsewhere under the Act.[26] However, there is a strong legislative inference that section

---

22  See Ryan Iwahashi, "How to Circumvent Technological Protection Measures without Violating the *DMCA*: An Examination of Technological Protection Measures under Current Legal Standards" (2011) 26 *Berkeley Technology Law Journal* 491 at 495–96.
23  381 F3d 1178 (Fed Cir 2004) [*Chamberlain*].
24  *Ibid* at 1196.
25  Above note 2, 17 USC § 1201(c)(1).
26  Moreover, as Hagen observes, the anti-circumvention provisions "potentially limit the ability of courts to give a technologically neutral interpretation of the *Copyright Act* whenever TPMs are used by copyright owners to favour themselves over rival disseminators and it is prohibited to circumvent the TPMs in the circumstances." See Gregory R Hagen, "Technological Neutrality in Canadian Copyright Law" in Michael Geist, ed, *The Copyright Pentalogy: How the Supreme Court of Canada Shook the Foundations of Canadian Copyright Law* (Ottawa: University of Ottawa Press, 2013) 307 at 309.

41 does exactly that. Unlike both the United States and Europe, there is no provision, like section 1201(c)(1) in the *DMCA*, affirming the rights and defences of users of works. More damning still, any reference to preserving such a balance is relegated to a regulation-enabling clause. Section 41.21 allows for the possible future prescription of activities that do not violate the access right, including those that "could adversely affect criticism, review, news reporting, commentary, parody, satire, teaching, scholarship or research that could be made or done in respect of the work ...."[27] It is clear that the government of the day was made aware of concerns about denying user rights through digital locks.[28] Yet rather than uphold these rights through a section 1201(c)(1)-type provision, it chose, instead, to address any concerns that might arise through regulation.[29] A purposive interpretation that read down the apparent intent and wording of a statute would not, however, be unprecedented even at the Supreme Court level.[30]

Under either interpretive approach, it cannot be the case that one who circumvents a technological protection measure to access or copy a work no longer under copyright would be liable under section 41. This would not be consistent with either the purpose of copyright (to extend monopoly rights indefinitely) or the language of section 41, which is rooted in the concept of the copyrighted work.

## 6) Manufacturers and Intermediaries

Makers and dealers of technological protection measures are regulated by the following:

> **41.1** No person shall
>
> ...

---

27   Section 41.21(2)(a)(iii).
28   *House of Commons Debates*, 41st Parl, 1st Sess, No 45 (14 November 2011) at 1710 (Hon Geoff Regan): "It does not make any sense that digital locks could supersede other rights that are guaranteed in the very same piece of legislation." In the same session, at 1045, Hon Christian Paradis: "Digital locks are important for encouraging innovation ... and consumers are still free to choose whether or not to purchase products with digital locks."
29   An earlier attempt at modernizing copyright legislation, Bill C-60, *An Act to amend the Copyright Act*, 1st Sess, 38th Parl, 2005, had TPM provisions that did not even contain an access right: see definition of TPM and s 34.02 in Bill C-60.
30   See *Kirkbi AG v Ritvik Holdings Inc*, 2005 SCC 65, discussed in Chapter 1.

(b) offer services to the public or provide services if
  (i) the services are offered or provided primarily for the purposes of circumventing a technological protection measure,
  (ii) the uses or purposes of those services are not commercially significant other than when they are offered or provided for the purposes of circumventing a technological protection measure, or
  (iii) the person markets those services as being for the purposes of circumventing a technological protection measure or acts in concert with another person in order to market those services as being for those purposes; or
(c) manufacture, import, distribute, offer for sale or rental or provide — including by selling or renting — any technology, device or component if
  (i) the technology, device or component is designed or produced primarily for the purposes of circumventing a technological protection measure,
  (ii) the uses or purposes of the technology, device or component are not commercially significant other than when it is used for the purposes of circumventing a technological protection measure, or
  (iii) the person markets the technology, device or component as being for the purposes of circumventing a technological protection measure or acts in concert with another person in order to market the technology, device or component as being for those purposes.

Given that acts of circumvention occur in private and are therefore extremely difficult to detect, targeting those who make and distribute services aimed at circumventing technological protection measures is critical to the goal of preventing their widespread proliferation. But it is not a blanket prohibition. For section 41.1(b), the services offered must be either "primarily" for the purpose of circumventing technological protection measures, marketed as being for that purpose, or have no other commercially significant purpose. Similarly, for section 41.1(c), makers, distributors, or purveyors will be liable if the technology is designed for circumvention, is marketed as such, or if it has no other commercially significant purpose. These requirements are disjunctive and not cumulative.

The effect of these provisions is tied, in a practical sense, to the interpretation of the access control right. If access control has a nexus with infringement, then the effect of sections 41.1(b) and (c) will be compromised as the purchase or use of circumvention technologies can always be ostensibly justified to facilitate user rights under the Act. If there is no nexus requirement, then there is less latitude to argue that the making or selling of a technological protection measure is for some other commercially significant purpose. However, that leeway may expand over time. Since technological protection measures on off-copyright works are beyond the scope of section 41, then a commercially significant demand to circumvent these formerly protected works may arise.

There are other ambiguities in sections 41.1(b) and (c) that have a critical impact on the scope of these provisions. First, the language may imply that the services or distribution of a circumvention technology must be commercial. Applying the maxim *noscitur a sociis* to section 41.1(c), the word "distribute" (which is otherwise broad enough to include not-for-profit dissemination) takes on a commercial flavour when it is informed by the language "manufacture," "import," "sale," and "rental." The word "service" in section 41.1(b) may also imply commercial activity especially when judged in light of the language "services are not commercially significant" and "markets those services" which appears later in the subsection. If intermediary activities must be commercial under sections 41.1(b) and (c), then freely offered information on TPM circumvention over the Internet would be shielded from liability. This, however, would likely be detrimental to the purpose of these provisions, and thus courts may choose to read "services" broadly so as to include not-for-profit dissemination.

There has been much controversy in the United States as to whether researchers or hobbyists who share circumvention information with each other over the Internet — for example, revealing vulnerabilities in a technology[31] — would be liable under this provision. To the extent that such information is in the development stage — that is, stops short of instructing one on "how to circumvent" — there is nothing in section 41 that would expose such persons to liability in Canada. Indeed, the activity would not cross the initial threshold of meeting the definition of circumvention.

---

31   See EFF, above note 17 at 4.

## 7) Remedies

Anti-circumvention measures are sometimes described as an extra layer of protection for copyright holders in the digital environment. Quite literally, this is true. Violation of section 41.1(a), (b), or (c) of the Act provides additional and independent grounds for a civil action, entitling the plaintiff to the full range of remedies as offered for copyright infringement. Thus, if circumvention leads to actual copyright infringement, there are two separate grounds of suit against a defendant: (1) traditional copyright infringement and (2) violation of anti-circumvention measures.

In general, contravening anti-circumvention is a strict liability offence. A plaintiff need not show actual or constructive knowledge that a defendant intended to circumvent a technological protection measure. This stands in contrast to European law, which identifies knowledge as an essential element in a circumvention cause of action. However, the Act mitigates the effects of strict liability in two situations. First, a plaintiff cannot choose statutory damages but has the burden to show actual damage if the circumvention is done for a private purpose.[32] Second, there is some protection for innocent infringers. A court may reduce or remit a damage award against a section 41(1) defendant who was not aware, and had no reasonable grounds for believing, she was violating section 41.1.[33] Furthermore, a plaintiff who sues a library, archive or museum, or educational institution that did not know, and had no reasonable grounds to believe, it was contravening section 41.1 will be limited to an injunction remedy.[34]

## 8) Exceptions

There are eight exceptions to the anti-circumvention measures outlined in section 41.1. These exceptions are for purposes of

- law enforcement and national security (section 41.11)
- interoperability of computer programs (section 41.12)
- encryption research (section 41.13)
- protection of privacy (section 41.14)
- computer or network security (section 41.15)

---

32  Section 41.1(3).
33  Section 41.19.
34  Section 41.2.

CHAPTER 5: TECHNOLOGICAL PROTECTION MEASURES AND RIGHTS MANAGEMENT INFORMATION

- accommodation of persons with perceptual disabilities (section 41.16)
- broadcasting undertakings (section 41.17)
- radio apparatus (section 41.18)

These exceptions are circumscribed though there remains room for interpretation of key terms and phrases. The US experience with similar exceptions may provide lessons on the perils associated with interpreting this language too narrowly. Here, we will consider two exceptions — the interoperability of computer programs and privacy — as examples.

From a consumer and competition perspective, the interoperability exception is a key provision as it addresses the ability to untether or unlock a device or software from proprietary technology tie-ins. For example, a technology company that makes computers may restrict consumers from downloading or accessing software in the marketplace that competes with its own. Interoperability is the exchange of information which, in this context, means creating compatibility of two or more technologies so that they may work together. The process of creating interoperable technologies requires access to, or copying of, information in a program. To the extent that technological protection measures restrict access or control copying, this activity potentially violates section 41.1 of the Act. Before considering the exception, one must bear in mind that not all efforts to interoperate technologies will *prima facie* constitute anti-circumvention liability. The *Lexmark International* and *Chamberlain* cases in the United States were both interoperability cases,[35] although for very different reasons, the plaintiffs in these cases failed to establish that a technological measure had been circumvented under language similar to section 41 of our Act (without resorting to the interoperability exception).

The key provisions in the interoperability exception are as follows:

> **41.12** (1) Paragraph 41.1(1)(*a*) does not apply to a person who owns a computer program or a copy of one, or has a licence to use the program or copy, and who circumvents a technological protection measure that protects that program or copy for the sole purpose of obtaining information that would allow the person to make the program and any other computer program interoperable.

---

35   See *Lexmark International*, above note 11; and *Chamberlain*, above note 23.

(2) Paragraph 41.1(1)(b) does not apply to a person who offers services to the public or provides services for the purposes of circumventing a technological protection measure if the person does so for the purpose of making the computer program and any other computer program interoperable.

(3) Paragraph 41.1(1)(c) does not apply to a person who manufactures, imports or provides a technology, device or component for the purposes of circumventing a technological protection measure if the person does so for the purpose of making the computer program and any other computer program interoperable and
(a) uses that technology, device or component only for that purpose; or
(b) provides that technology, device or component to another person only for that purpose.

(4) A person referred to in subsection (1) may communicate the information obtained under that subsection to another person for the purposes of allowing that person to make the computer program and any other computer program interoperable.

The exception is circumscribed by the following limitations.

First, it applies only to those who circumvent a "computer program" that they own (or license). The corresponding provision in the United States has interpreted the term "computer program" (similarly defined in the US Code) restrictively so as not to include DVDs.[36]

Second, those who circumvent technological protection measures must do so for the "sole purpose" of obtaining information to facilitate interoperability. In the US case of *Universal City Studios v Reimerdes*, efforts to create interoperability between DVDs and Linux machines ran afoul of the sole purpose requirement because the circumvention technology could also be used to decrypt and play movies on Windows technology (and for which there were authorized devices available).[37] The "sole purpose" requirement, in fairness, should be based on the intention of the circumventer, not on the possible uses that might be made of the resulting interoperability technology. Notably, only a "purpose"

---

36  *Universal City Studios v Reimerdes*, 82 F Supp 2d 211 at 218 (SDNY 2000). The court, however, based its interpretation on legislative history which, it said, showed that the interoperability provision applies only to computer programs and not movies.
37  *Universal City Studios v Reimerdes*, 111 F Supp 2d 294 at 320 (SDNY 2000) [*Reimerdes*].

requirement is made for service providers, and for makers and distributors (though for the latter class, there is some obligation to ensure that it is used for that purpose). This should mean that multiple purposes of an interoperability technology will not bring someone outside the exception if the primary purpose is legitimate.

Third, section 41.12(4) appears to authorize the dissemination of legitimate interoperability information to others. However, the literal language of the provision limits this dissemination exception to the one who develops the interoperable technology and no other. In *Reimerdes*, defendants who posted anti-circumvention interoperability information were not saved by a similar US provision since they were not the ones who created the technology.[38] This interpretation, while likely unavoidable in light of the wording of section 41.12(4), severely limits the potential to disseminate interoperability information as widely as possible.

The privacy exception provides as follows:

> **41.14** (1) Paragraph 41.1(1)(a) does not apply to a person who circumvents a technological protection measure if
> (a) the work, performer's performance fixed in a sound recording or sound recording that is protected by the technological protection measure is not accompanied by a notice indicating that its use will permit a third party to collect and communicate personal information relating to the user or, in the case where it is accompanied by such a notice, the user is not provided with the option to prevent the collection and communication of personal information without the user's use of it being restricted; and
> (b) the only purpose of circumventing the technological protection measure is to verify whether it permits the collection or communication of personal information and, if it does, to prevent it.
>
> (2) Paragraphs 41.1(1)(b) and (c) do not apply to a person who offers services to the public or provides services, or manufactures, imports or provides a technology, device or component, for the purposes of circumventing a technological protection measure in accordance with subsection (1), to the extent that the services, technology, device or component do not unduly impair the technological protection measure.

---

38  *Ibid.*

Again, this exception is limited in its scope. Technological protection measures that collect personal information on a user and either do not provide notice of doing so or do not allow a user to opt out may be legitimately disabled. Under section 41.14(1)(b), it is also permissible to circumvent for the purpose of ascertaining whether personal information is being collected. However, the circumvention is limited to the sole purpose of protecting privacy. Thus, for example, users of virtual private networks that use proxy servers to hide their Internet protocol addresses may (assuming there is contravention of section 41.1) find safe harbour in this provision if privacy is their only goal. However, if the virtual private network is also the basis for accessing content in another jurisdiction, then this would seem to bring this activity outside the exception. The rules for service providers, makers, and distributors of such anti-circumvention devices are both less demanding (no requirement to ensure the legitimacy of their use) and more demanding (not to unduly impair the technological protection measure) than in some of the other exceptions.

## C. RIGHTS MANAGEMENT INFORMATION

Rights management information (RMI) is information attached to a work which identifies the author, owner, or terms and conditions that might apply to use of the work or a neighbouring right. A 1995 US White Paper likened rights management information to a "license plate for a work on the information superhighway, from which a user may obtain important information about a work. The accuracy of such information will be crucial to the ability of consumers to find and make authorized uses of copyrighted works . . . . Reliable information will also facilitate efficient licensing and reduce transaction costs for licensable uses of copyrighted works."[39]

The obligation to provide effective protection of rights management appears in article 12 of the *WIPO Copyright Treaty* (*WCT*). This international obligation is implemented through section 41.22 of the Act:

> **41.22** (1) No person shall knowingly remove or alter any rights management information in electronic form without the consent of the owner of the copyright in the work, the performer's performance or the sound

---

39   Efroni, above note 3 at 337–38.

recording, if the person knows or should have known that the removal or alteration will facilitate or conceal any infringement of the owner's copyright or adversely affect the owner's right to remuneration under section 19.

Unlike TPM circumvention, liability for altering or removing rights management information has intent requirements. There must be an intent to remove or alter the information as well as knowledge (real or construed) that such an act will "facilitate or conceal" infringement or "adversely affect" the remuneration right. A secondary obligation is imposed on vendors, distributors, importers, broadcasters, and Internet transmitters of such works. Again, the obligation is to not knowingly commit listed acts in connection with a work that one actually or constructively knows has had its rights management information altered or removed.[40] As with technological protection measures, contravention of either of these obligations entitles a copyright owner to a cause of action for which all infringement remedies are available.

Section 41.22 is restricted to rights management information in electronic, or digital, form. This conjures up images of hacking into a work by tampering with its underlying code. However, commonplace acts, such as the posting of user-generated content, run the risk of contravening rights management protection. Consider that in the US case of *Murphy v Millennium Radio Group, LLC*, the posting of a photo onto a website that cut off the name of the copyright owner was found to contravene the *DMCA*.[41] Indeed, under section 41.22 of the Canadian Act, there seems little doubt that such an act would constitute removal of rights management information in electronic form:

The scope of protected information is as follows:

(4) In this section, "rights management information" means information that
(a) is attached to or embodied in a copy of a work, a performer's performance fixed in a sound recording or a sound recording, or appears in connection with its communication to the public by telecommunication; and
(b) identifies or permits the identification of the work or its author, the performance or its performer, the sound recording or its maker or

---

40   Section 41.22(3).
41   650 F3d 295 (3d Cir 2011).

the holder of any rights in the work, the performance or the sound recording, or concerns the terms or conditions of the work's, performance's or sound recording's use.

Article 12 of the *WCT* clarifies that rights management information includes "any numbers or dots that represent such information."[42] Thus, the removal or alteration of digital rights information in the code that underlies the work also runs afoul of section 41.22.

There may be some uncertainty about where, or the means by which, rights management information must appear in relation to the work in order to be protected. Section 41.22(4)(a) uses broad language: "attached to or embodied in a copy of a work" or "appears in connection with its communication to the public by telecommunication." The proximity of the rights management information in relation to the work has been controversial in US law, where rights management information is defined in similarly broad terms.[43] For example, would a hyperlink at the bottom of a web page "appear in connection" with a work? The proximity question also bears directly on the *mens rea* component to the cause of action: can one knowingly remove something that he does not know exists? A reasonable balance should be struck between notice and access to users, on the one hand, and not making such requirements unduly cumbersome or unreasonable in a given context, for example, detailed terms and conditions posted on the same web page as the work. As one commentator has suggested,

> Copyright owners should post [RMI] in accessible locations so that users may know the parameters of the use of the work. They should not play a game of "gotcha." And users should come to expect to look for [RMI] and be held accountable for following the terms of use if they want to avoid fraud in the marketplace, especially on the Internet, where inauthentic and unauthorized copies can flourish. Use of a clearly marked and accessible hyperlink on a webpage containing a copyrighted work meets the needs of both parties.[44]

---

42  Above note 1, art 12(2).
43  That is, as being "conveyed in connection" with a work. See, generally, Russell W Jacobs, "Gutters and Hyperlinks: The *DMCA* and Proper Position of Copyright Management Information" (2013) 11 *Northwestern Journal of Technology and Intellectual Property* 163.
44  *Ibid* at 172.

Finally, rights management information has sometimes been associated in the literature with the invasion of privacy. This is because "IP phone home" technologies can be implanted in digital products such that rights holders are able to monitor user behaviours. There is nothing in the Act that permits this! More than that, as we saw in section 41.14 above, it is perfectly legal to access a work to determine whether it is tracking personal information and if so, to disable it. Moreover, users can take additional comfort in the fact that privacy legislation makes it illegal for commercial organizations to collect, use, or disclose personal information without the express consent of the individual concerned.[45]

\* \* \* \* \*

It is not just a little controversial that Canada has implemented a system of anti-circumvention measures that are apparently stronger than in the United States. This is because the US *DMCA* anti-circumvention measures caused a great deal of concern in terms of their unintended consequences of, for example, stifling innovation and restricting competition. These unintended consequences now drive result-oriented and inconsistent decisions that have made it difficult to make coherent sense of the provisions. With a stronger regime in place — and most notably an apparent access right — it seems likely that Canadian copyright law will encounter similar problems.

---

45   See the *Personal Information Protection and Electronic Documents Act*, SC 2000, c 5 [*PIPEDA*], for example.

CHAPTER 6

# User Rights

## A. INTRODUCTION

The apparent emphasis of the *Copyright Act*, and its pre-millennial interpretation by courts, has been on the nature of the monopoly rights granted to authors, and their exploitation by owners. During the past fifteen years or so, however, there has been a seismic interpretive shift by Canadian courts in the way that key provisions of the Act (particularly the so-called exceptions to copyright infringement) are to be understood. Key to this shift is a new perspective which sees user rights of works as contributing to, rather than diminishing, the goals of copyright policy. Beginning with the Supreme Court decisions in *Théberge v Galerie d'Art du Petit Champlain inc* and *CCH Canadian Ltd v Law Society of Upper Canada*[1] copyright law has been as much concerned with upholding the rights of purchasers and users of content as with protecting the legitimate interests of copyright holders.

The concept of user rights is potentially broad and may include elements that are in the public domain available for all to use, for example, the use of the idea behind a work. It may also include exhaustion rights afforded to purchasers of copyrighted works. These aspects of user rights are discussed in Chapter 2. Here, the focus is on the legitimate uses of copyrighted works during the term of the monopoly under fair

---

1  2002 SCC 34 [*Théberge*]; 2004 SCC 13 [*CCH*].

dealing (sections 29–29.2) and the specific exceptions recited thereafter in sections 29.21–32.2. The difference between these two sets of user rights is pronounced. Fair dealing is a broadly conceived right whereas the specific exceptions are unusually detailed and condition laden. It makes sense, as discussed in Chapter 2, to treat the specific exceptions as offering clear guidance to users as to how to definitively avoid infringing copyright. Failure to meet the exact terms of these exceptions should not be understood as infringement but as signalling the need to analyze the use in terms of whether it constitutes infringement and if so, whether fair dealing is a defence.

## B. FAIR DEALING

The fair dealing exceptions, listed in sections 29–29.2, are the centrepiece of user rights under the Act. Section 29 states: "Fair dealing for the purpose of research, private study, education, parody or satire does not infringe copyright." Additional exceptions are made for criticism and review, and news reporting with the further requirement that the dealing attributes the source and, if given, author, performer, maker, or broadcaster of the work or neighbouring right.[2] It is important to note that the use of copyrighted material must be characterized as fitting one of these purposes to be eligible for fair dealing. In *CCH*, the Supreme Court recast fair dealing as an "integral part of the *Copyright Act*" and not merely as a defence.[3] Further: "The fair dealing exception, like other exceptions in the *Copyright Act*, is a user's right. In order to maintain the proper balance between the rights of a copyright owner and users' interests, it must not be interpreted restrictively."[4] In *CCH*, the Supreme Court set out a two-step inquiry to determine fair dealing, namely, to assess (1) whether the dealing was for an allowable purpose and (2) whether it was fair.[5]

### 1) Allowable Purposes

The reason for the dealing must fit within one or more of eight allowable purposes: research, private study, education, parody, satire, review,

---

2   See ss 29.1 & 29.2.
3   *CCH*, above note 1 at para 48.
4   Ibid.
5   Ibid at para 50.

criticism, or news reporting. Education, parody, and satire were added through the *Copyright Modernization Act*, or *CMA*. The exact contours of the education exception are not clear. The addition of parody and satire is welcome as it settles two erstwhile problems in the law. First, it avoids the need to fit parody or satire under criticism and thus be bound by attribution requirements that are neither appropriate nor necessary for this form of comedy.[6] Second, it avoids the problematic distinction, apparent in US law, between parody (which ridicules the work) and satire (which ridicules some larger social phenomenon).[7]

The Supreme Court has repeatedly affirmed that the fair dealing purposes are to be given "a large and liberal interpretation in order to ensure that users' rights are not unduly constrained."[8] In *CCH*, the Court was not prepared to limit the research exception to non-commercial uses or private contexts.[9] Therefore, lawyers who conduct research to advise clients and other for-profit legal services may avail themselves of the exception. The full breadth of this "large and liberal" interpretation of the allowable purposes for fair dealing became even more apparent in *Society of Composers, Authors and Music Publishers of Canada v Bell Canada* and *Alberta (Education) v Canadian Copyright Licensing Agency (Access Copyright)*.[10]

---

6   For example, in *Michelin v CAW — Canada*, [1997] 2 FC 306 (FC), the trial court refused (wrongly) to characterize parody as criticism. The attribution requirements are in s 29.1 and require that, if a work is criticized the source and author (or equivalent) of the work must be cited. As many have criticized, such a requirement is not needed for parody which, to be effective, conjures up the work it is referencing; moreover, it would be awkward to make such an attribution in a parody.

7   See *Campbell v Acuff-Rose Music, Inc*, 510 US 569 (1994) [*Acuff-Rose*]; where parody is an allowable fair use while satire is not. In that case, a rap song poked fun at the banal innocent lyrics of "Pretty Woman" which the court characterized as a parody. Arguably, the rap song could just as easily have been characterized as a satire mocking the relative innocence of a music composition from this age, of which "Pretty Woman" would be an example.

8   *CCH*, above note 1 at para 51. In *CCH*, the fair dealing purpose was "research." There is no convincing reason why a large and liberal interpretation would not be given to all eight fair dealing purposes. Indeed, subsequent caselaw has confirmed this: see *Warman v Fournier*, 2012 FC 803 at para 31, where "news reporting" was given a large and liberal interpretation; and *Re Collective Administration in Relation to Rights under Sections 3, 15, 18, and 21*, [2015] CBD No 2 at para 240 [*Rts under ss 3, 15, 18, and 21*]: "... all of the purposes enumerated in sections 29–29.2 of the *Act* must receive a large and liberal interpretation."

9   *CCH*, above note 1 at para 51.

10  2012 SCC 36 [*Bell*]; 2012 SCC 37 [*Alberta Education*].

In *Bell*, research for the purpose of fair dealing was advanced in connection with an online music sampling service that allowed consumers to listen to thirty to ninety second clips of songs before deciding whether or not to purchase. SOCAN (Society of Composers, Authors and Music Publishers of Canada) argued first, that the purpose of the dealing should be viewed from the perspective of the service provider trying to sell music file downloads, and second, that allowable research must result in a creative or added-value output. The Supreme Court rejected both arguments. Research, as understood in section 29, "can be piecemeal, informal, exploratory, or confirmatory" and "for no other purpose except personal interest."[11] Moreover, as a user right, research is to be understood from the end-user's perspective, which, in this case, was the consumer listening to the previews.[12]

Similarly, in *Alberta Education*, where teacher-created course packs for student dissemination were under consideration, the court adopted a liberal, end-user perspective on research and private study under section 29. Rather than considering the use as instruction, which was not at the time an allowable purpose, the court viewed teachers as facilitators of research and private study of the student end-users.[13] As it stated in *Bell*, there is "a relatively low threshold for the first step so that the analytical heavy-hitting is done in determining whether the dealing was fair."[14] More recent authority even suggests that fair dealing need not be the sole or predominant purpose so long as it is one of the purposes of the dealing.[15]

Although the threshold is low, it must still be possible to characterize some element of the dealing as connected to a permitted purpose. A pre-*CCH* case illustrates the point nicely. In *Productions Avanti Ciné-Vidéo Inc v Favreau*, the Quebec Court of Appeal refused to characterize the borrowing of elements from the plaintiff's television series in the production of an adult film as parody. In a concurring opinion, Rothman J observed that the purpose of the dealing was not to parody the plain-

---

11   *Bell*, above note 10 at para 22.
12   *Ibid* at paras 29 & 30. Moreover, previews trigger purchases that lead to increased dissemination of works and compensation for owners, thus advancing copyright's other interests (at para 30).
13   *Alberta Education*, above note 10 at para 23. Education as an exception was added after this case was decided.
14   *Bell*, above note 10 at para 27.
15   *Rts under ss 3, 15, 18, and 21*, above note 8 at paras 243–46.

tiff's work but to exploit its popularity "by appropriating its characters, costumes and decor as a mise-en-scène."[16] Elaborating on the distinction between parody and outright exploitation, he continued:

> Parody normally involves the humorous imitation of the work of another writer, often exaggerated, for the purposes of criticism or comment. Appropriation of the work of another writer to exploit its popular success for commercial purposes is quite a different thing.[17]

## 2) Criteria for Assessing Fairness

Once an allowable purpose of the dealing is found, the second step is to assess whether the dealing is "fair." The *CCH* court offered a non-exhaustive list of six factors that courts may look at to make this determination: (1) the purpose of the dealing, (2) the character of the dealing, (3) the amount of the dealing, (4) alternatives to the dealing, (5) the nature of the work, and (6) the effect of the dealing on the work. The Court indicated that these factors may not arise in every case of fair dealing.[18]

The *purpose of the dealing*, already found to be permissible under the first step, appears repetitive at the second stage for assessing fairness. Courts have maintained that this is not, in fact, the case. In *CCH*, purpose as a fairness consideration had two dimensions: an "objective assessment" of the user's "real purpose or motive" in using the work, and as a way to determine a more specific goal of the dealing, for example, whether it is for commercial or non-commercial reasons (the latter being inherently more fair).[19] On the first issue, the concern appears to be whether an allowable purpose is being used to shield truly infringing behaviour. As the *Alberta Education* court stated, in the context of teacher-initiated copying for student course packs, if "the copier hides behind the shield of the user's allowable purpose in order to engage in a separate purpose that tends to make the dealing unfair, that separate purpose will also be relevant to the fairness analysis."[20]

---

16 (1999), 177 DLR (4th) 568 at para 8, Rothman J.
17 *Ibid* at para 10.
18 Above note 1 at para 53.
19 *Ibid* at para 55. On purpose as goal of the dealing, see *Rts under ss 3, 15, 18, and 21*, above note 8 at para 259ff.
20 *Alberta Education*, above note 10 at para 22.

In *CCH* and subsequent caselaw, "reasonable safeguards" put in place to ensure that the use is faithful to the permitted purpose has weighed heavily under this factor. In *Bell*, for example, the fact that the previews were streamed (not downloaded), short, and of lesser quality compared with purchased downloads ensured that they would not be a substitute for purchasing music but would fulfill only a research function.[21] By the same token, when Netflix argued that free subscriber trials of its streamed content (movies and TV shows), which contains musical works in audiovisual format, was akin to free music previews in *Bell*, the Copyright Board balked:

> ... the analogy between free previews and free trials is weak. In a free preview, the customer can hear a portion of a musical work in a degraded format. In a free trial, the customer can hear complete musical works, to the extent that such works are fixed in the audiovisual work being watched.[22]

For *character of the dealing*, the courts consider the extent to which the work is disseminated and whether or not copies are eventually destroyed.[23] For example, the less a work is distributed and the more likely such copies are to be destroyed after use, the more likely the dealing will be judged fair. In *Bell*, the court seemed to conflate destruction with extent of dissemination: "The fact that each file [streamed preview] was automatically deleted meant that copies could not be duplicated or further disseminated by users."[24] The *Bell* court, however, was notoriously silent about the extent of dissemination caused by the preview service as it relates to character of the dealing. Still, it may be inferred from that court's statements on technological neutrality that massive Internet dissemination of the work will not work against the fairness of the dealing — at least insofar as the purpose of the use justifies it. The Copyright Board is probably correct in suggesting that these factors — extent of dissemination and destruction of copies made — must be judged in light of the purpose of the dealing:

---

21   *Bell*, above note 10 at para 35.
22   *Re Collective Administration of Performing and of Communication Rights*, [2014] CBD No 3 at para 60. It is interesting that diminished format was considered controlling and not impermanence or both.
23   *CCH*, above note 1 at para 55.
24   *Bell*, above note 10 at para 38.

Where the character of the dealing helps ensure that the work will be used for a permitted purpose, this would tend to make the dealing fair; where works are unnecessarily kept, or distributed unnecessarily, and where such acts risk that other unfair dealing will occur, this would tend to make the dealing unfair. For example, by its very nature, news reporting and criticism may result in works being widely disseminated .... Penalizing such dealings for achieving their goal would go contrary to the enumerated purposes of the fair dealing provisions.[25]

In gauging acceptable standards for character of the dealing, the *CCH* court indicated that custom or practice in a trade or industry may be relevant.[26] In *Century 21 Canada Limited Partnership v Rogers Communications Inc*, the plaintiff argued that the defendants' failure to abide by a "robot exclusion standard" on the Internet was evidence that the character of the dealing was unfair. Essentially, the argument was that the defendant did not disclose the identity of its robots to the Internet community so that measures could be taken to prevent the defendant's robots from accessing and copying the plaintiff's web pages. By not abiding by this Internet custom or practice, in other words, the defendant's dealing with the work was unfair. The court rightly rejected this argument by observing that the "Robot Exclusion Standard addresses how the copyrighted material was acquired, not how it was used" and thus, this was not relevant to fair dealing.[27]

The *amount of the dealing* pertains to the quantitative borrowing of the work, as well as the importance of the work.[28] Quantitative taking is assessed on an individual-per-dealing basis. Thus, it is the amount of each song that is streamed in an individual streaming experience that is measured, not the amount of streaming that occurs *in the aggregate*. Here is where the court in *Bell* references technological neutrality in that measuring aggregate use would disadvantage fair dealings over the Internet as compared with other media.[29] As well, the fairness of the dealing will depend on the purpose for which the work is being used. In some cases, it is justifiable to use an entire work, for example,

---

25 *Rts under ss 3, 15, 18, and 21*, above note 8 at paras 300–1.
26 Ibid.
27 2011 BCSC 1196 at para 253 [*Century 21*].
28 *CCH*, above note 1 at para 56.
29 See discussion of technological neutrality in Chapter 1.

for private research, while for other purposes, for example, criticism, this may not be the case.[30] Thus far, courts have not considered the relevance of the "importance of the work" nor has there been any suggestion that the amount taken should be assessed on a qualitative basis.[31]

The fourth factor, *alternatives to the dealing*, considers whether using a copyrighted work is reasonably necessary to achieve the purpose.[32] The implication is that if a non-copyrighted alternative is available, then the dealing will less likely be considered fair. It is not a reasonable alternative, for example, to require students to purchase copies of a book as an alternative to copying, when only a small amount of the book is to be reproduced.[33] Nor is it reasonable to expect lawyers from across Ontario to attend a Toronto library to read a case rather than have it copied.[34] Other than hardship created by the alternative, effectiveness of other measures also seems to be relevant. In *Bell*, for example, it is not an effective alternative to base music sampling on album artwork, descriptions, and reviews — or return policies — as opposed to streamed previews.[35] In *Century 21*, released before *Bell* was decided, the trial court held that the defendants might have acquired the information about property listings for their meta search website by other means than copying from the plaintiff's website.[36] However, doing this would seem an onerous requirement not proportionate to the purpose of the dealing, which is to aggregate property listings from multiple websites as a convenient research tool for end-users.

The *nature of the work* refers to issues such as whether the work is confidential and whether or not it has been published. Use of the former would tilt the analysis towards "unfair" whereas contributing to the dissemination of the latter would have the opposite effect. It is interesting that this factor considers matter external to copyright law per se. It is not clear why or how protecting privacy interests or confidential information fits with the goals of copyright law, which are to

---

30  *CCH*, above note 1 at para 56.
31  Qualitative assessment was rejected in *Rts under ss 3, 15, 18, and 21*, above note 8 at paras 315–25.
32  *CCH*, above note 1 at para 57.
33  *Alberta Education*, above note 10 at para 32.
34  *CCH*, above note 1 at para 69.
35  *Bell*, above note 10 at paras 45 & 46.
36  *Century 21*, above note 27 at para 262.

encourage creation and dissemination of works.[37] Moreover, it creates tensions within copyright law itself. In particular, the right to publish a work is a right of the author, yet Canadian copyright law seems to suggest that a use that involves publishing an unpublished work will more likely be considered fair. In fact, in *Warman v Fournier*, publication of an unpublished work militated in favour of fair dealing, without considering the author's right of the publication.[38] To the extent the dealing promotes dissemination or purchase of published works, this favours fairness of the dealing. Thus, in *Bell*, music previews facilitate the identification of a work which could then be purchased.[39]

Finally, *the effect of the dealing on the work* considers whether, and the extent to which, the use competes with the original work in the marketplace.[40] Beginning with *CCH*, courts insist that evidence of lost profits caused by the competing use be tendered into evidence. Courts will not make inferences about negative market effects. Some uses are, in fact, complementary to sales of the original work, which tends to make the dealing fair. In *Bell*, for example, the previews did not compete with the original but facilitated sales of the previewed work.[41] By contrast, in *Century 21* (decided before *Bell*), the trial court ruled that a meta search website that copied works from a real-estate company website weighed against fairness of the dealing, even though the court acknowledged that the primary purpose of the plaintiff's website was to facilitate real-estate sales.[42] The situation in *Century 21* is analogous to *Bell* in that the meta search website was complementary to the plaintiff's business: it increased dissemination of the works, which was ultimately beneficial to the plaintiff. As such, this part of *Century 21* appears wrongly decided.

---

37  The relationship has not been articulated. This is not to suggest that these goals are irreconcilable. We can imagine that an author would be encouraged to create a work (say, a private journal) on the assurance that the law would not require her to disclose it — thus creating incentive. The goal of dissemination might later be achieved by publication of the work after the author's death.
38  Above note 8 at para 33.
39  *Bell*, above note 10 at para 47.
40  *CCH*, above note 1 at para 59.
41  *Bell*, above note 10 at para 48.
42  *Century 21*, above note 27 at para 275.

## 3) Fair Dealing in the Digital Context

Some general trends emerge from the above analysis of the caselaw on fair dealing. First, the threshold for meeting one of the eight enumerated purposes of fair dealing is low and will be considered in a broad and purposive manner. What this means is that the focus will not be on the status of the person who copies or disseminates the works but on the substantive purpose of the dealing, including its ultimate end use. Second, it is useful to consider the fairness factors in a proportional relationship to the permitted purpose of the dealing. In other words, whether an amount borrowed from a work or the extent of its dissemination is to be considered fair will often be justified, as it should, relative to the reason for doing so. Third, custom or practice in an industry can be relevant and useful evidence going to fairness of the dealing. In this regard, users in various creative and educational sectors of the economy should be encouraged to develop authoritative codes of best practices for fair dealing.[43] Fourth, uses that are mainly complementary to sales of the original work should weigh towards fairness of the dealing, even if there is a theoretical or small probability of competition.

There are three additional observations that might be made in connection with digital technologies in particular. First, where feasible and warranted (again, relative to the purpose), dealings will more likely be considered fair if digital copies are destroyed or reasonable safeguards are in place to limit the possibility of downstream infringement. Reasonable safeguards will probably also include measures that, where possible, ensure that the dealing promotes use of the work, for example, meta news search engines such as Google News or Huffington Post that link directly to the web page of the source publication so as not to divert ad revenue.

Second, the threshold for alternatives to the dealing is particularly high in the digital context since often an efficient and equally effective real-space second choice is lacking. It makes little sense to require users to obtain musical previews in any other way than by sample clips over the Internet; as well, it is unduly time-consuming and cumbersome

---

43   See Patricia Aufderheide & Peter Jaszi, *Reclaiming Fair Use: How to Put Balance Back in Copyright* (Chicago: University of Chicago Press, 2011), which tells the story of how documentary filmmakers (and others) developed codes of best practices as a way to authoritatively guide users on fair use in the United States.

to require the operators of meta search engines to manually compile information. The goals of copyright, which include the wide dissemination of works and the facilitation of fair dealing uses such as research, suggest that technological efficiencies should be embraced rather than discouraged in favour of the least infringing option.

Finally, and most important, the impact of widespread dissemination of the work through the Internet as affecting the *character of the dealing*, which might have skewed fair dealing analysis in this context, has been neutralized. The application of the principle of technological neutrality to this digital fact means that the Internet is to be embraced as a tool of dissemination. Moreover, the neutralization of this digital fact appears to be one of general application so long as widespread dissemination can be justified vis-à-vis the purpose of the dealing.

A distinction should be made between two kinds of digital uses: conventional uses and digitalization uses. The distinction becomes clear when we consider mass digitization projects which endeavour to create comprehensive digital repositories of works. Such projects "operate on the basis of routine, automatic, and indiscriminate copying of works en masse, for which no authorization can be realistically sought."[44] They may enable one or more of three purposes: (1) preservation of works, such as digitization of rare books; (2) access to works by enabling the public to use a centralized database of works; and (3) computation, for example, analytics and data mining.[45] Mass digitization projects can enable either conventional or digitalization uses of a work or both kinds of uses.

Conventional uses are those that are functionally equivalent to real-space dealings with a work except that they are created with digital technologies or appear in a digital environment such as the Internet. These are new expressive uses of a work. Thus, when Google Books permits users to review a small snippet from a book as a preview to possible purchase, it is using the work for a new purpose of facilitating research.[46] A digitalization use is one where digital technologies are

---

44   Maurizio Borghi & Stavroula Karapapa, *Copyright and Mass Digitization: A Cross Jurisdictional Perspective* (Oxford: Oxford University Press, 2013) at 19. Mass digitization involves two separate reproductions of the work: a scanned image file of each page and a corresponding text file.
45   *Ibid* at 11ff.
46   Indeed, the snippet and search functions of Google Books were found to come within fair use of US copyright law: see *Authors Guild v Google, Inc*, No 13-4829-cv (2d Cir, October 16, 2015) [*Google*].

employed to achieve some functional result, such as meta-analyzing works for new information. These are new digitalization uses of the work, quite removed from new expressive activity. In Chapter 2, I suggest that the making of non-consumptive copies, of which digitalization uses is one category, is outside the scope of copyright. If that is not the case, then fair dealing must be considered.

It is difficult to imagine anything but the most generous interpretations of the fair dealing provisions insofar as digitization projects serve any of the above-mentioned three purposes: preservation, access, or computation. Each activity, in its own way, facilitates the research, private study, and education purposes of fair dealing. To the extent that such projects facilitate research for end-users and promote dissemination and sales of the original work, such uses generally appear fair. Even the amount of the dealing — copying of entire libraries of works — may be justified in facilitating access to works provided appropriate safeguards are in place. To the extent that the use is purely computational, the case for fairness of the dealing is even stronger for three reasons. First, this kind of activity is far removed from the goals and legitimate interests normally associated with copyright. Second, copying of entire libraries is justified by the purpose of the dealing: to create a comprehensive database from which to retrieve content or meaningful data. Massive copying of entire works is, in other words, proportionate to the purpose. Third, since their purposes are entirely different computational uses are more likely to be complementary to, not competitive with, the original expressive use.

While the above analysis applies to Canadian fair dealing principles, it is striking that US courts have used similar reasoning in their fair use rulings in mass digitization cases.[47] Whether the facts involved search engines, which displayed copyrighted content in some form, or data mining, which does not, US courts have embraced these projects as meeting an important public interest of access to information. In *Kelly v Arriba Soft Corp*, where a search engine returned smaller and lower-resolution thumbnails of original images found on websites, the court found that the defendant's use constituted an entirely different purpose than the original image, that is, "... improving access

---

47   336 F3d 811 (9th Cir 2003) [*Arriba Soft*]; *Perfect 10, Inc v Amazon*, 508 F3d 1146 (9th Cir 2007) [*Perfect 10*]; *AV v iParadigms*, 562 F3d 630 (4th Cir 2009); *Authors Guild, Inc v HathiTrust*, 755 F3d 87 (2d Cir 2014) [*HathiTrust*].

to information on the internet versus artistic expression."[48] These uses, moreover, have been considered so transformative and important that any commercial element associated with them has been marginalized relative to the importance of the purpose.[49]

These cases uniformly found that digital copying of entire works was essential to the purpose undertaken. In *Authors Guild, Inc v HathiTrust*, where entire libraries were digitized to facilitate full-text searches (but never to display any content), the court found it "reasonably necessary" and "not excessive" to copy all the books in their collections.[50] Of course, the fairness of mass copying of entire works in *HathiTrust* and *Arriba Soft* is proportionately connected to the purpose, the creation of a comprehensive full-text search function for books and of a search tool on the web, respectively. Despite these generous interpretations, it would be wrong for users to be too cavalier in how they deal with works. In *Arriba Soft*, for example, the court emphasized that the works did not serve the same purpose and did not compete with the original, since the quality of the thumbnail image was lower than the original. This comment suggests the importance of reasonable safeguards being put in place to avoid substitutability with the original or other unfair uses.

## C. EXCEPTIONS OUTLINED IN SECTIONS 29.21 TO 32.2

The above fair dealing exceptions exist alongside a number of specifically tailored exceptions contained in sections 29.21 to 32.2 of the Act. The exceptions can be pleaded in the alternative so that if a use fails for some reason as fair dealing, then a defendant may still resort to one of the other exceptions in the Act or vice versa.[51] Failure to meet the specific terms of these exceptions does not automatically infer infringement. In other words, the exceptions are not necessarily comprehensive treatments concerning liability of the activity in question; rather, they offer greater certainty for users who seek to avoid committing infringement.[52] Where the specific terms or conditions are not met,

---

48  *Arriba Soft*, above note 47 at 819.
49  See, for example, *ibid* at 818; and *Perfect 10*, above note 47 at 1166.
50  *HathiTrust*, above note 47 at 98. See also *Google*, above note 46 at 21 for a similar holding.
51  *CCH*, above note 1 at para 49.
52  See discussion in Chapter 1.

courts must consider whether the act in question constitutes infringement and (if pleaded) whether fair dealing is a defence.

## 1) User-Generated Content

One of the most interesting additions to the *Copyright Act* by way of the *Copyright Modification Act* was the inclusion of section 29.21, "non-commercial user-generated content," or UGC. The basic thrust of the provision is to except from copyright infringement the making of new works through remixing of existing content, so long as a number of conditions are met. As Scassa notes, this exception reflects "the shifting realities of cultural production and dissemination"[53] inasmuch as "digital technologies empower users of digital works to interact in new ways with copyright-protected content; at the same time, the proliferation of new and modified content from non-professional sources has undermined the traditional content intermediaries, creating a radically transformed context for the dissemination of information and cultural content."[54] While the UGC exception is sometimes referred to as the "YouTube exception," thereby conjuring up images of amateurish videos of children dancing to copyrighted music in the background, the range of activities potentially encompassed by this provision is wide and may include culturally significant and innovative creations.[55]

The provision reads as follows:

> **29.21** (1) It is not an infringement of copyright for an individual to use an existing work or other subject-matter or copy of one, which has been published or otherwise made available to the public, in the creation of a new work or other subject-matter in which copyright subsists and for the individual — or, with the individual's authorization, a member of their household — to use the new work or other subject-matter or to authorize an intermediary to disseminate it, if

---

53  Teresa Scassa, "Acknowledging Copyright's Illegitimate Offspring: User-Generated Content and Canadian Copyright Law" in Michael Geist, ed, *The Copyright Pentalogy: How the Supreme Court of Canada Shook the Foundations of Canadian Copyright Law* (Ottawa: University of Ottawa Press, 2013) 431 at 431.
54  Scassa, *ibid* at 432.
55  See *ibid* at 434 referencing fan fiction mashups, video game modifications, and parodic and satirical uses of existing works, or the creation of apps based on government data compilations as examples.

(a) the use of, or the authorization to disseminate, the new work or other subject-matter is done solely for non-commercial purposes;

(b) the source — and, if given in the source, the name of the author, performer, maker or broadcaster — of the existing work or other subject-matter or copy of it are mentioned, if it is reasonable in the circumstances to do so;

(c) the individual had reasonable grounds to believe that the existing work or other subject-matter or copy of it, as the case may be, was not infringing copyright; and

(d) the use of, or the authorization to disseminate, the new work or other subject-matter does not have a substantial adverse effect, financial or otherwise, on the exploitation or potential exploitation of the existing work or other subject-matter — or copy of it — or on an existing or potential market for it, including that the new work or other subject-matter is not a substitute for the existing one.

The cumulative requirements of this provision are many. The introductory wording outlines four requirements pertaining to the scope of non-commercial user-generated content covered. The first requirement is that the user-creator must be an "individual." While this should exclude corporate entities,[56] the provision extends to collaborations between two or more persons based on a purposive reading of the provision and section 33(2) of the *Interpretation Act*.[57] Second, the existing work[58] must already have been published or publicly disseminated. Third, unless the creation is a neighbouring right, "new work" implies that the originality requirements of skill and judgment must be satisfied. (Ironically, this could be a challenging requirement for YouTube videos of the kind indicated above.) Fourth, the user-creator is given a right of use in the resulting new work. *Use* is defined in section 29.21(2) of the *Copyright Act* as the rights of an owner (economic rights under section 3). Instead of a general authorization right, as per section 3, however, the user-creator has the right to authorize an intermediary to disseminate the new work.

---

56  *Ibid* at 436.
57  RSC 1985, c I-21, s 33(2): "Words in the singular include the plural, and words in the plural include the singular."
58  Again, a purposive reading and s 33(2) of the *Interpretation Act* suggest that user-creators should be able to draw on one or more works in their creation.

There are four additional conditions outlined in the enumerated paragraphs of section 29.21. First, the use of the new work (or its dissemination) must be done "solely" for non-commercial purposes. It is sensible that the purpose of the use should be assessed from the perspective of the user-creator.[59] The word "solely" suggests that a commercial purpose of any kind will bring the use outside the exception. It is unclear whether user-generated content initially made for a non-commercial purpose is transformed into a commercial purpose if, for example, the creator later profits from the new work. Trickier still is the characterization of a commercial purpose. Scassa illustrates the points nicely:

> It is clear from the business world that "free" does not necessarily mean non-commercial. Free content may be a means of self-promotion, or it may build or enhance reputation with a view to professional or other advancement. In some cases, the fame or notoriety that leads to commercial benefits may be entirely unanticipated, but may nevertheless flow from the dissemination of UGC.[60]

The second and third conditions are relatively straightforward. Subparagraph (b) imposes an attribution requirement to the work or neighbouring right where reasonable in the circumstances to do so. Subparagraph (c) requires that the existing work or copy thereof not infringe copyright.

Fourth, and perhaps most controversially, use or dissemination must not have a "substantial adverse effect, financial or otherwise" on the exploitation or potential exploitation of the work or neighbouring right or its markets. The threshold of "substantial," to some extent, offsets the wide breadth of this condition. However, while it is understandable that substantial adverse *financial* effects would be a condition for user-generated content, it is less clear why other such effects, for example, reputational, are also prohibited. This has clear implications for parodic or satirical uses that may, through ridicule, lessen the attractiveness of the existing work. It may also be difficult to anticipate or control the consequences of user-generated content for an existing work, thus creating uncertainty as to whether a particular piece of user-generated content fits within this exception.

---

59   Scassa, above note 53 at 441.
60   *Ibid* at 441–42.

Finally, the reference to *potential* in reference to exploitation of, or markets for, the existing work, exposes a tension between creator and user rights.[61] The tension is the overlap between an owner's right to exploit uses or markets for their work with a user's right to deal fairly with a work for an enumerated purpose. For example, parody may simultaneously be conceived as both a derivative right of the owner and a legitimate purpose of fair dealing for a user of a work.[62] At a minimum, courts should be satisfied that there is concrete evidence indicating an intention on the part of the owner to exploit a work in a way similar to the user-generated content before invoking potential exploitation or market as a basis for denying the application of this exception.

## 2) Private Copy Exceptions

The *Copyright Modification Act* introduced three new private copy exceptions. These exceptions pertain to the making of (1) a single copy of a work or neighbouring right for private purposes, (2) a backup copy of a work or neighbouring right, and (3) copying of a broadcast for later viewing. Strict conditions are in place to ensure that the first copy (or access) is legally obtained or purchased, and that such copies are used only for a narrowly defined purpose and not otherwise disseminated. Controversially, the right to make private copies under these provisions does not extend to a work or neighbouring right that is locked by anti-circumvention measures. Thus, the private copy exceptions do not effectively exist for works protected by technological protection measures (TPMs). These regimes exist alongside, but do not replace, the increasingly irrelevant private copying regimes under Part VII of the Act.[63]

The private copy exception for personal use is set out in section 29.22(1), which reads:

---

61 This tension is implicit also in the sixth factor in the fairness analysis for fair dealing.
62 A famous instance of this is the US case of *Acuff-Rose*, above note 7. Fair use for the purpose of parody was made through a rap version of the song "Pretty Woman" by Roy Orbison. The plaintiff tried to argue that this use supplanted its derivative right to exploit a rap version of the song. There was, however, no evidence of any intention on the part of the plaintiff to exploit this right.
63 See s 29.22(3).

It is not an infringement of copyright for an individual to reproduce a work or other subject-matter or any substantial part of a work or other subject-matter if

(a) the copy of the work or other subject-matter from which the reproduction is made is not an infringing copy;

(b) the individual legally obtained the copy of the work or other subject-matter from which the reproduction is made, other than by borrowing it or renting it, and owns or is authorized to use the medium or device on which it is reproduced;

(c) the individual, in order to make the reproduction, did not circumvent, as defined in section 41, a technological protection measure, as defined in that section, or cause one to be circumvented;

(d) the individual does not give the reproduction away; and

(e) the reproduction is used only for the individual's private purposes.

It is significant that section 29.22(1)(a) refers to the copy from which the reproduction is made, the initial copy. This suggests that private copying does *not* apply to works that are streamed or otherwise telecommunicated. Section 29.22(1)(e) implies, when read alongside section 29.24, that the copy made can be used and need not lie dormant as a backup copy in case the original becomes in some way unusable. Section 29.22(1)(b) is aimed at ensuring that the initial copy is purchased or otherwise legally obtained, not borrowed or rented. Presumably, "rent" also includes a licensing arrangement to the extent that it is a time-limited, less-than-full-value "transfer" of the work to which the private copying exception is not intended to apply.

Section 29.22(1)(b) also ensures that the copy is placed on a medium or device that is owned (or authorized to be used) by the person who purchased the original. Sections 29.22(2) and (3) clearly demarcate between mediums subject to the Part VII regime (interpreted to apply to copies made on mediums separate from devices onto which copies are played, for example, CDs and tape cassettes), on the one hand, and other types of digital storage to which section 29.22 applies, on the other.[64] Finally, under section 29.22(4), the private copy must be destroyed if the initial copy is given away, rented, or sold. This means that

---

64 Section 29.22(2). See *Canadian Private Copying Collective v Canadian Storage Media Alliance*, 2004 FCA 424 for the interpretation of medium and device under Part VII (also discussed in Chapter 3).

the exception would not apply to someone who keeps a copy of a CD that she has resold in a second-hand market.

The backup copy exception is set out under section 29.24(1):

> It is not an infringement of copyright in a work or other subject-matter for a person who owns — or has a licence to use — a copy of the work or subject-matter (in this section referred to as the "source copy") to reproduce the source copy if
> (a) the person does so solely for backup purposes in case the source copy is lost, damaged or otherwise rendered unusable;
> (b) the source copy is not an infringing copy;
> (c) the person, in order to make the reproduction, did not circumvent, as defined in section 41, a technological protection measure, as defined in that section, or cause one to be circumvented; and
> (d) the person does not give any of the reproductions away.

The apparent intent of this section is to allow software consumers the ability to back up source copies during the time that they own or have a licence to use software. However, the wording of the section is obviously broader than that as it applies to all works and neighbouring rights. The backup copy exception has many of the same conditions to safeguard against dissemination as does section 29.22.[65] One important distinction between private copy and backup exceptions is that the latter can be used and enjoyed only if the source copy becomes unusable. Consumers who own the initial copy may therefore make two copies — one copy for private use and enjoyment, and a second backup copy of the initial copy (which can be used only if the initial copy becomes unusable).

Finally, section 29.23(1) permits copying for the purpose of time-shifting broadcast content:

> It is not an infringement of copyright for an individual to fix a communication signal, to reproduce a work or sound recording that is being broadcast or to fix or reproduce a performer's performance that is being broadcast, in order to record a program for the purpose of listening to or viewing it later, if

---

65 See also ss 29.24(2) & (3): the backup copy becomes the source copy if the latter becomes unusable; and all backup copies must be destroyed if the person ceases to own or have a licence to use the original.

(a) the individual receives the program legally;
(b) the individual, in order to record the program, did not circumvent, as defined in section 41, a technological protection measure, as defined in that section, or cause one to be circumvented;
(c) the individual makes no more than one recording of the program;
(d) the individual keeps the recording no longer than is reasonably necessary in order to listen to or view the program at a more convenient time;
(e) the individual does not give the recording away; and
(f) the recording is used only for the individual's private purposes.

This "PVR exception" is of limited value to most consumers who now stream content on-demand, for which copying is not permitted under this exception. Specifically, section 29.23(2) does not apply to on-demand service, meaning "a service that allows a person to receive works, performer's performances and sound recordings at times of their own choosing."

## 3) Educational Institutions

The term "educational institution" is defined in section 2 of the Act to mean, essentially, a publicly sanctioned non-profit institution engaged in preschool, elementary, secondary, or post-secondary education, or professional or vocational training. The exceptions generally apply to educational institutions and persons acting under their authority. Section 29.3 prescribes that, for some exceptions, the activity engaged in may not be "carried out with motive or gain." That same section also states that an educational institution, library, archive, or museum does not have a motive for gain when it recovers costs associated with acts taken under these exceptions. The exceptions for educational institutions tend to be quite specific and condition-laden. At the end of this section, a brief overview of the balance of these exceptions not specifically discussed below will be listed. There are two exceptions that are particularly relevant to digital copyright: (1) distance learning and (2) use of work or neighbouring right available on the Internet for educational purposes.

The use of the Internet as a means to offer lessons and instruction to the public at large has created enormous opportunities for distance learning initiatives. Increasingly, educational institutions, such as universities, are offering courses online. At the University of Alberta, for example, massive open online courses (MOOCs) on various topics are offered to the public at large and to students for credit. Such courses allow persons located around the world to access, be graded upon, and receive credit for course content. Section 30.01 of the Act attempts to address the copyright implications associated with the offering of such courses. The provision, however, is among the most poorly drafted in the Act, and its terms do not obviously make sense.

Section 30.01 defines "lesson" as the use of a work or neighbouring right for a lesson, text, or examination that would not "otherwise be an infringement of copyright but is permitted under a limitation or exception under this Act." The rather odd inclusion of this tailing phrase is likely due to the fact that the definition of lesson is explicitly referenced in section 27.22 in prescribing liability for secondary infringement. In other words, the statute clarifies that use of a lesson within the parameters of user rights is not an infringement of section 29.22. Infringement will result, however, if a person commits an act described in section 27.22 in connection with a lesson.

Section 30.01(3) permits educational institutions to: telecommunicate a "lesson" for educational purposes so long as it is directed only at students enrolled in the course; make a copy of the lesson for these purposes; and do anything else necessary to facilitate these acts. However, section 30.01(2) states that the section should not be understood as permitting any of these acts if their use in the lesson constitutes an infringement of copyright. Again, the only sensible interpretation of this provision is that an act which would constitute infringement under section 27.22 is not saved by virtue of the fact that it is being used for distance learning purposes.

The distance learning exception applies when the lesson is for a course in which a student is enrolled, wherever he or she may be located. Moreover, section 30.01(4) deems a distance learner who meets the criteria in section 30.01(3)(a) to be "a person on the premises of the educational institution." This therefore may extend other educational institution exceptions (which have an "on campus" nexus requirement) to distance learning courses. The final two subsections should also be noted. Section 30.01(5) allows distance learners the latitude to time-shift their access to the lesson by copying it, provided they destroy the copy within a relatively short time frame. Section 30.01(6) imposes a number of safeguard measures on educational institutions to ensure that works embodied in lesson copies are ultimately destroyed and not improperly disseminated.

Subject to conditions, section 30.04 allows educational institutions to use (in various ways) works or other subject matter found on the Internet. In doing so, educational institutions must attribute the source and author (or equivalent) of the work or other subject matter. However, the work or other subject matter, or Internet sites on which it is available, must not be accessed by circumventing a technological protection measure. Moreover, the exception does not apply if a "clearly visible notice — and not merely the copyright symbol" is posted on the site prohibiting the act in question. Finally, the exception does not apply if the educational institution "knows or should have known" the work was made available through the Internet without the copyright owner's consent. The breadth of this exception likely depends on how strictly the constructive knowledge requirement of this last condition is interpreted.

Educational institutions are also entitled to the following exceptions:

- certain rights of use of a work or other subject matter in the classroom, and for tests or examinations, so long as the work or other subject matter is not "commercially available" (a defined term in section 2 which includes the availability of a collective management society licence) "in a medium that is appropriate" for the purposes (section 29.4)
- public performance of a work or other subject matter, including the playing of movies or live broadcast of a work, if it occurs on the premises of the educational institution, is not for profit, and is for an audience consisting primarily of students, instructors, or certain other personnel of that educational institution (section 29.5)
- copying (at the time of telecommunication) and later performance of a news program (but not a documentary) for educational purposes before primarily students on the premises of an educational institution (section 29.6)
- copying (at the time of telecommunication) of a work or other subject matter and keeping the copy for thirty days pending a decision as to whether to publicly perform the work at an educational institution (section 29.7)

- the publication of certain "short passages from literary works" by educational institutions under a number of strict conditions (section 30)
- the exercise of certain rights in connection with a reprographic reproduction licence between an educational institution and a collective management society (section 30.03)

### 4) Libraries, Archives, or Museums (LAM)

The term "library, archive or museum" (LAM) is broadly defined in section 2 to mean a non-profit organization which maintains "a collection of documents and other materials that is open to the public or to researchers." LAM exceptions fall into one of three categories of permitted copying: to preserve works, to facilitate patron research, and to facilitate interlibrary loans for the purpose of research.

In the first category, under section 30.1, libraries, archives, and museums are permitted to make a copy, for the purpose of maintaining or managing a permanent collection, of a work or other subject matter where it is, *inter alia*, damaged or deteriorating or the format of the existing copy is obsolete, so long as an appropriate copy is not otherwise "commercially available."[66]

In the second category, under section 30.2, libraries, archives, and museums are protected against infringement insofar as they facilitate the fair dealing rights of others under sections 29 and 29.1.[67] More specifically, a single reprographic reproduction of a "scholarly, scientific, or technical periodical" or newspaper or other periodical at least one year old is also permitted for the purpose of a requesting patron's research or private study.[68] This exception appears to be extended to digital copies by virtue of section 30.2(5.01). The third category as per section 30.2(5), directed at interlibrary loans, permits a library, archive, or museum to do acts in the second category for another LAM's patron. To the extent that an interlibrary loan requires the making of a digital copy to satisfy a patron request at another library, this is permitted so long as the

---

66 Sections 30.01(1) & (2). See definition of "commercially available" in s 2.
67 Section 30.2.
68 Section 30.2(2). The LAM must also inform the patron about the limited use that may be made of the article: s 30.2(4).

"providing library"[69] ensures that strict safeguards are in place: these include that any such copy is not used for more than five days.

An archive is permitted to make a copy of a deposited unpublished work (and to allow researchers to make a copy) under specified conditions outlined in section 30.21. There are special provisions directed specifically at Library and Archives Canada (section 30.5) and for machines installed in educational institutions and libraries, archives, and museums (section 30.3). This latter regime insulates these entities from copyright liability for the installation of copy-facilitating machines, such as photocopiers, on their premises and under certain conditions. But this applies only if there is a reprographic reproduction licence in place, whether individually negotiated or as set by royalty or tariff by the Copyright Board, between the institution and the relevant collective society.

### 5) Computer Programs

The section 30.6 group of exceptions permits the purchaser or licensee of software or computer programming to make a copy of the program for the purpose of

- facilitating compatibility with a computer (section 30.6(a))
- having a backup copy (section 30.6(b))
- facilitating interoperability with another program (section 30.61)
- doing legitimate encryption research (section 30.62)
- supporting legitimate network or computer security research (section 30.63)

Of course, important conditions are attached to each of these exceptions. One point of uncertainty is the relationship between section 30.6(b) and section 29.24. Both pertain to the making of backup copies though with different conditions attached. For example, the latter permits use of the backup copy only if the initial copy is unusable

---

69  It is difficult to know which library is the "providing library" in an interlibrary loan arrangement: see Margaret Ann Wilkinson, "Filtering the Flow from the Fountains of Knowledge: Access and Copyright in Education and Libraries" in Michael Geist, ed, *In the Public Interest: The Future of Canadian Copyright Law* (Toronto: Irwin law, 2005) 331 at 361, in connection with an similarly ambiguous provision in an earlier bill.

whereas there is no such limitation in the former. Another example is the prohibition against circumventing technological protection measures in section 29.24, which does appear in section 30.6(b). Where such a conflict arises in the legal operation of these provisions, it is likely that a court would apply the principle of statutory interpretation which gives precedence to the later provision (section 29.24) over the earlier one (section 30.6(b)).

**6) Incidental Use/Temporary Copy**

Section 30.7 creates an exception for the incidental and non-deliberate inclusion of a work or other subject matter in the making of a new work or other subject matter. For this provision to have any meaningful breadth, the non-deliberate requirement must be read more generously than merely assessing whether the author had knowledge that the work or other subject matter is present in the work. For example, a documentary filmmaker who films a subject on a downtown street should not be required to remove all copyrighted logos that might appear outside stores and restaurants.

Section 30.71 provides that it is not infringement to make a copy of a work or other subject matter if "reproduction forms an essential part of the process," the only purpose is to facilitate a non-infringing use, and the copy is expunged after completion of the technological process. This provision appears to insulate incidental digital copying, e.g., to effect a licensed broadcast such as in *Canadian Broadcasting Corp v SODRAC*,[70] from copyright infringement so long as the copies are destroyed after use. The only possible ambiguity in this provision is the use of the word "essential." There is every reason to expect that courts will interpret this word purposively, much like the Supreme Court construed "necessary" in connection with the common carrier exception in *Society of Composers, Authors and Music Publishers of Canada v Canadian Assn of Internet Providers*,[71] to permit copying that is integral to technological economy and efficiency. Any stricter interpretation, e.g., "essential" as indispensible, would not only render the exception pointless,

---

70   2015 SCC 57. See Chapter 1.
71   2004 SCC 45.

but would favour analogue production methods over encouragement of technological innovation.

## 7) Ephemeral Copies

Ephemeral (or temporary) copies can be also be made by a "programming undertaking" or a "broadcasting undertaking" as those terms are defined in the Act. These provisions are in place to allow such entities to make temporary copies as a means to effectuate licensed broadcasts of a work or other subject matter. Under section 30.8, a programming undertaking may fix or reproduce a live performer's performance or work (but not a cinematographic work) or a sound recording performed at the same time if it has a corresponding permission or licence to telecommunicate the work, performer's performance, or sound recording. Strict conditions on use of the fixation and copy are in place and, unless the copy is deposited in an "official archive" as being of "exceptional documentary character," the copy must be destroyed within thirty days. The breadth of the exception is narrowed considerably by the limitation in section 30.8(8); the section does not apply when there is a licence available for the work or other subject matter from a corresponding collective management society.

Under section 30.9, a broadcasting undertaking is permitted to reproduce a sound recording, performer's performance, or work embodied in a sound recording if it owns or has a licence to use, and has a licence to telecommunicate, the corresponding copy. Again, there are strict conditions on use of such reproductions, and they must be destroyed, at the latest, within thirty days of the making of the copy. There is no requirement to seek a licence from a collective society, if available, although if copies authorized by this provision are ultimately retained, a royalty must be paid the copyright owner.

## 8) Retransmission

This exception, found in section 31, outlines the parameters within which a signal — defined as that which "carries a literary, dramatic, musical or artistic work and is transmitted for free reception by the public" by terrestrial radio or TV station — may be retransmitted. The most important condition is that such a retransmission is "lawful under the *Broadcast Act*." The retransmission exception does not apply to Internet broadcasts.[72]

## 9) Perceptual Disabilities

Section 32 outlines exceptions pertaining to persons with *perceptual disabilities*, a term that is broadly defined in section 2. The exceptions include the permissibility of making reformatted copies of works and sound recordings to accommodate a perceptual disability and performance of a literary or dramatic work in sign language. Section 32(3) provides that these exceptions do not apply to reformatted works or sound recordings that are "commercially available." These exceptions also do not apply to cinematographic works nor does section 32 "authorize the making of large print books."[73] The balance of section 32 is concerned with the sending of reformatted copies of a work for the benefit of persons with a "print disability" located outside Canada.

## 10) Statutory Obligations

These exceptions under section 32.1 facilitate the disclosure of information and records that may be required by statute. At times, the section refers to "disclose" which, on a purposive interpretation, must include any act that might constitute infringement and not just copying. The exceptions pertain to specific statutory regimes, including disclosure of records under the *Access to Information Act*.[74] In *Geophysical Service Inc v Antrim Energy Inc*, this exception was cited in support of the disclosure of purported copyrighted information by the federal government.[75] However, the court correctly noted that the disclosure by the federal government was not pursuant to an access-to-information request, and thus this exception did not apply. It is possible that other statutory obligations that may implicate copyright exist and are not specified under

---

72   The s 31(2) exemption does not apply to a "new media transmitter," as defined in s 31(1) and which refers to CRTC, Exemption Order for New Media Broadcasting Undertakings CRTC 1999-197 (17 December 1999), online: www.crtc.gc.ca/eng/archive/1999/PB99-197.htm. See discussion of what constitutes an Internet broadcast in Chapter 3.
73   Section 32(2).
74   RSC 1985, c A-1.
75   2015 ABQB 482.

this category of exception. If that is the case, one wonders if the purposes of the exception would be better served by a general immunity from copyright liability for acts taken pursuant to an obligation under statute.

## 11) Miscellaneous Exceptions

These exceptions are truly deserving of the miscellaneous categorization and consist of the following acts that are deemed non-infringing:

- the author but no longer owner of an artistic work to reuse a mould, cast, sketch, plan, model or study so long as he or she does not "repeat or imitate the main design of a work" (section 32.2(1)(a))
- to reproduce an architectural work or publicly situated sculpture in a painting, drawing, engraving, photograph, or cinematographic work (section 32.2(1)(b))
- to make or publish a report of a public lecture for the purpose of news reporting except under specific conditions (section 32.2(1)(c))
- to "read or recite in public a reasonable extract from a published work" (section 32.2(1)(d))
- to make or publish a report on a public "address of a political nature" for the purpose of news reporting (section 32.2(1)(e))
- for a person who has commissioned a photograph or portrait for personal purposes, to use it for private or non-commercial purposes unless there is an contrary agreement with the owner of the copyright in the work (section 32.2(1)(f))
- to undertake various kinds of performances at agricultural fairs without motive of gain (section 32.2(2))
- for religious, educational, charitable, or fraternal organizations to engage in various public acts "in furtherance of a religious, educational or charitable objective" (section 32.2(3))

*****

The breadth of the fair dealing "exception" has expanded enormously over the past dozen years or so as the Supreme Court has consistently set the purpose threshold at a low level and has been generous in ensuring that digital uses and dissemination of works are not unduly burdened by liability concerns. The prospect for many controversial uses of works in the digital age — including computational uses exemplified in Google Books and HathiTrust — is bright under Canadian copyright law. The fair dealing provisions will no doubt continue to evolve as new technological uses are considered by courts. On the other hand, the other exceptions are less amenable to change over time due to their specificity. Still, there are interpretive ambiguities and controversies associated with these provisions as well. It bears repeating that these exceptions exist to guide users seeking to ensure that their actions will not constitute infringement. But there remains ample room for acts that do not meet the conditions of these exceptions to still be considered non-infringing.

CHAPTER 7

# Internet Intermediaries

## A. INTRODUCTION

Internet intermediaries provide the tools through which people communicate with one another in cyberspace. In terms of their legal treatment under the *Copyright Act*, they may be grouped into four functional categories: (1) service providers that offer connectivity to the Internet (network services), (2) the digital space for hosting content on web pages (digital memory), (3) search engines that facilitate the location of desired content (information location tools), and (4) sites that exist to enable file transfers of content (infringement enablers). In respect of the first three categories, these services are integral to the operation of the Internet and, in connection with copyright goals in particular, they offer the opportunity to legally disseminate works on an unprecedented scale. The dark side, from the perspective of copyright holders, is that intermediaries also facilitate the dissemination of infringing content, also on an unprecedented scale. To target the uploaders and distributors of infringing content is an unworkable solution: the cost of locating and suing each infringer on the Internet is too high. For these reasons, Internet intermediaries have always been (and continue to be) the focus of efforts by copyright holders to extract compensation for their role in facilitating, and indirectly benefiting from, the dissemination of pirated content. But the same problem of scale that prevents copyright holders from effectively pursuing those responsible for uploading pirated content also impedes the ability of intermediaries to monitor or remove it.

Through various mechanisms, legal systems have devised ways in which copyright owners and intermediaries are to share the burden of addressing infringement on the Internet. There are two parts to these regimes: (1) the copyright owner monitors for, and notifies intermediaries about, specific acts of infringement and (2) when notified, an intermediary faces certain obligations to address infringing activities. Beyond this, intermediaries are generally not held accountable for copyright infringing activities that occur *in the aggregate* through their services. Put another way, most intermediary activities are viewed as "content neutral" until and unless an intermediary becomes aware of specific acts of infringement and fails to respond.

Before the *Copyright Modernization Act,* or *CMA,* the law in this area was based on the decision in *Society of Composers, Authors and Music Publishers of Canada v Canadian Assn of Internet Providers,*[1] a case which considered liability of Internet service providers as intermediaries. The *CMA* modified that regime by instituting a "notice and notice" system that, unlike in the US "notice and takedown" regime, has no bearing on whether an intermediary is to be held liable for copyright infringement per se. The *CMA* also added a patchwork of provisions that address questions of liability for service providers in their various capacities. As was the case with the specific exceptions outlined in Chapter 6, these provisions are detailed and, at times, condition laden.

Section B will offer necessary background by analyzing the *CAIP* case as well as briefly considering the US regime under the *Digital Millennium Copyright Act.*[2] Section C then analyzes the new provisions of the *Copyright Act* which regulate various Internet intermediary functions. Section D considers the relationship between these new provisions and the authorization right under which intermediaries were formerly regulated.

## B. BACKGROUND

Internet intermediaries are a natural and relatively easy target for copyright holders seeking to rectify online infringement. However, copyright

---

1  2004 SCC 45 [*CAIP*].
2  Pub L No 105-304, 112 Stat 2860 (1998) (codified in scattered sections of 17 USC) [*DMCA*].

holder concerns are not the only interests at play on the Internet. Policy-makers and courts have been vigilant in ensuring that the efficiency and economy of the Internet as a tool of information exchange is not unduly encumbered. In the copyright sphere, in particular, the Internet offers enormous potential to disseminate works. As the Supreme Court observed in *CAIP*: "The capacity of the internet to disseminate 'works of the arts and intellect' is one of the great innovations of the information age. Its use should be facilitated rather than discouraged . . . ."[3] Indeed, this policy goal drives much of the analysis in that case, to which we now turn.

## 1) The Issues in *CAIP*

This case was an appeal on legal issues relevant to SOCAN's efforts to extract compensation from Internet service providers for facilitating, and indirectly benefiting from, massive online infringement through music file-sharing. Two issues relevant here were whether Internet service providers (1) qualified for safe harbour protection against infringement as mere providers of telecommunication services, or (2) were liable for "authorizing" infringement. In this case, the legal treatment of Internet service providers' activities was judged according to the function under consideration, for example, hosting or network services.[4] This functional approach was continued in the *CMA* amendments to the Act.

### a) Safe Harbour Considerations

The first issue in *CAIP* was whether, and if so which, ISP functions fit within the telecommunication services "safe harbour" in section 2.4(1), which provides

> . . . a person whose *only act* in respect of the communication of a work or other subject-matter to the public consists of *providing the means of telecommunication necessary* for another person to so communicate the work or other subject-matter does not communicate that work or other subject-matter to the public . . . .[5]

The Court interpreted "means" expansively so as to capture many Internet intermediary services:

---

3   Above note 1 at para 40.
4   *Ibid* at para 102.
5   Section 2.4(1)(b) [emphasis added].

> "The 'means,'" as the Board found, "... are not limited to routers and other hardware. They include all software connection equipment, connectivity services, hosting and other facilities and services without which such communications would not occur" (p. 452). I agree. So long as an Internet intermediary does not itself engage in acts that relate to the content of the communication, i.e., whose participation is content neutral, but confines itself to providing "a conduit" for information communicated by others, then it will fall within s. 2.4(1)(b).[6]

The Court then considered various intermediary functions. Caching is the practice of storing temporary copies on a server for the purpose of economizing and speeding up Internet transmissions.[7] Here, SOCAN argued that the safe harbour did not apply to this activity since it was not "necessary" for the provision of telecommunication services. Adopting a purposive interpretation of section 2.4(1)(b) and the word "necessary," in particular, the Court found that "necessary" means "reasonably useful" and includes caching since this enhances the efficiency and economy of the Internet.[8]

In terms of hosting services, the Court observed:

> [T]he *Copyright Act*, as a matter of legislative policy established by Parliament, does not impose liability for infringement on intermediaries who supply software and hardware to facilitate use of the Internet. The attributes of such a "conduit", as found by the Board, include a lack of actual knowledge of the infringing contents, and the impracticality (both technical and economic) of monitoring the vast amount of material moving through the Internet, which is prodigious.[9]

The main significance of this passage is that it affirms that hosting services also fall under safe harbour so long as the provider is unaware of specific acts of infringement. The foregoing analysis suggested that network services (including caching and hosting) are protected under the safe harbour to the extent that they function as passive, content-neutral conduits of information. The noted exception to this is when an Internet service provider receives notice of a specific act of infringement in respect of a hosting function.

---

6   *CAIP*, above note 1 at para 92.
7   See *ibid* at para 23.
8   *Ibid* at paras 114–15.
9   *Ibid* at para 101.

## b) The Authorization Right

A separate ground of infringement, to which the safe harbour does not generally apply, is the copyright holder's right to "authorize" section 3 uses of the work. To the extent that an intermediary is involved in the process of transmitting infringing content it may, depending on the circumstances, be viewed as authorizing infringement. As discussed in Chapter 3, the Supreme Court considered the meaning of "authorizing" copyright infringement in both *CAIP* and *CCH Canadian Ltd v Law Society of Upper Canada*.[10] In *CCH* the Court set down two principles. First, authorization *may* arise where there is a "sufficient degree of indifference" in terms of facilitating an infringement by a third party. Second, there is a presumption against authorization based on the mere provision of technology, but this may be rebutted by a relationship of control.

In *CAIP*, the Supreme Court affirmed that Internet service providers do not "authorize" infringement by merely providing connectivity. Again, the mere provision of technology, which can be used for infringing and non-infringing purposes, is not enough to establish infringement of the authorization right. However, liability may attach if ISP activities "cease to be content neutral, e.g. if it has notice that a content provider has posted infringing material on its system and fails to take remedial action."[11] The Court later suggests that a failure to respond to a notice and takedown procedure *might* constitute authorization. However, it was noncommittal on this point:

> [N]otice of infringing content, and a failure to respond by "taking it down" may in some circumstances lead to a finding of "authorization". However, that is not the issue before us. Much would depend on the specific circumstances. An overly quick inference of "authorization" would put the Internet Service Provider in the difficult position of judging whether the copyright objection is well founded, and to choose between contesting a copyright action or potentially breaching its contract with the content provider. A more effective remedy to address this potential issue would be the enactment by Parliament of a statutory "notice and take down" procedure as has been done in the European Community and the United States.[12]

---

10    2004 SCC 13 [*CCH*].
11    *CAIP*, above note 1 at para 124.
12    *Ibid* at para 127.

The upshot seems to be that knowledge of specific acts of infringement would be necessary to implicate an Internet service provider for authorization infringement, whether or not it takes the form of a notice and takedown procedure.

## 2) The US Notice and Takedown Regime

The US notice and takedown system insulates service providers from liability so long as, when notified by a copyright holder (or otherwise becoming aware) of specific acts of infringement, they act quickly to remove the content.[13] The regime also provides for a counter-notification system, by which subscribers may object to removal of their content on the basis that it does infringe copyright.[14] Where that happens, the material is to be reposted unless the service provider receives notice by the copyright owner that it has initiated injunction proceedings. The fast removal of the content is, in the vast majority of cases, a complete defence to copyright infringement.[15] Efforts to bring Internet service providers outside this "safe harbour" based on the refusal by a service provider to implement available technological measures to proactively prevent copyright infringement have failed.[16]

This safe harbour has, however, been eroded in other ways.[17] If a service provider is willfully blind as to the occurrence of specific acts and does nothing to remove the offending content, it will be outside the safe harbour.[18] Furthermore, in severe cases, intermediaries that engage in activities that actively encourage copyright infringement in the aggregate may also be outside the harbour, even if it cannot be proven that they were aware of specific acts of infringement.[19] This appears to be an adoption of the rule in *Metro-Goldwyn-Mayer Studios Inc v Grokster* that, "one who distributes a device with the object of promoting its use

---

13   See *DMCA*, above note 2, 17 USC § 512(c).
14   *Ibid*, § 512(g).
15   See *Viacom International v YouTube*, 676 F3d 19 at 41 (2d Cir 2012) [*Viacom*].
16   See *ibid*, where these arguments failed.
17   See Eric Goldman, "How the *DMCA*'s Online Copyright Safe Harbor Failed" (2014) 3 *National Taipei University of Technology Journal of Intellectual Property Law and Management* 195 at 197.
18   *Viacom*, above note 15 at 34–35, citing *Metro-Goldwyn-Mayer Studios Inc v Grokster*, 545 US 913 (2005) [*Grokster*].
19   *Viacom*, above note 15 at 37–38.

to infringe copyright as shown by clear expression or other affirmative steps taken to foster infringement, is liable for the resulting acts of infringement by third parties."[20] Under US law, this is known as "contributory infringement."[21]

A number of features of the US regime pose an interesting contrast to the parallel provisions under the Canadian Act. First, the notice and takedown regime places more responsibility on service providers, who must act to remove content and engage in a process of counter-notification with subscribers. The notice and notice regime, by contrast, is decidedly less cumbersome and exists as an independent obligation unconnected to determinations of infringement. Second, the US safe harbour is not a defence for those who actively encourage infringement by third parties, even in the absence of knowledge of specific acts. Under the Canadian regime, a separate ground of infringement has been established against those who offer services over the Internet primarily for the goal of enabling acts of infringement.

## C. THE *CMA* AMENDMENTS

### 1) The Notice and Notice Regime

The notice and notice regime set up under section 41.25 of the Act applies to service providers that offer either connectivity through the Internet or the digital memory for others to host content; it also applies to information location tools.[22] These categories appear to capture the full ambit of passive conduits of content-neutral information on the web. Notice and notice works in the following way. First, the copyright owner must send a notice of claimed infringement to any person who offers such a service. The notice must include the identity of the claimant, the work or other subject matter that is claimed to have been infringed, the nature of the infringement as well as when it occurred, the claimant's

---

20  *Grokster*, above note 18 at 936–37, Souter J.
21  See Sheldon Halpern, *Copyright Law: Protection of Original Expression* (Durham, NC: Carolina Academic Press, 2002) at 552. Contributory infringement occurs where "one who, with knowledge of the infringing activity, induces, causes, or materially contributes to the infringing conduct of another, may be held liable as a 'contributory' infringer." There is also vicarious liability in US copyright law based on relationship of control. Authorizing infringement, under Canadian law, seems to embrace both of these kinds of liability.
22  Section 41.25(1).

right or interest in the work or other subject matter, and the electronic location of the infringed work.[23] Upon receiving a notice that complies with these requirements, the recipient is to (1) forward the notice to the person hosting the site where the infringing content is found and (2) retain identifying information about the person hosting the site for a period of six months to a year.[24] The penalty for failure of an intermediary to abide by the notice and notice requirements is statutory damages in an amount between $500 and $10,000.

This notice and notice regime is decidedly less cumbersome than the notice and takedown regime that exists in the United States. However, compliance with the US regime offers a safe harbour, subject to some limitations, from claims of infringement against Internet intermediaries.[25] By contrast, sections 41.25 and 41.26 do not reference copyright infringement and, therefore, do not seem to act as a safe harbour against it. Rather, these provisions read as if they set out independent obligations on service providers, over and above any liability that may exist for copyright infringement. In other words, a service provider that complies with notice and notice may not necessarily be free from liability for copyright infringement.

Although the Act sets out the required contents of the notice to be forwarded to a service provider, it does not prevent copyright holders from including other information. This has led to some abuses by copyright trolls who include "demand letters" in their notices:

> Certain anti-piracy groups have already been using the regime questionably by forcing ISPs into relaying notices containing inaccurate legal information and threatening users with fines higher than possible under the *Act*, without proof that the user is responsible for the alleged copyright infringement.[26]

The worst excesses of this practice are not allowed under the US *DMCA*. Under that regime, a copyright holder is prevented from making mate-

---

23   Section 41.25(2)
24   Section 41.26. The service provider or search engine may charge a fee for this service.
25   The language of the *DMCA*, above note 2, 17 USC § 512(c) makes that clear: "A service provider shall not be liable ... for infringement of copyright" for offering host services to a subscriber.
26   Pierre-Christian Collins Hoffman, "Non-commercial Online Copyright Infringement in Canada: The Challenge of Balancing the Copyright Owners' Interests against Those of Internet Users" (2014–15) 16 *Internet and E-Commerce Law in Canada* 1 at 4.

rial misrepresentations about whether material or an activity is infringing.[27] Furthermore, in any takedown notice, a complaining party must have a good faith belief that the activity is infringing, including that it is not fair use.[28] These prohibitions are not in place under Canadian law nor is there an enabling clause under section 41.26 that would allow Cabinet to address abuses by regulation.

## 2) Network (or Connectivity) Services

Categorized as an "exception" in the Act, section 31.1 protects content-neutral network services providers against claims of infringement.

> (1) A person who, in providing services related to the operation of the Internet or another digital network, provides any means for the telecommunication or the reproduction of a work or other subject-matter through the Internet or that other network does not, solely by reason of providing those means, infringe copyright in that work or other subject-matter.

The terms "operation of the Internet" and "digital network" are not defined, though this language is broad enough to include the various services suggested in *CAIP*.[29] Section 31.1 is both an expansion, as well as retraction, of the rule set out in *CAIP*. It broadens protection against all acts of infringement, not just against the section 3(1)(f) telecommunication right. But, while section 31.1(2) is a codification of the *CAIP* rule on caching, section 31.1(3) sets out conditions that do not appear in that case:

> (2) Subject to subsection (3), a person referred to in subsection (1) who caches the work or other subject-matter, or does any similar act in relation to it, to make the telecommunication more efficient does not, by virtue of that act alone, infringe copyright in the work or other subject-matter.
> 
>    (3) Subsection (2) does not apply unless the person, in respect of the work or other subject-matter,

---

27   *DMCA*, above note 2, § 512(f).
28   *Ibid*, § 512(c)(3)(A)(v). See also *Lenz v Universal Music*, 801 F3d 1126 (9th Cir 2015).
29   See above note 6 (save and except the reference to "hosting" which is dealt with under digital memory provider, ss 31.1(4) & (5)).

[183]

(a) does not modify it, other than for technical reasons;
(b) ensures that any directions related to its caching or the doing of any similar act, as the case may be, that are specified in a manner consistent with industry practice by whoever made it available for telecommunication through the Internet or another digital network, and that lend themselves to automated reading and execution, are read and executed; and
(c) does not interfere with the use of technology that is lawful and consistent with industry practice in order to obtain data on the use of the work or other subject-matter.

The protections under section 31.1 are, understandably, not afforded to network services of the kind targeted under section 27(2.3) (services primarily for the purpose of enabling acts of copyright infringement).[30]

### 3) Digital Memory Providers (Hosting)

Providers of "digital memory," an undefined term in the Act, are also eligible for safe harbour protection. Sections 31.1(4) and (5) provide as follows:

> (4) Subject to subsection (5), a person who, for the purpose of allowing the telecommunication of a work or other subject-matter through the Internet or another digital network, provides digital memory in which another person stores the work or other subject-matter does not, by virtue of that act alone, infringe copyright in the work or other subject-matter.
>
> (5) Subsection (4) does not apply in respect of a work or other subject-matter if the person providing the digital memory knows of a decision of a court of competent jurisdiction to the effect that the person who has stored the work or other subject-matter in the digital memory infringes copyright by making the copy of the work or other subject-matter that is stored or by the way in which he or she uses the work or other subject-matter.

This is a codification of the content-neutral rule in *CAIP* though, like for network services, protection is extended to all grounds of infringement, not just the telecommunication right.

---

[30] Section 31.1(6).

Section 31.1(5) states that if, upon becoming aware of a court decision that a site is infringing, a digital storage provider fails to act, that failure will take it outside the safe harbour. A good case can be made that specific knowledge short of a court-sanctioned finding of infringement should not, in any circumstance, bring hosts outside this exception. This provision, as read in context with the notice and notice regime, suggests a legislative intention that intermediaries are not to be placed in the position of making infringement determinations. To give full effect to this policy choice, it would make sense to extend protection against all unproven (i.e., not judicially made) allegations of infringement, even when such allegations are specific.

### 4) Information Location Tools (Search Engines)

An "information location tool" is broadly defined under section 41.27(5) to mean "any tool that makes it possible to locate information that is available through the Internet or another digital network." The paradigmatic case is a search engine, such as Google, that allows a user to enter words or phrases that return a list of search results from web pages on the Internet. Section 41.27 sets out the conditions under which these intermediaries are insulated from liability for copyright infringement:

> In any proceedings for infringement of copyright, the owner of the copyright in a work or other subject-matter is not entitled to any remedy other than an injunction against a provider of an information location tool that is found to have infringed copyright by making a reproduction of the work or other subject-matter or by communicating that reproduction to the public by telecommunication.[31]

Rather than create an exception for infringement, this provision achieves a similar practical result by limiting the remedy available to a copyright holder to an injunction only.

Section 41.27 sets out the conditions for eligibility, including that copies be made or cached, or telecommunicated, for information location purposes only and that any copies made are not to be modified unless for technical reasons.[32] The immunity granted under this section

---

31   Section 41.27(1).
32   Section 41.27(2).

does not extend to services under section 27(2.3) that exist primarily to facilitate acts of infringement. The balance of section 41.27 deals with the parameters of granting an injunction. Though it is the only remedy available under this section, its operation is highly circumscribed. Under section 41.27(4.1), the court is to balance competing considerations of harm to the plaintiff if the injunction is not granted against the burden imposed on the search engine if the injunction is granted.

## 5) Services That Enable Infringement (Peer-to-Peer Sharing)

Websites that exist "primarily for the purpose of enabling acts of infringement" and through which it can be proven that specific acts of infringement occurred are liable for copyright infringement under section 27(2.3).

> It is an infringement of copyright for a person, by means of the Internet or another digital network, to provide a service primarily for the purpose of enabling acts of copyright infringement if an actual infringement of copyright occurs by means of the Internet or another digital network as a result of the use of that service.

Both evidence of aggregate infringement and of specific acts of infringement are required to satisfy this section. In determining whether a service exists primarily to facilitate acts of infringement, a court may consider criteria outlined under section 27(2.4):

> In determining whether a person has infringed copyright under subsection (2.3), the court may consider
> (a) whether the person expressly or implicitly marketed or promoted the service as one that could be used to enable acts of copyright infringement;
> (b) whether the person had knowledge that the service was used to enable a significant number of acts of copyright infringement;
> (c) whether the service has significant uses other than to enable acts of copyright infringement;
> (d) the person's ability, as part of providing the service, to limit acts of copyright infringement, and any action taken by the person to do so;
> (e) any benefits the person received as a result of enabling the acts of copyright infringement; and

## CHAPTER 7: INTERNET INTERMEDIARIES

(f) the economic viability of the provision of the service if it were not used to enable acts of copyright infringement.

The low threshold language of section 27(2.4) suggests that this provision is designed to give courts maximum flexibility to make infringement findings against such websites. For example, section 27(2.4)(a) refers to "implicitly" marketing or promoting the website as one that will enable infringement. If a BitTorrent site offers customers "free, unlimited downloading," might a court infer this as an implicit pitch for users to commit copyright infringement via unlimited (read: indiscriminate) downloading? Furthermore, the knowledge requirement in section 27(2.4)(b) pertains merely to a "significant" number of acts of infringement via the service. Finally, in terms of low threshold language, section 27(2.4)(e) refers to "any benefits" — presumably direct or indirect — that may be received for offering such services.

To the extent that the factor analysis generally weighs against a service, a court will look to measures taken by the service to limit infringement under section 27(2.4)(d) to help bring it back on side. Depending on the severity of the enablement, courts will likely expect, at the very least, a notice and takedown regime and, likely in serious cases, more proactive technical measures taken by the service to identify and remove copyrighted content. Section 27(2.4)(f) refers to the economic viability of the service if it were not used for infringement purposes, though it is unclear whether courts will make inferences or require evidence under this factor. While section 27(2.4)(c) should favour peer-to-peer sites insofar as non-copyrighted material will likely be shared to a significant extent, it stands alone among the other factors that will weigh against such services.

This basis for copyright infringement appears to be directed at the many BitTorrent sites whose business model depends on file sharing of copyrighted content. However, it will be interesting to see how services that enable copyright infringement on a large, but still much lesser, scale will fare under this provision. For example, the website Pinterest allows users to upload and share information about various topics, a significant portion of which is subject to copyright. To the extent that much information posted on these sites is subject to copyright, it seems that the sites would need to both discourage the uploading of such content among its subscribers and take proactive measures to identify and remove it when it does appear, to avoid liability under this provision.

## D. THE STATUS OF AUTHORIZATION LIABILITY FOR INTERNET INTERMEDIARIES

A critical question remains. Is this patchwork of provisions intended as a complete regime of Internet intermediary liability, or is there still room for a finding of infringement based on "authorizing" acts of infringement under section 3? This question is a difficult one to answer. On the one hand, there is an apparent policy choice to remove intermediaries from the task of assessing the validity of copyright infringement allegations. This is implied in the notice and notice regime, and is explicit in the shield given to hosting services (requiring them to act only when there is a court order). The notice and notice regime does not contemplate that intermediaries should do anything more than send along notifications to alleged infringers. It most certainly does not ask them to make judgments about infringing content or to remove the content in any prescribed circumstance. Moreover, the *Copyright Modernization Act* added a provision that imposes liability on a host of a website that facilitates infringement in the aggregate under section 27(2.3). In light of all this, there appears little room left for "authorizing" infringement. In particular, what kind of knowledge, and/or what kind of ensuing failure to act, would qualify?

On the other hand, like many other exceptions to copyright infringement, these are specific responses to certain functions, or activities, of Internet intermediaries. As new potentially infringing acts, or intermediary functions, emerge, these provisions will not provide answers. Much as sections 30.08 and 30.09 addressed a single-copy-for-broadcast incidental copying, and did not contemplate the kind and degree of incidental copying that occurred in *Canadian Broadcasting Corp v SODRAC*,[33] so too these exceptions may be out of date in a decade or so. Courts may then have to resort to assessing liability under the authorization right rather than try to fit uncontemplated technologies into specifically worded exceptions. In other words, the authorization right still exists to address acts or functions not addressed in these exceptions.

\* \* \* \* \*

Canada has taken a unique approach to Internet intermediary liability. The thrust of this approach is to impose few obligations on these

---

[33] 2015 SCC 57.

intermediaries, other than to forward notices to purported infringers. Moreover, to the extent that an intermediary service acts as a content-neutral passive conduit of information, it continues to be protected under the Act. The scope of hosting activities caught under section 27(2.3) is an interesting question that will, no doubt, be fertile ground for infringement litigation.

CHAPTER 8

# International Dimensions

## A. INTRODUCTION

This chapter examines the public and private international law dimensions of copyright. There are a number of provisions in the *Copyright Act* which are intended to fulfill our obligations under international law. These include the national treatment rule, which extends a principle of non-discrimination towards works of foreign provenance, as well as (in the digital context) anti-circumvention measures. Much of this chapter is devoted to private international law — a field concerned with private disputes with multi-jurisdictional elements — and the way in which it has been adapted to copyright infringement over the Internet. Canadian rules on jurisdiction, choice of law, and judgment enforcement are generally not well developed in the Internet context and are even less developed as they apply to copyright infringement. In response, I offer a framework through which the rules on jurisdiction and choice of law might be developed. The chapter ends with a discussion of proposed principles for managing the problem of ubiquitous infringement over the Internet.

## B. PUBLIC INTERNATIONAL LAW

Each sovereign state determines the copyright rules applicable within its jurisdiction. Public international law — in particular, treaty law — sets minimum standards that signatory governments are to implement in their national legislation. These provisions relate to, among many others, the minimum duration of the copyright term.[1] As many treaty obligations are broadly stated, there is much scope left for how national governments choose to implement these standards. Thus, user rights such as fair dealing or fair use (or in international copyright treaty language, "limitations" or "exceptions") vary significantly from country to country. For our purposes, the "Internet" treaties of the World Intellectual Property Organization (WIPO)[2] are the most significant as they establish certain minimum standards for protecting copyrighted works in the digital context. The most prominent of these is the addition of the "making available right" and the obligation on states to provide adequate legal measures to combat the circumvention of technological protection measures placed on copyrighted works.[3]

Beyond minimum standards, copyright treaties typically impose a national treatment rule to be applied to works of foreign provenance. In other words, signatory states are required to afford the same legal treatment to works of foreign origin as they do to domestic works. There is an inclusive basis for capturing foreign works, and related subject matter, under these treaties and as reflected in Canadian copyright law. Recognizing that "treaty country" as defined in the Canadian *Copyright Act* encompasses countries that are World Trade Organization (WTO) members, which includes most countries in the world, section 5 offers protection to works whose author is a citizen or resident of a treaty country and, in more limited circumstances, where first publication occurs in a treaty country.[4] Therefore, original works made in most countries of the world are afforded Canadian copyright protection the moment they are created. Foreign works are thus subject to Canadian rules on copyright within Canada. Similarly, generous rules for recognizing foreign works on the basis of the national treatment

---

1  See, for example, *Berne Convention for the Protection of Literary and Artistic Works*, Can TS 1998 No 18 [*Berne Convention*]; *Agreement on Trade-Related Aspects of Intellectual Property* (1994) IIC 209 [*TRIPS Agreement*].
2  *WIPO Copyright Treaty*, Can TS 2014 No 20 [*WCT*]; and *WIPO Performances and Phonograms Treaty*, Can TS 2014 No 21 [*WPPT*].
3  See *WCT*, above note 2, arts 8 and 11, respectively. The "making available" right is implemented under s 2.4(1.1), and anti-circumvention measures appear under s 41.1, of the *Act*.
4  See ss 5(1)(a) and (c).

principle are in effect for performers' performances,[5] makers of sound recordings,[6] the right of equitable remuneration,[7] and broadcasts[8] in connection with various treaty regimes.

## C. PRIVATE INTERNATIONAL LAW

Private international law refers to the body of rules by which national courts determine their ability to hear and resolve disputes that have multi-jurisdictional elements. It is comprised of three distinct areas of study: (1) Jurisdiction: When will a court take jurisdiction to hear a case? (2) Choice of law: Which law does a court apply to resolve the dispute? (3) Enforcement of foreign judgments: Under what circumstances will a court recognize and enforce a foreign judgment? For example, if I upload copyrighted content onto YouTube from my home in Edmonton, could the US rights holder sue me for infringement in New York, where it carries on business, or does it have to sue me in Alberta? And if either court takes jurisdiction, will it apply Canadian copyright law, US copyright law, or both? Finally, if the New York court takes jurisdiction and renders a judgment against me, can that judgment be enforced against me and my assets in Alberta?

Academic interest in, and judicial decisions concerning, the relationship between intellectual property and private international law has grown in recent years. Indeed, the topic has provoked detailed treatment in edited volumes and reports by legal think tanks.[9] However, it is still an area with many unanswered questions compared with more developed subject matter such as tort and contract. As well, there are no treaties that establish common rules for multi-jurisdictional intellectual property actions either globally or in the North American context. One of the

---

5   Sections 15(2)–(4).
6   Sections 18(2)–(4).
7   Sections 20(1.1) & 20(1.2).
8   Section 21(2).
9   See the global study in Toshiyuki Kono, ed, *Intellectual Property Law and Private International Law* (Oxford: Hart, 2012); and James J Fawcett & Paul Torremans, *Intellectual Property and Private International Law*, 2d ed (New York: Oxford University Press, 2011). See also American Law Institute, *Intellectual Property: Principles Governing Jurisdiction, Choice Of Law, and Judgments in Transnational Disputes* (St Paul, MN: American Law Institute, 2008) [ALI]; European Max Planck Group for Conflict of Laws in Intellectual Property, *Conflict of Laws in Intellectual Property: The CLIP Principles and Commentary* (Oxford: Oxford University Press, 2013) [CLIP].

most challenging issues is the problem of ubiquitous infringement, or the possibility that a single act on the Internet may lead to simultaneous infringements in multiple countries (and subject to corresponding multiple copyright laws), as in the YouTube example above. This problem demands modification of established rules of private international law in a way that ensures the fair, predictable, and efficient resolution of global and otherwise unwieldy infringement actions. The issue of ubiquitous infringement will be addressed in Section D, below in this chapter.

Causes of action in copyright may be based on various grounds, such as breach of contract for licensing arrangements, validity, or infringement. The basis for the cause of action, and how it is characterized by a court, may invite consideration of different connecting factors that may materially affect whether a court can hear the case and which law is applied.[10] This chapter will focus on copyright *infringement*, in particular, the right to make copies (the reproduction right) and the right to communicate to the public by telecommunication (the telecommunication right). One of these rights is engaged when a defendant uploads infringing content onto the Internet for either download (reproduction right) or streaming (telecommunication right). It is not uncommon for such transmissions to occur across two or more jurisdictions. These particular activities and rights are the focal point of the following analysis.

## 1) Jurisdiction

For a Canadian court to hear a case concerning copyright infringement, it must satisfy itself that it has (1) subject matter jurisdiction over the dispute and (2) personal jurisdiction (or jurisdiction *simpliciter*) over the parties. Subject matter jurisdiction is related to choice of law in that it asks which country's copyright law has been infringed. In other words, what if a Canadian court is presented with the allegation that another country's copyright law (say, that of the United States) has been infringed? Should a Canadian court determine rights that have been granted by foreign legislation? There is no judicial authority on this point in Canadian law.[11]

---

10   For example, in choice of law, the most real and substantial connection is the connecting factor for contracts, but *lex loci delicti* (place of the wrong) is the rule for tort.
11   Joost Blom, "Canada" in Kono, above note 9 at 444.

There are, however, two opposing schools of thought. On the one hand, *lex loci protectionis* (law of the protecting country) holds that redress should occur in the courts of the country whose copyright law has been infringed. This approach is rooted in the highly territorial nature of intellectual property rights as reflected in international treaties,[12] as well as the idea that such rights are conferred by statute and should properly be adjudicated within the sovereign jurisdiction of the granting state.[13] On the other hand, a recent trend recognizes that intellectual property rights are, in substance, private and that, in order to facilitate international commerce, it is efficient and expedient for courts to adjudicate and enforce foreign intellectual property rights if jurisdiction is otherwise satisfied.[14] Most recently, after a lengthy consideration of many factors, the UK Supreme Court, in *Lucasfilm v Ainsworth*, decided that there is no good reason not to adjudicate foreign copyright law in cases where a court would otherwise take and assume jurisdiction.[15] To save the cost of multiple proceedings and ensure efficient resolution of disputes, it seems reasonable that Canadian courts should follow this lead and allow themselves the competence to adjudicate all copyright claims, whether foreign or domestic, connected to a single transaction in otherwise appropriate circumstances.

The second, and usually more common, issue is whether a court has *personal* jurisdiction over the parties. Here, the distinction to be made is between the existence of jurisdiction, or jurisdiction *simpliciter*, and the exercise of jurisdiction after consideration of *forum conveniens* factors, that is, whether another forum is more appropriate for the hearing of the dispute. For jurisdiction *simpliciter*, the standing of a plaintiff to

---

12  See, for example, *Berne Convention*, above note 1, art 5(2), which states that "... the means of redress afforded to the author to protect his rights shall be governed exclusively by the laws of the country where protection is claimed."
13  See, for example, *Lucasfilm Ltd v Ainsworth*, [2009] EWCA Civ 1328 at para 175: "Infringement of an IP right (especially copyright, which is largely unharmonised) is essentially a local matter involving local policies and local public interest. It is a matter for local judges."
14  Joost Blom, "The Private International Law of Intellectual Property" (2010) 26 *Canadian Intellectual Property Review* 67 at 76 [Blom, "Private International Law"]. See also ALI Principles, referred to in Toshiyuki Kono & Paulius Jurcys, "General Report" in Kono, above note 9 at 36.
15  *Lucasfilm Ltd v Ainsworth*, [2011] UKSC 39. See also Blom, "Private International Law," above note 14 at n 65, citing two New York district court cases where US courts assumed subject matter jurisdiction over foreign copyright infringement claims.

bring an action in her jurisdiction of choice is not usually a problem.[16] Moreover, a court has jurisdiction over a defendant who is present or resident in, or submits to (whether by agreement or conduct), a jurisdiction. Agreement to submit might take the form of a jurisdiction selection clause that appears in an online shrink-wrap contract stipulating that "... the parties agree that any dispute arising under this contract shall be resolved in the courts of Ontario." In other words, a defendant who is located in, or consents to, a particular forum gives that forum's court jurisdiction to hear the case.

Courts may also take jurisdiction over an out-of-province (or *ex juris*) defendant in situations where there is a real and substantial connection between the dispute and the forum. In other words, a plaintiff may sue in a jurisdiction where the defendant is not located if it is determined that there is a real and substantial connection between that jurisdiction and the facts giving rise to the cause of action. There are two perspectives on this test. On the one hand, a copyright owner plaintiff should have access to the courts in a forum (usually where he lives or carries on business) where his right has been significantly affected by an infringement. On the other hand, it may be unfair to subject a defendant to a forum unless he could reasonably be expected to answer for his conduct in that forum. In ideal cases, real and substantial connection can be justified by both perspectives. But what of the case where the defendant infringes a copyright whose owner suffers damage in some far-off jurisdiction? Should that defendant be hauled into the plaintiff's choice of jurisdiction if she neither knew (subjectively) nor could reasonably be expected to know (objectively) where the copyright owner would likely suffer damage?

The Supreme Court of Canada has not provided a clear answer to this question. In *Club Resorts Ltd v Van Breda*, the Court emphasized the importance of predictability in the real and substantial connection test. In its view, the real and substantial connection test is an objective inquiry that considers the contacts between the subject matter of the litigation and the forum,[17] which may presumptively present in certain situations (discussed below).[18] The Court did, however, state that pre-

---

16   The plaintiff submits to the jurisdiction of the court to which it files its statement of claim. However, a plaintiff may not have standing in some exceptional cases.
17   2012 SCC 17 at para 82 [*Van Breda*].
18   *Ibid*.

sumptive connecting factors "*generally* point to a relationship between the subject matter of the litigation and the forum such that it *would be reasonable to expect that the defendant would be called to answer legal proceedings in that forum.*"[19] The implication is that if the defendant could not reasonably be expected to know of the circumstances justifying the plaintiff's choice of jurisdiction, then there cannot be a real and substantial connection with that forum. In the context of global access to content over the Internet, any more generous basis for a plaintiff's choice of jurisdiction would seem unfair to the defendant.[20] So, if I upload a song of a locally known Ontario-based artist on an Ontario-based record label, I would expect to be sued in Ontario for infringement; I would not expect to account for my actions in Quebec even if some harm to the copyright interest is suffered in that province.

In fact, there is some basis for believing that the Supreme Court would be reluctant to establish jurisdiction on the sole basis of harm suffered in a jurisdiction.[21] The *Van Breda* court found that certain connecting factors justifying service on an out-of-province defendant were presumptive, including when either a tort is committed, or a person carries on business, in the jurisdiction.[22] As to the former ground, the

---

19   *Ibid* at para 92 [emphasis added]; see also para 97.
20   In *Geophysical Service Inc v Arcis Seismic Solutions Corp*, 2015 ABQB 88 [*Geophysical Service*], the court emphasized the importance of this factor in finding that it is reasonable to expect that a defendant who communicates seismic data to oil companies purportedly in violation of copyright would have to answer for its conduct in the energy capital of Canada: at para 5, and also paras 42–44.
21   For torts committed in Europe, jurisdiction can be established in the "place where the harmful event occurred or may occur" (EC, Council Regulation (EC) No 44/2001 of 22 December 2000, *Jurisdiction, recognition and enforcement of judgments in civil and commercial matters (Brussels I)*, art 5(3)). This has been interpreted to include the place where the alleged damage occurs. In *Pez Hejduk v EnergieAgenur.NRW GmbH*, C-441/13 (22 January 2015) (ECJ) [*Pez Hejduk*], this basis for jurisdiction was applied to copyright infringement. The European Court of Justice held that, to satisfy this basis for jurisdiction, the defendant did not need to direct or target her activity to that jurisdiction. It is enough that a defendant's activity causes harm in a member state to give that country's court jurisdiction over the copyright infringement action. Interestingly, the facts in *Pez Hejduk* were such that the defendant could reasonably expect to be hauled into the Austrian court chosen by the plaintiff as this was both where the plaintiff lived and where the subject matter of the copyright was located. See also *Pinckney v KDG Mediatech AG*, C-170/12 (3 October 2013) (ECJ).
22   These would be in addition to provincial rules of court elaborating additional bases for real and substantial connection in respect of *ex juris* defendants.

Court indicated that damage sustained in a jurisdiction, without more, will not likely justify the assumption of jurisdiction:

> The use of damage sustained as a connecting factor may raise difficult issues. For torts like defamation, sustaining damage completes the commission of the tort and often tends to locate the tort in the jurisdiction where the damage is sustained. In other cases, the situation is less clear. The problem with accepting unreservedly that if damage is sustained at a particular place, the claim presumptively falls within the jurisdiction of the courts of the place, is that this risks sweeping into that jurisdiction claims that have only a limited relationship with the forum. An injury may happen in one place, but the pain and inconvenience resulting from it might be felt in another country and later in a third one. As a result, presumptive effect cannot be accorded to this connecting factor.[23]

The concern here is to safeguard a defendant from being hauled into a jurisdiction that, from her perspective, has only a limited (and likely unforeseeable) connection with the forum. By parity of reasoning, harm suffered through infringing acts that arise by reason of access to content in a jurisdiction will, on its own, serve as an inadequate basis for jurisdiction.

Encouraging on this front, as well, is the following excerpt of the *Van Breda* court on carrying on business as a presumptive ground:

> Active advertising in the jurisdiction or, for example, the fact that a Web site can be accessed from the jurisdiction would not suffice to establish that the defendant is carrying on business there. The notion of carrying on business requires some form of actual, not only virtual, presence in the jurisdiction, such as maintaining an office there or regularly visiting the territory of the particular jurisdiction. But the Court has not been asked in this appeal to decide whether and, if so, when e-trade in the jurisdiction would amount to a presence in the jurisdiction. With these reservations, "carrying on business" [in the Ontario rules of civil procedure] may be an appropriate connecting factor.[24]

This *dictum* discourages the assumption of jurisdiction by reason of a mere virtual presence, or even active advertising in the forum.

---

23   *Van Breda*, above note 17 at para 89.
24   *Ibid* at para 87.

However, in *Equustek Solutions Inc v Jack*,[25] the British Columbia Court of Appeal was asked to grant an injunction against Google to stop it from delivering search results of the BC defendant's website. The court was willing to assume jurisdiction over Google even though it had no physical presence of any kind in the province. Specifically, Google was held to be carrying on business in the province by advertising BC businesses to BC end-users through the use of its proprietary web crawler software (which also took place in British Columbia). If a distinction is to be made between active advertising in a jurisdiction and the kind of online activity engaged in by Google in *Equustek*, it is a fine one. Or, to put it another way, *Equustek* seems to suggest not much more than active advertising is required for a court to establish jurisdiction.

There is no presumptive factor identifying copyright infringement actions per se in *Van Breda* though the Court emphasized that the presumptive connecting factors cited therein are non-exhaustive and will evolve based on treatment of the connecting factor in caselaw, legislation, and private international law more generally as well as "similarity of the connecting factor with recognized presumptive connecting factors." It is not difficult to imagine that analogies might be made between copyright infringement and tort or property law in terms of establishing "new" presumptive connecting factors.[26] However, in two copyright decisions[27] released since *Van Breda*, courts have preferred (wrongly) to consider jurisdiction *simpliciter* for copyright infringement on the basis of the choice of law rule in *Society of Composers, Authors and Music Publishers of Canada v Canadian Assn of Internet Providers*.[28]

In *Davydiuk v Internet Archive Canada*, the plaintiff brought an action for copyright infringement in the Federal Court of Canada against the defendant owner of the Wayback Machine, which archives web content. The plaintiff sought to have his pornographic movies deleted from the

---

25 2015 BCCA 265 [*Equustek*], leave to appeal to SCC granted, [2015] SCCA No 355 (hearing scheduled for November 2016).

26 Consider, for example, *Composers, Authors & Publishers Association of Canada Ltd v Kvos Inc*, [1963] SCJ No 6, where copyright infringement was characterized as a tort committed in Canada since copyrighted communications were specifically targeted to Canadian TV viewers.

27 The cases are *Davydiuk v Internet Archive Canada*, 2014 FC 944 [*Davydiuk*], discussed below, and *Geophysical Service*, above note 20.

28 2004 SCC 45 [*CAIP*]. See discussion of this case, which was about choice of law, not jurisdiction, below.

archived content but the defendant ultimately refused to do this. The primary defendant was a US non-profit company located in San Francisco using servers in the United States. The Wayback Machine copied the disputed content from a Canadian porn site for its archive and, at least in the case of the plaintiff, transmitted it back to Canada. Using the *CAIP* test, the court found that reaching into Canada to archive the web pages (even if done automatically), and more particularly, the fact that the plaintiff was able to have them transmitted back to Canada was enough for real and substantial connection.[29] This thin basis for jurisdiction *simpliciter* was buttressed by a connection between Internet Archive and its wholly owned subsidiary, Internet Archive Canada.[30]

Strictly speaking, *Van Breda* sets out the basis for establishing new presumptive connecting factors for jurisdiction *simpliciter* while *CAIP* addressed the issue of the legislative reach of the *Copyright Act*. Nevertheless, both use a real and substantial connection test. Still, care must be taken by courts to be mindful of whether the defendant's conduct could reasonably be expected to bring her within the jurisdiction of the forum court. In the aftermath of the dicta in *Van Breda*, it seems likely that Canadian courts will require more than just access to copyright infringing content on the Internet as a basis for jurisdiction. The connection between the cause of action and the forum should be strong enough to infer a reasonable expectation of the defendant of being sued in that forum.

It is routinely the case that two or more forums will possess jurisdiction under one of the above bases. So, for example, in the *Davydiuk* case, both Canada and California (as the place of the primary defendant's business) had jurisdiction. Since it is not in anyone's interests to have parallel proceedings in two or more separate places, courts select one using the doctrine of *forum conveniens*. If raised by a defendant, this doctrine asks a court to consider whether, notwithstanding the existence of jurisdiction, it is more appropriate to stay the action in favour of another forum possessing jurisdiction. The purpose of the

---

29   *Davydiuk*, above note 27 at paras 32–34.
30   In addition to being a wholly owned subsidiary and at the complete control of its parent corporation, Internet Archive Canada promotes the archive service and can post and modify content without Internet Archive's permission: see *ibid* at para 23. This factor, however, seems more relevant to carrying on business in the jurisdiction than to copyright infringement per se.

doctrine is to ensure that both parties are treated fairly and the process for resolving the litigation is efficient in individual cases.[31] The Supreme Court has affirmed that the defendant has the burden to show that another forum is *clearly* more appropriate after a consideration of various factors. The exact formulation varies in each jurisdiction although in substance the factors to be considered are as follows:

(a) the comparative convenience and expense for the parties to the proceedings and their witnesses in litigating in the court or in any alternative forum;
(b) the law to be applied to issues in the proceeding;
(c) the desirability of avoiding multiplicity of legal proceedings;
(d) the desirability of avoiding conflicting decisions in different courts;
(e) the enforcement of an eventual judgment; and
(f) the fair and efficient working of the Canadian legal system.[32]

These factors are to be assessed on a global basis and there is not one that, in theory or in practice, is determinative. The first factor usually favours the less wealthy party. In *Davydiuk*, for example, this factor weighed in favour of Canada being the forum because the plaintiff was a man of modest means whereas the defendant was relatively wealthy such that it could absorb the expense of defending the action in Canada.[33] Obviously, choice of law will favour the forum that is familiar with applying its own laws although this should not normally have undue weight as courts are experienced in applying foreign laws to resolve disputes.[34] The desirability of avoiding multiple proceedings as well as

---

31 *Van Breda*, above note 17 at para 105.
32 Uniform Law Conference of Canada, *Canadian Jurisdiction and Proceedings Transfer Act*, s 11(2). Noticeably absent from this factor analysis is loss of juridical advantage. In *Amchem Products Inc v British Columbia (Workers' Compensation Board)*, [1993] 1 SCR 897, the Supreme Court indicated that juridical advantage or disadvantage should flow from the degree of connection between the dispute and the parties. This factor is still relevant: see *Éditions Écosociété Inc v Banro Corp*, 2012 SCC 18 at para 63, where the juridical disadvantage to the plaintiff of having the action barred due to missing the limitation period in Quebec as compared to the disadvantage to the defendant of certain procedural protections in Quebec favoured a finding of Ontario as *forum conveniens*.
33 *Davydiuk*, above note 27 at para 47.
34 Such unusual situations might include where a forum is unfamiliar with a particular cause of action: *Young v Tyco International of Canada Ltd*, 2008 ONCA 709 at para 59. Blom, "Private International Law," above note 14 at 74, suggests that if a civil action involves infringement of foreign copyright law, then it will usually be clearly

conflicting decisions, while central to concerns underlying the *forum conveniens* doctrine, is also not determinative. The Supreme Court has affirmed that Canadian courts should not stand down to assertions of jurisdiction in foreign courts that are not otherwise *clearly* more appropriate.[35] Moreover, in *Davydiuk*, the fact that the US *Digital Millennium Copyright Act* "takedown" regime was available to the plaintiff (and the defendant had complied with the plaintiff's request in the past) did not prevent the Canadian forum from being the *forum conveniens*. The inability to enforce an eventual judgment in the jurisdiction where the defendant has its assets will have a bearing on whether it is worthwhile to continue the Canadian proceedings. However, even in such a case, the Supreme Court has upheld the Canadian jurisdiction as *forum conveniens*.[36] This review of *forum conveniens* factors confirms the highly contextualized nature of the inquiry.

### 2) Choice of Law

As previously discussed, a Canadian court must be satisfied it has subject matter jurisdiction over the dispute. If the dispute concerns infringement under the Canadian copyright legislation, then this jurisdictional requirement is satisfied. However, it remains unclear whether a Canadian court will adjudicate claims of *foreign* copyright infringement.[37] In other words, a court may engage in a choice of law — or applicable law — analysis at the stage of assessing jurisdictional competence to determine whether Canadian copyright or foreign copyright infringement is at issue.[38]

In terms of identifying infringement of Canadian copyright law, the leading case is *CAIP*. In that case, the performing rights collective was

---

more appropriate to stay the action in favour of the foreign forum. However, this makes choice of law essentially determinative of the question of *forum conveniens* in respect of a kind of law that a Canadian forum is familiar with.

35  *Teck Cominco Metals Ltd v Lloyd's Underwriters*, 2009 SCC 11.
36  See *Breeden v Black*, 2012 SCC 19 at para 35, where the Court acknowledged that a defamation judgment would not be enforceable in Illinois, but that the plaintiff should not be deprived of his right of vindication by proceeding with the action in the place of his most substantial reputation. In the caselaw thus far, no independent or particular meaning has been ascribed to the last factor. It may be that courts will consider issues relevant to *forum conveniens* not captured in the other factors.
37  See Section C(1), above in this chapter, on subject matter jurisdiction.
38  But see *Preston v 20th Century Fox Canada Ltd*, [1990] FCJ No 1011 (TD), where a court did not address the issue of subject matter jurisdiction.

seeking a tariff (to compensate the music publishing industry) on Internet services based on the argument that illegal music downloading comprised a sizable portion of Internet activity at that time. The Supreme Court responded by framing the issue in jurisdictional terms. What is the reach of Canada's copyright legislation when acts of uploading, hosting, transmission, and downloading of music files occur in, and across, two or more jurisdictions? The Court emphasized the territorial application of the *Copyright Act*, which is best achieved by determining whether a transmission has a real and substantial connection with Canada. Moreover,

> [i]n terms of the Internet, relevant connecting factors would include the *situs* of the content provider, the host server, the intermediaries and the end user. The weight to be given to any particular factor will vary with the circumstances and the nature of the dispute.[39]

In other words, there must be a real and substantial connection between the activity in question and the territorial jurisdiction of Canada, based on relevant connecting factors, to trigger consideration of copyright infringement under the Canadian Act.

The *CAIP* Court, however, was not clear about whether the real and substantial connection analysis, or the identified connecting factors, applied to all grounds of copyright infringement. Ostensibly, the Court was considering the vague, and geographically non-specific, "right to communicate to the public by telecommunication" in the context of music file-sharing.[40] The geographical location of a "communication" in the Internet context is notoriously diffuse. Communication is a process that involves a sender, a receiver, and a medium of delivery which, in the Internet context, implicates a number of possible intermediaries and points of transmission. As such, the real and substantial connection test under this ground of infringement becomes more contextualized than it might be for other types of infringing activity.

It is worth considering whether more predictable choice of law rules could be devised for copyright infringement. For the reproduction right, courts might choose to focus on identifying the place where a download is completed under this ground of infringement. In other words, the place where the human comprehensible copy occurs is the *locus*

---

39 Above note 28 at para 61.
40 See, for example, *ibid* at paras 45 and 79–83.

of the infringement no matter the means or geographical route of the transmission.[41] This would mean that Canadian copyright law would apply to those who download a copy of a work while located in Canada. It would also mean that those who upload files for others to copy would not commit infringement since the "making available" right, after the decision in *Entertainment Software Association v Society of Composers, Authors and Music Publishers of Canada*,[42] is limited to streaming activities, not copies. To plug this gap, courts may choose to retain the option of imposing liability on uploaders of files for copy through a real and substantial connection test in relation to reproduction right.

The rule in *CAIP* should be changed as it relates to the telecommunication right. In *Entertainment Software*, the Supreme Court rejected the very premise of the *CAIP* decision by re-characterizing this right as a performance right and thus not applicable to Internet downloads (or music file-sharing, in particular). While this seems to insulate Canadian viewers of streamed content from copyright infringement regardless of its provenance, it remains unclear which uploaders of the content will be held liable. For example, if I am an offshore commercial operation that streams content over the Internet that is accessible in Canada, should I be subject to Canadian copyright law?

Although there is no caselaw on point in Canada, English courts have found liability for offshore BitTorrent sites and other Internet content providers on the basis that the copyrighted content is *targeted* to viewers in the United Kingdom. This targeting approach is a multi-factorial analysis that considers both the degree of access by UK end-users and efforts made to attract these users to the website. Thus, in *British Sky*

---

41  The locus of infringement approach has support in Canadian patent law. See *Domco Industries Ltd v Mannington Mills Inc* (1988), 23 CPR (3d) 96 (FCTD), aff'd (1990), 29 CPR (3d) 481 (FCA), where infringement of the exclusive right to "sell" under the Canadian Act did not apply to a transfer which occurred in the United States. See also Blom, "Private International Law," above note 14 at 83. This common sense understanding of the reproduction right was articulated in the English case *1967 Ltd v British Sky Broadcasting Ltd*, [2014] EWHC 3444 at para 12 (Ch) [*British Sky Broadcasting*]:

> When the user of a Target Website selects a torrent file in order to obtain a copy of particular content, and downloads the associated content files, the user copies the content contained in those content files on his or her computer. If the content files comprise a copyright work and the user does not have the licence of the copyright owner, he or she infringes the copyright in that work.

42  2012 SCC 34 [*Entertainment Software*].

*Broadcasting*, targeting was found where the defendant websites (1) were presented in English, (2) had a large number of visitors from the United Kingdom, (3) offered a large number of albums on the UK Top 40 chart, and (4) directed much advertising at the United Kingdom.[43] It is notable that this case did not consider whether the defendant websites employed geo-blocking software as a means of preventing access in the United Kingdom. The upshot of the targeting approach is that, if a website does not take measures to seek or solicit business from a particular jurisdiction, it should not be subject to its copyright law. Thus, a reasonable balance is achieved such that content providers can predict the jurisdictions in which they must seek copyright clearance while the rights of copyright holders in those markets are protected.

Furthermore, new grounds of infringement have been added to the Canadian Act which should require consideration of other factors, not just the locations of the content provider, end-user, host server, and intermediaries. Consider section 27(2.3) which creates liability for digital services that primarily enable acts of infringement. In making this determination, a court is asked to consider under section 27(2.4)

(a) whether the person expressly or implicitly marketed or promoted the service as one that could be used to enable acts of copyright infringement;

(b) whether the person had knowledge that the service was used to enable a significant number of acts of copyright infringement;

(c) whether the service has significant uses other than to enable acts of copyright infringement;

(d) the person's ability, as part of providing the service, to limit acts of copyright infringement, and any action taken by the person to do so;

(e) any benefits the person received as a result of enabling the acts of copyright infringement; and

(f) the economic viability of the provision of the service if it were not used to enable acts of copyright infringement.

---

43 *British Sky Broadcasting*, above note 41 at para 21. See also *Omnibill (PTY) Ltd v EGPSXXX Ltd*, [2014] EWHC 3762 (IPEC), where, on different facts, the court similarly looked at factors relevant to UK end-user access and efforts to attract customers in the United Kingdom.

One might imagine a situation where an offshore BitTorrent site, which has host server, content provider, and intermediary locations mostly or entirely outside Canada, might still be subject to liability of this provision if it was exclusively, or even largely, targeted to a Canadian market.

With these developments since *CAIP*, it will be interesting to see whether Canadian courts continue to apply the real and substantial connection test, and if so, how they do it. If it does survive, it must be revised to account for different grounds of infringement. This change is necessary because a particular ground of infringement may suggest the pre-eminence of a particular connecting factor or factors, or even the creation of new connecting factors. The test, if it is to remain relevant, should be reformulated as follows: copyright liability under the Act occurs where there is a real and substantial connection between the activity, the territorial limits of Canadian jurisdiction, *and the ground for infringement under consideration*. Moreover, the relevance of the connecting factors will similarly depend on the infringement right at issue. In some cases, such as the telecommunication right or even for services that enable infringement, it might make more sense to substitute real and substantial connection with a targeting approach.

### 3) Recognition and Enforcement of Foreign Judgments

In which circumstances will a forum court enforce a foreign order against a judgment debtor? Or put another way, if I am served *ex juris* with a copyright infringement action commenced in another jurisdiction, do I need to be concerned that, if I do not defend the action, an ensuing order might be enforced against me and my assets where I live? Under the old common law rules, there was a fairly straightforward answer to these questions. A Canadian court will enforce an order against a judgment debtor who is properly served in the foreign jurisdiction or who somehow submits to the jurisdiction of that court. Submission can take many forms, including via a forum selection clause in a contract or the taking of any step to defend the action on the merits.[44] Under these rules, if you were neither served in nor submitted to the foreign jurisdiction, any order resulting from that action could not be enforced against you in your home jurisdiction in Canada.

---

44   It is not submission, however, to challenge the *jurisdiction* of the court so long as the merits of the action are not in any way raised or addressed.

The basis for enforcing a foreign judgment in Canada was expanded interprovincially in *Morguard Investments Ltd v De Savoye*,[45] then internationally in *Beals v Saldanha*.[46] In *Morguard*, the Supreme Court held that a province may enforce the judgment of another province within Canada against an *ex juris* defendant, provided there is a real and substantial connection between that other province and the subject matter of the action. The main rationale for this rule was the need to accommodate the interjurisdictional flow of commerce and people within a federation to ensure stability and predictability of transactions.

In a surprising move, the Supreme Court extended the real and substantial connection jurisdictional basis for enforcing judgments to the international arena. In *Beals*, the issue was whether a Florida default judgment against Ontario defendants could be enforced in Ontario. Since the action stemmed from the sale of the defendant's Florida property, there was a real and substantial connection between the subject matter of the action, the defendants, and the jurisdiction, thus justifying enforcement in Ontario. Particular emphasis was placed on the importance that a defendant not be subjected to court orders from remote jurisdictions:

> [A] defendant can reasonably be brought within the embrace of a foreign jurisdiction's law where he or she has participated in something of significance or was actively involved in that foreign jurisdiction.[47]

Thus, an Ontario website that targets its pirated movie sales to New York customers will have a New York judgment enforced in Ontario since there is a real and substantial connection between the defendant, the action, and the issuing forum.[48] However, after *Van Breda*, mere virtual presence in a jurisdiction or access to content in a jurisdiction, even if it results in some harm to the copyright interest of the owner, will not constitute a real and substantial connection. In cases where a real and substantial connection is not clear, an *ex juris* defendant should dispute the jurisdiction of the court and, if unsuccessful, defend the action lest a default judgment be enforced against them in their home province.

---

45  (1990), 76 DLR (4th) 256 (SCC) [*Morguard*].
46  2003 SCC 72 [*Beals*].
47  *Ibid* at para 32.
48  See *Disney Enterprises Inc v Click Enterprises Inc*, [2006] OJ No 1308 (SCJ).

The enforcement of foreign judgments by a receiving court, under common law rules, traditionally extended only to money judgments. However, there are oftentimes remedies that successful plaintiffs seek to enforce other than damages; these include injunction (that the defendant refrain from future infringing activity) and accounting for profits (money owed to the plaintiff through the wrongful gains of the defendant). The Supreme Court, in *Pro Swing Inc v Elta Golf Inc*,[49] indicated that it would be willing to enforce non-monetary judgments in the right circumstances. In broad terms, the concern is to balance a broader scope of enforcement remedies in an increasingly interconnected world with a need to preserve scarce court resources in the supervision of a more demanding set of remedies. It seems that the more final and the less demanding the non-monetary order, the more likely a court will be convinced to enforce it.

## D. UBIQUITOUS INFRINGEMENT

In a 2008 non-Internet Federal Court of Canada case, *Kent v Universal Studios Canada Inc*,[50] a stay of proceedings was requested by the defendant on the basis that a parallel proceeding, generated from the same facts, had been brought in the United States. The plaintiff in the Canadian action was alleging infringement of his copyright in a newscast that appeared in a movie that had been distributed in both Canada and the United States. The defendant, an affiliate of the US action defendant, argued that the US court was *forum conveniens*. The existence of parallel proceedings in the United States (and the problems pertaining thereto) relating to the same facts was not enough to satisfy the court to stay the action. To the contrary, the court found that a determination of the US action would have no bearing on whether Canadian copyright law had been infringed:

> A determination in the U.S. Action of whether there has been infringement will not necessarily be determinative of the outcome in Canada. In this action, Mr. Kent must demonstrate that, under *Canadian* law, he is the owner of the copyright in issue and that Universal Canada has performed one or more of the specific acts set out in the *Copyright*

---

49  2006 SCC 52.
50  2008 FC 906.

Act. While there will have to be determinations in the U.S. Action of copyright action such determinations will be made under U.S. copyright law.... Copyright law is statutory law and there are both subtle and not so subtle differences between U.S. copyright law and Canadian law.... These differences ... militate against a stay of this action being granted.[51]

The case is notable for a number of reasons. First, there is an assumption by the Canadian court that the US court either will not (or should not) consolidate infringement proceedings and apply Canadian copyright law to acts of infringement occurring in Canada. In other words, courts are presumed to have subject matter jurisdiction to apply their own copyright law and no other. Second, the court correctly observes that there is unavoidable variation in the specific copyright laws of different countries. So, even if proceedings were to be consolidated in one court, there is the problem of identifying the locus of each discrete act of infringement and applying the local copyright law to its resolution. Third, the case concerned infringement occurring in a Hollywood motion picture, and it would likely have been open to the plaintiff to bring actions in various jurisdictions around the world, based on the pervasive distribution of such films.

This last point, in particular, illustrates the problem of ubiquitous infringement. As Fawcett and Torremans describe it:

> Unregistered rights such as copyright exist globally, and posting copyright material on a website without permission of the right holder therefore potentially constitutes an infringement in every single country in the world. Such ubiquitous infringement could give a form of jurisdiction to courts of every single country and for each country. But to have separate actions for marginal amounts in every country in the world would be unworkable. One state needs to have jurisdiction over the infringements committed in a number of different States. Thus there is a need for private international law to provide a tool to consolidate cases.[52]

Conversely, protections offered under local law may be largely inadequate in the Internet context. For example, as Blom explains, the

---

51  *Ibid* at paras 25, 26, and 29 [emphasis in original].
52  Above note 9 at 549.

unique protection offered in Canada's copyright law for user-generated content that is uploaded onto the Internet is not a defence in other jurisdictions where the content is accessed.[53]

The issue of ubiquitous infringement has generated much academic debate; it has also been addressed in reports dealing with intellectual property and private international law. Key reports have been issued by the American Law Institute, or ALI[54] and the European Max Planck Group on Conflict of Laws in Intellectual Property, or CLIP.[55]

Both the ALI and CLIP reports allow for the possibility of a court applying foreign copyright law in circumstances of ubiquitous infringement.[56] The CLIP Principles are more circumscribed in this respect, requiring that there be both a substantial connection between the forum and either the infringing activities or the harm caused *and* an absence of substantial effect in the place where the infringer is habitually resident.[57] The effect of applying this principle seems to be that the infringer's place of habitual residence should, in most instances, be the natural forum for resolution of infringement claims on a global basis.

In terms of establishing *personal* jurisdiction over an *ex juris* defendant, both reports *generally* seem to emphasize the importance of the defendant engaging with the forum in some meaningful way. The defendant must have "substantially acted, or taken substantial preparatory acts, to initiate or to further an alleged infringement."[58] The ALI Comment to this provision indicates that these acts are intentional engagements with a forum, for example, the defendant operates "a website in a forum on which it has placed infringing material."[59] This is even more clearly suggested in the provision, found in both sets of principles, that establishes jurisdiction over defendants who direct, or target, infringing activities to the forum.[60]

---

53   Joost Blom, "Private International Law Aspects of User-Generated Content" (2014) 26 *Intellectual Property Journal* 205 at 212.
54   ALI, above note 9.
55   CLIP, above note 9.
56   ALI, above note 9, s 211; CLIP, above note 9, art 2:203(2).
57   *Ibid*.
58   ALI, above note 9, s 204; CLIP, above note 9, art 2:202(2) — very similar language.
59   ALI, above note 9, Comment to s 204 (np).
60   *Ibid*, s 204(2); CLIP, above note 9, art 2:202(2)(b). The ALI Comment provides as follows: "The connotation of 'directs' is less predatory than 'targets,' but is intended to retain an element of intentionality. The inquiry ... is an objective one. The question is whether it is reasonable to conclude from the defendant's behavior that defen-

The CLIP Principles add one further jurisdictional basis over an *ex juris* defendant not found in the ALI Principles: "the activity by which the right is claimed to be infringed has substantial effect within . . . the territory of that state."[61] Arguably, this provision does not require the defendant to knowingly engage with a particular forum. For example, a defendant may substantially act, and direct, her activities to her home jurisdiction, believing her use of copyright material is protected under local fair dealing provisions. However, if the use of that material is not protected under Japanese fair dealing law, there might be a substantial negative effect on the copyright holder's right in that forum which would justify a Japanese court taking jurisdiction. The inclusion of this provision is questionable given the possibility of a defendant being subject to a jurisdiction to which it could not reasonably have anticipated.

For choice of law, both reports affirm the principle of *lex protectionis*, that is, applying the copyright law of each state for which protection is sought,[62] with an important exception for cases of ubiquitous infringement.[63] In such cases, both sets of principles indicate that the law of the state or states with a close or the closest connection to the infringement should be applied.[64] There are important points of divergence between the two sets of factors for determining close connection. The American Law Institute lists the location of the parties, the centre of their relationship if any, the extent of activities and the investment of the parties, and the principal markets to which parties directed activities. The commentary provides the following justification: "Because intellectual property rights are intended to create incentives to innovate, the States most closely connected to that objective are those where the parties resided, made their investment decisions, expected to exploit their work, and (where relevant) entered into a relationship."[65] This justification suggests a possible bias towards the place where the copyright holder's

---

dant sought to enjoy the benefits of engaging with the forum." The Comment then considers more specific factors helpful to this inquiry and provides a list of activities that are *not* intended to come within this provision.
61   CLIP, above note 9.
62   ALI, above note 9, s 301; CLIP, above note 9, art 3:601(1).
63   *Ibid*, art 3:602. The CLIP Principles also provide that *lex protectionis* does not apply to *de minimis* infringement in a jurisdiction but rather must meet the thresholds found for personal jurisdiction over an *ex juris* defendant.
64   ALI, above note 9, s 321; CLIP, above note 9, art 3:603.
65   ALI, above note 9, Comment to s 321 (np).

marketing activities with respect to the work are centred, which would unduly favour the contacts made by the copyright holder.

In contrast, the CLIP Principles have a slight bias in favour of the *locus* of the defendant. The factors for determining closest connection are as follows:

- (a) the infringer's habitual residence;
- (b) the infringer's principal place of business;
- (c) the place where substantial activities in furthering of the infringement in its entirety have been carried out;
- (d) the place where the harm caused by the infringement is substantial in relation to the infringement activity in its entirety.[66]

These factors seem to favour the law either where the defendant is located or where she has engaged in meaningful activity with a jurisdiction or would likely foresee the effects of her activities, and for this reason, is more consistent with Canadian law. Once a court accepts jurisdiction and has chosen the law or laws to be applied to a case of ubiquitous infringement, it may proceed, where infringement is so found, to assess damages for infringements occurring outside the court's jurisdiction.[67] However, it is not clear whether such an assessment would include infringements in all jurisdictions where harm occurs, or those where the harm is most substantial, or only to which the choice of law applies.

\* \* \* \* \*

Principles of private international law continue to be modified to meet the particular challenges of copyright infringement on the Internet, in particular, the inherent cross-border dimension of many content transmissions as well as the scale of content dissemination. The law continues to evolve in this area as established principles are tested and reinterpreted to meet this new reality. In the aftermath of *Van Breda*, Canadian courts are now wrestling with the concept of carrying on business (as a basis for asserting jurisdiction over an out-of-province

---

66 CLIP, above note 9, art 3:603(2).
67 *Barrick Gold Corp v Lopehandia*, 2004 CarswellOnt 2258 at paras 44 & 45, where the Ontario Court of Appeal increased the general damages amount for a defamation in part on the basis that the Internet caused transborder loss of reputation. *Australian Broadcasting Corp v Waterhouse* (1991), 25 NSWLR 519 (CA), endorsed this principle in respect of one court assessing all damages arising from a defamation action occurring in all jurisdictions within the federation of Australia.

defendant) in a way that balances concerns of ubiquitous liability for Internet defendants with a jurisdiction's ability to regulate matters within its territory. Similarly, the choice of law rule in Canada for copyright infringement should probably be changed to a targeting approach in connection with the most substantial means of online infringement — via streaming services and intermediaries that exist to facilitate acts of infringement.

# Table of Cases

1967 Ltd v British Sky Broadcasting Ltd, [2014] EWHC 3444 (Ch) ............. 204–5
671122 Ontario Ltd v Sagaz Industries Canada Inc, 2001 SCC 59 ................. 104–5

Agfa Monotype v Adobe Systems, 404 F Supp 2d 1030 (ND Ill 2005) ............. 127
Alberta (Education) v Canadian Copyright Licensing Agency
  (Access Copyright), 2012 SCC 37 ............................................. 147, 148, 149, 152
Amchem Products Inc v British Columbia (Workers' Compensation
  Board), [1993] 1 SCR 897, 102 DLR (4th) 9, 1993 CanLII 124 ..................... 201
American Broadcasting Cos v Aereo, Inc, 573 US ___ (2014) ............................... 92
Apple Computer Inc v Mackintosh Computers Ltd, [1987] 1 FC 673,
  18 CPR (3d) 129, [1987] FCJ No 916 (CA), aff'd [1990] 2 SCR 209,
  30 CPR (3d) 257, [1990] SCJ No 61 ................................................................ 47, 57
Astral Media Radio Inc v Society of Composers, Authors and Music
  Publishers of Canada, 2010 FCA 16 ...................................................................... 91
Ateliers Tango argentin Inc c Festival d'Espagne & d'Amérique latine
  Inc, [1997] RJQ 3030, 84 CPR (3d) 56, [1997] JQ no 3693 (CS) .................... 53
Australian Broadcasting Corp v Waterhouse (1991), 25 NSWLR 519 (CA) ........ 212
Authors Guild v Google, Inc, No 13-4829-cv (2d Cir 2015) ........................... 155, 157
Authors Guild, Inc v HathiTrust, 755 F3d 87 (2d Cir 2014) ........ 58, 62, 63, 156, 157
AV v iParadigms, 562 F3d 630 (4th Cir 2009) ...................................................... 156

Barrick Gold Corp v Lopehandia (2004), 71 OR (3d) 416,
  2004 CarswellOnt 2258, 2004 CanLII 12938 (CA) ......................................... 212
Beals v Saldanha, 2003 SCC 72 .............................................................................. 207

Bishop v Stevens, [1990] 2 SCR 467, 1990 CanLII 75 .................................. 22, 60, 61
Blacklock's v Canadian Vintners Association, 2015 CanLII 65885
    (ON SCSM) ........................................................................................................ 131
Bleistein v Donaldson Lithographing Co, 188 US 239 (1903) ........................ 52, 53
BMG Canada v John Doe, 2004 FC 488, aff'd 2005 FCA 193 ....................... 119, 120
Boudreau v Lin (1997), 150 DLR (4th) 324, 75 CPR (3d) 1, [1997]
    OJ No 3397 (Gen Div) ...................................................................................... 83
Breeden v Black, 2012 SCC 19 ............................................................................... 202
British Columbia Automobile Assn v Office and Professional
    Employees' International Union Local 378, 2001 BCSC 156 ................. 47–48

Campbell v Acuff-Rose Music, Inc, 510 US 569 (1994) .................................. 147, 161
Canadian Artists' Representation v National Gallery of Canada,
    2014 SCC 42 ................................................................................................. 38, 108
Canadian Broadcasting Corp v SODRAC 2003 Inc,
    2015 SCC 57 ............................... 3, 21, 22, 26, 36–38, 41, 59, 60, 63, 109, 169, 188
Canadian Private Copying Collective v Canadian Storage
    Media Alliance, 2004 FCA 424 ................................................................ 94, 162
Capitol Records v ReDigi, US Dist Ct Southern Dist of NY,
    12 Civ 95 (RJS) .................................................................................................. 75
CCH Canadian Ltd v Law Society of Upper Canada,
    2004 SCC 13 ...................... 11, 14, 24, 31, 32, 34–35, 51–52, 79, 80, 127, 145, 146,
    147, 148, 149, 150, 151, 152, 153, 157, 179
Century 21 Canada Limited Partnership v Rogers Communications
    Inc, 2011 BCSC 1196 ................................... 53, 59, 104, 107, 108, 111, 151, 152, 153
Chamberlain Group v Skyline Technologies, 381 F3d 1178
    (Fed Cir 2004) ............................................................................................ 132, 137
Cinar Corporation v Robinson, 2013 SCC 73 ................................... 65–66, 67, 68
Club Resorts Ltd v Van Breda, 2012 SCC 17 ..... 196–97, 198, 199, 200, 201, 207, 212
Compo Co v Blue Crest Music, 1979 CanLII 6 (SCC) ............................................. 16
Composers, Authors & Publishers Association of Canada Ltd v Kvos Inc,
    [1963] SCR 136, 37 DLR (2d) 1, [1963] SCJ No 6 ............................................ 199
Copyright Act, ss 70.2 and 70.15 (Re), [2012] CBD No 11 ..................................... 63
Crookes v Newton, 2011 SCC 47 ............................................................................ 82
Davydiuk v Internet Archive Canada, 2014 FC 944 ................... 109, 200, 201, 202
Delrina Corp (cob Carolian Systems) v Triolet Systems Inc (1993),
    47 CPR (3d) 1, 9 BLR (2d) 140, [1993] OJ No 319 (Gen Div),
    aff'd (2002), 58 OR (3d) 339, 17 CPR (4th) 289, [2002]
    OJ No 676 (CA) ................................................................................... 48, 50, 67
Disney Enterprises Inc v Click Enterprises Inc (2006), 267 DLR
    (4th) 291, [2006] OTC 321, [2006] OJ No 1308 (SCJ) .................................. 207

## Table of Cases

Domco Industries Ltd v Mannington Mills Inc (1988), 24 FTR 234,
23 CPR (3d) 96, [1988] FCJ No 1133 (TD), aff'd (1990),
107 NR 198, 29 CPR (3d) 481, [1990] FCJ No 269 (CA) ................................ 204

Éditions Écosociété Inc v Banro Corp, 2012 SCC 18 ............................................ 201
Enrietti-Zoppo v Colla (2007), 63 CPR (4th) 377, [2007] OJ No 5183
(Sm Cl Ct) ................................................................................................................ 83
Entertainment Software Association v Society of Composers,
Authors and Music Publishers, 2010 FCA 221, rev'd
2012 SCC 34 ........................... 19, 20, 36, 37, 38, 41, 57, 60, 62, 71, 72, 73, 94, 204
Equustek Solutions Inc v Jack, 2015 BCCA 265 ................................................... 199
Euro-Excellence Inc v Kraft Canada Inc,
2007 SCC 37 ................................................................ 27, 29, 73–74, 107, 108, 117

Feist Publications, Inc v Rural Telephone Service Company,
111 S Ct 1282, 499 US 340 (1991) ........................................................................ 52
Francis, Day & Hunter Ltd v 20th Century Fox (1939), [1940] AC 112,
[1939] UKPC 68 ................................................................................................... 45
FWS Joint Sports Claimants v Canada (Copyright Board) (1991),
[1992] 1 FC 487, 36 CPR (3d) 483, [1991] FCJ No 501 (CA) ........................... 45

Geophysical Service Inc v Antrim Energy Inc, 2015 ABQB 482 ....................... 171
Geophysical Service Inc v Arcis Seismic Solutions Corp,
2015 ABQB 88 ............................................................................................. 197, 199
Gould Estate v Stoddart Publishing Co, 1996 CanLII 8209
(Ont Ct Gen Div), aff'd (1998), 30 OR (3d) 555,
80 CPR (3d) 161, [1998] OJ No 1894 (CA) ......................................... 16, 48, 50

Hager v ECW Press Ltd (1998), [1999] 2 FC 287, 85 CPR (3d) 289,
[1998] FCJ No 1830 (TD) ................................................................................ 50–51
Harmony Consulting Ltd v GA Foss Transport Ltd,
2011 FC 340 ................................................................................................. 53, 116

IMS Inquiry Management Systems, Ltd v Berkshire Information
Services, Inc, 307 F Supp 2d 521 (SDNY 2004) ......................................... 130–31

Jacobsen v Katzer, 535 F3d 1373 (Fed Cir 2008) ............................................ 113–14

Kelly v Arriba Soft Corp, 336 F3d 811 (9th Cir 2003) .................................... 156–57
Kent v Universal Studios Canada Inc, 2008 FC 906 ...................................... 208–9
Kirkbi AG v Ritvik Holdings Inc, 2005 SCC 65 ......................... 27, 28, 29, 133

[217]

Labrecque (O Sauna) c Trudel (Centre Bellaza, senc), 2014 QCCQ 2595..........105
Lenz v Universal Music, 801 F3d 1126 (9th Cir 2015)................................183
Lexmark International v Static Control Components, 387 F3d 522
    (6th Cir 2004) .................................................................................. 128, 137
Lucasfilm Ltd v Ainsworth, [2009] EWCA Civ 1328 ............................................195
Lucasfilm Ltd v Ainsworth, [2011] UKSC 39......................................195

Metro-Goldwyn-Mayer Studios Inc v Grokster, 545 US 913 (2005).......... 180, 181
Michelin v CAW — Canada (1996), [1997] 2 FC 306,
    1996 CanLII 11755 (FC)..................................................................147
Morguard Investments Ltd v De Savoye, [1990] 3 SCR 1077,
    76 DLR (4th) 256, 1990 CanLII 29 ................................................. 207
Murphy v Millennium Radio Group, LLC, 650 F3d 295 (3d Cir 2011)...............141

Neudorf v Nettwerk Productions Ltd, 1999 CanLII 7014 (BCSC)....................... 55
Nils Svensson and Others v Retriever Sverige AB (13 February 2014),
    C-466/12 (Court of Justice of the European Union
    (Fourth Chamber))................................................................. 81
Nova Productions Ltd v Mazooma Games Ltd and Others,
    [2006] EWHC 24 (Ch) .................................................................. 45, 55

Omnibill (PTY) Ltd v EGPSXXX Ltd, [2014] EWHC 3762 (IPEC)...................... 205

Perfect 10, Inc v Amazon, 508 F3d 1146 (9th Cir 2007) ...............................156, 157
Pez Hejduk v EnergieAgenur.NRW GmbH, C-441/13
    (22 January 2015) (ECJ).....................................................................197
Pinckney v KDG Mediatech AG, C-170/12 (3 October 2013) (ECJ) ...................197
Pinto v Bronfman Jewish Education Centre, 2013 FC 945..................................90
Preston v 20th Century Fox Canada Ltd (1990), 38 FTR 183,
    33 CPR (3d) 242, [1990] FCJ No 1011 (TD).................................................. 202
Prise de Parole Inc c Guerin (1995), 104 FTR 104, 66 CPR (3d) 257,
    [1995] FCJ No 1583 (TD) ............................................................. 83
Pro Swing Inc v Elta Golf Inc, 2006 SCC 52...............................................208
Productions Avanti Ciné-Vidéo Inc v Favreau, [1999] RJQ 1939,
    177 DLR (4th) 568, [1999] JQ no 2725 (CA) ............................................148–49

Re Collective Administration in Relation to Rights under
    Sections 3, 15, 18, and 21, [2015] CBD No 2 ..................................................147
Re Collective Administration of Performing and of Communication
    Rights, [2014] CBD No 3..............................................................150
Re:Sound v Fitness Industry Council of Canada, 2014 FCA 48........................ 91

Re:Sound v Motion Picture Theatre Associations of Canada,
   2012 SCC 38 .................................................................................................. 90
Red Label Vacations Inc (redtag.ca) v 411 Travel Buys Limited
   (411travelbuys.ca), 2015 FC 18 .................................................................. 59
Reproduction of Sound Recordings, Re, 2008 CarswellNat 516
   (Copyright Board) ...................................................................................... 94
Riggs v Palmer, 115 NY 506 (1889) ................................................................. 27
Rizzo & Rizzo Shoes Ltd (Re), [1998] 1 SCR 27, 1998 CanLII 837 ............... 22
Robertson v Thomson Corp, [2001] OTC 723, 15 CPR (4th) 147,
   [2001] OJ No 3868 (SCJ) ..................................................................... 69, 70
Robertson v Thomson Corp, 2006 SCC 43 ....................... 31–32, 34, 45, 58, 70
Rogers Communications Inc v Society of Composers, Authors
   and Music Publishers of Canada, 2012 SCC 35 ............... 32–33, 34, 37, 39,
   41, 59, 60, 61, 71, 72, 73

Sega Enterprises Ltd v Galaxy Electronics Pty Ltd, [1996] FCA 761 ............. 55
Sirius Canada Inc v CMRRA/Sodrac Inc, 2010 FCA 348 ......................... 71, 80
Snow v Eaton Centre Ltd (1982), 70 CPR (2d) 105, [1982]
   OJ No 3645 (HCJ) ....................................................................................... 83
Society of Composers, Authors and Music Publishers of Canada v
   Bell Canada, 2012 SCC 36 .......... 30, 31, 32, 33–34, 41, 147–48, 150, 151, 152, 153
Society of Composers, Authors and Music Publishers of Canada v
   Canadian Assn of Internet Providers, 2004 SCC 45 ....... 6, 7, 14, 19, 25, 31, 34,
   35–36, 37, 39, 40, 41, 60, 61, 71, 79, 80, 81, 126, 176, 177–80, 183, 184, 199, 200,
   202, 203, 204, 206
Sony Corp of America v Universal City Studios, 464 US 417 (1984) ................ 80

Teck Cominco Metals Ltd v Lloyd's Underwriters, 2009 SCC 11 .................. 202
Théberge v Galerie d'Art du Petit Champlain inc,
   2002 SCC 34 ................... 3, 16, 23, 24, 25, 27, 28, 29, 48, 57, 75, 77–78, 109, 145
TMTV, Corp v Mass Productions, Inc, 645 F3d 464 (1st Cir 2011) ................ 66
Tokatlidis v MxN Media Corp, [2009] OJ No 6030 (SCJ) .............................. 87
Tremblay v Orio Canada Inc, 2013 FC 109 ............................................. 105, 107

Universal City Studios v Reimerdes, 111 F Supp 2d 294 (SDNY 2000) ....... 138–39
Universal City Studios v Reimerdes, 82 F Supp 2d 211 (SDNY 2000) ............ 138
Universal Studios v Corley, 273 F3d 429 (2d Cir 2001) ............................ 124–25
University of London Press Ltd v University Tutorial Press Ltd,
   [1916] 2 Ch 601 .......................................................................................... 52

Viacom International v YouTube, 676 F3d 19 (2d Cir 2012) ....................... 180

Voltage Picture LLC v John Doe, 2014 FC 161 .................................................. 120
Voyeur Dorm, LC v City of Tampa, 265 F3d 1232 (11th Cir 2011) ..................... 18

Warman v Fournier, 2012 FC 803 ............................................................... 147, 153
Winkler v Roy, 2002 FCT 950 ........................................................................... 115

Young v Tyco International of Canada Ltd, 2008 ONCA 709 ..................... 201–2

# Index

Abella, Justice, 22, 37
Access control right. *See also* Circumvention; *Digital Millenium Copyright Act (DMCA)*, Section 1201 provision
    definition by Act, 131–32
    interpretation of, 135
    nexus requirement, 132–33, 135
    US interpretation, 132
*Access to Information Act*, 171
Advertising, 198–99
Amazon Kindle store, 77
American Law Institute, 210–11
Anti-circumvention measures. *See also* Circumvention; *Copyright Modernization Act*; Technological protection measures (TPMs); World Intellectual Property Organization (WIPO)
    access control, 125, 126
    authorial incentive versus user rights, 127
    burden of proof for violations, 136
    copy control, 125, 127
    copyright interests, balancing, 7, 126–27
    exceptions to, 126, 136–39
    general intermediary liability rules, 126
    international, 124, 125. *See also* Copyright law, international
    Internet, adapting legal doctrine for, 14, 126. *See also* Internet, impact on copyright law; Internet intermediaries
    Internet intermediaries, and creation of, 5. *See also* Internet intermediaries
    interoperability information, dissemination of, 139
    introduction of, 4–5, 124
    language interpretation, 10, 125
    rationalization for, 124
    remedies for violation of, 136
    targets of, 125–26
    technological protection measures (TPMs), and, 10, 126, 127
    US Green Paper, 124, 126
    user privacy, and, 140
Apple iTunes store, 77
Authored works. *See also* Authorization rights for authors; Computer programs, authoring using; Copyright, conditions for obtaining; Internet intermediaries; Moral rights; Non-consumptive uses of works; Substantial taking

compilations or collective works, treatment of, 45
creativity, role of in determining rights, 46, 51–52
definition of, 43, 44–45
digital context, adapting to, 44–45
rights given under Act, 43–44, 56. *See also* Non-consumptive uses of works; Substantial taking
works of joint authorship, 55
intention of joint authors requirement (US), 55–56
wiki creations, challenge of, 56
Authorial incentive, 1. *See also* Anti-circumvention measures; Copyright law interests, reconciling conflicts
authorial rights, 1, 153
compensation, proper, 24, 26, 51, 62
content sharing, impact of, 15, 64
economic impact on, 5
infringement, creating through acts of, 119–20
just rewards, 24, 26, 51, 62
right to copy, and, 62
Authorization rights for authors, 56
"authorizing" infringement, 79
endorsement of defamatory material, 82
hyperlinking as republication of material, 82
hyperlinking to copyrighted material, 81–82, 142
intermediary activities, 78–79

Binnie, Justice, 23, 27–28, 75, 77–78
BitTorrent, 11, 187, 204, 206
British Columbia Court of Appeal, *Equustek Solutions Inc v Jack*, 199
*Broadcasting Act*, 92, 170
Broadcasts. *See also* Neighbouring rights
broadcast incidentals, 26, 37, 38, 58, 60, 96, 163–64, 170–71. *See also* Non-consumptive uses of works
broadcaster, definition of, 92
broadcasting undertaking, 92
broadcasts by educational institutions, copying rights for, 93, 95, 96, 164–65
communication signal, definition of, 92
protection under Act, scope of, 92, 193
streaming broadcasts, subscription services, 92–93

*Canada GST Cases*, index, copyright, 52
Casual expression, lack of copyright protection for, 50
Circumvention
definition of, 130, 135
detection, difficulty of, 134
password protection, circumventing, 131
TPMs, overcoming, 130, 133, 134
Collaborative works, 83, 112, 122
Collective management, 9, 85–86, 101–2. *See also* Broadcasts; Collective management societies; *Copyright Modernization Act*; Neighbouring rights; Society of Composers, Authors and Music Publishers (SOCAN)
authored work copyrights, 86. *See also* Authored works
copyrights and collective societies chart, 101–2
function of, 93
general regime, 93
licensing fees, 93
musical performing rights, 93. *See also* Performance rights; Performers' performances
private copying, 93
retransmissions of distant signals, 95, 96
tariffs, importance of for claiming infringement, 93–94, 95
Collective management societies, 9, 97–100, 167
Collective works, 45–46, 70. *See also* Authored works
Compilations, 45–46. *See also* Authored works
Computer programs, authoring using, 43, 45

# Index

broad definition of "computer program," 47
challenges posed by, 47
characterizing as a work, 47, 48
computer-assisted works versus computer-generated works, 54–55
copyright protection for, 47–48, 67–68
databases, 45
infringement analysis, 47
multimedia works, 46, 47
Conflict of Laws in Intellectual Property (CLIP), 210–12
Content-sharing. *See* BitTorrent, Infringement, copyright; YouTube
Contract law. *See also* Licensing
    breach of contract, conditions for, 109
    breach of the covenant, 114
    clear language, importance of, 109
    "contracting out" of Act provisions, 109–10
    relationship to copyright to, 108–9
    user exceptions, 110
    website terms of use agreements, 109, 111–12. *See also* Licensing
Copyright, conditions for obtaining, 43, 44
    authorial originality versus creative originality, 51–53
    authorship requirement, 54–56
    fixation requirement, 48–49, 96. *See also* Digitization
    general categories of works defined in Act, 44–45, 46
    original expressive content requirement, 49–54
    pre-digital versus digital requirements, 43
*Copyright Act*. *See also Copyright Modernization Act*
    amendment (1997), 21, 60–61, 94
    collective management provisions, 9
    court interpretations of, 3
    exceptions, 11. *See also* Fair dealing
    exhaustion rights for consumers, lack of legislation on, 75–76
    fair dealing provisions, 21. *See also Copyright Act*, Section 29
    private copy levy on blank media, 94
    Section 2, 92, 164, 166, 168, 171, 177–78
    Section 3, 16–19, 23, 27–28, 31–33, 36, 56–57, 71–73, 74, 78, 94, 131, 159, 183. *See also* Reproductions; Technological neutrality; Telecommunication, definition of
    Section 5, 192
    Section 13, 104, 106–7, 109
    Section 15, 86, 94
    Section 16, 89
    Section 18, 90, 94
    Section 19, 93
    Section 20, 93
    Section 21, 94
    Section 27, 11, 74, 165, 184, 186–87, 189, 205. *See also* Internet intermediaries
    Section 28, 89
    Section 29, 95, 146, 157, 159–60, 161–3, 164–67. *See also* Fair dealing; User rights
    Section 30, 21, 37–38, 60–61, 165, 167, 169, 170
    Section 31, 95, 170–71, 182, 184–85
    Section 32, 171, 172
    Section 33, 160
    Section 34, 114
    Section 39, 115, 117
    Section 41, 7, 10, 124–25, 127, 130, 131–34, 136–39, 143, 181–83, 185–86. *See also* Anti-circumvention measures; Circumvention; Technological protection measures (TPMs)
    Section 53, 114
    Section 77, 116
Copyright Board
    buffering, characterization as copying, 80–81
    incidental copies, 63
    "orphan works," statutory licences issued for, 116
    tariffs, setting of, 93, 94, 95, 150, 169
    telecommunication rights, 71

Copyright contracts
  employee to employer ownership, 104–5
  open-source licensing, 10
  website terms of use, 10
Copyright infringement. *See* Infringement, copyright
Copyright law, international. *See also* Anti-circumvention measures; World Intellectual Property Organization (WIPO)
  private law
    accounting for profits, 208
    adjudicating domestic claims, 195–96, 209
    adjudicating foreign claims, 195, 202, 206–8, 209
    adjudicating out-of-province claims, 196, 197–98, 212–13
    carrying on business, and, 198, 212–13
    causes of action, 194, 200
    choice of law, 193, 194, 202–13
    *ex juris* defendants, 196, 206–7, 210–11
    fair dealing, and, 211
    foreign judgments, enforcement of, 193, 197–98, 206–8
    *forum conveniens*, use of, 200–2, 208–9
    injunction, 208
    intellectual property rights, and, 193, 195, 211–12
    jurisdiction, 193, 194–202
    law of the protecting country, 195
    modifications of, 194, 212–13
    real and substantial connection test, 196–98, 203, 204, 206, 207, 210
    reproduction rights, 194
    targeting approach, 204–5, 206, 207, 210, 213
    telecommunication rights, 194, 206
    ubiquitous infringement, 194, 208–12, 213
  public law
    fair dealing, and, 192
    implementation of, 192–93
    national treatment rule, 191
    treaty law, 191–92
Copyright law interests. *See also* Anti-circumvention measures
  balancing of, 2–4, 7–8, 23–24, 110, 155. *See also* Digital technology, evolution of; Technological neutrality
  reconciling conflicts, 1–2. *See also* Statutory rules, drafting of
Copyright legislation
  failure to adapt to digital age realities, 6–7
  measuring success of, 2
*Copyright Modernization Act*
  codification of judicially created rules, 7, 16
  controversial aspects of, 10
  creation of, 7
  fair dealing exceptions, 147
  Internet intermediaries, liability of, 7, 78, 176, 188
  moral rights protections, extension to performers' performances, 89, 193
  private copying in digital formats, allowance of, 95
  remaining ambiguities post-creation, 7. *See also* Statutory interpretation
  secondary infringement provision, new, 117
  streaming content provision, 72–73
Copyright ownership. *See also* Copyright registration
  contracts. *See* Copyright contracts
  copyright registration, and, 115
  employer ownership of employee copyright, 104–5
  first owner, definition in Act, 103–4
Copyright registration. *See also* Copyright ownership
  benefits of, 114
  copyright ownership, and, 114
  evidence, absence of, 115
  infringement remedies, protection for, 115

# Index

"orphan works," problem of, 115–16
   protection under *Copyright Act*, no requirement for, 114, 115
   review process, lack of, 115

Data mining, 9, 58, 155, 156
Digital locks. *See* Technological protection measures (TPMs)
*Digital Millenium Copyright Act (DMCA)*, 10, 141, 176, 182–83
   "notice and takedown" regime, 202. *See also* Internet intermediaries
   Section 1201 provision, 132–33
   unintended consequences of, 143
   US courts, interpretation of by, 124
Digital technology, evolution of
   copyright balance, challenges to, 4–5, 7–8, 13–14. *See also* Technological neutrality
Digitization. *See also* Dissemination; Internet, impact on copyright law
   copy-dependent technologies, adoption of, 22, 37, 63
   copyright law adaption to, 14, 49. *See also* Anti-circumvention measures
   mass projects, 155, 156
   problems presented by, 14–15, 44, 49
Dissemination, 1–2. *See also* Digitization; Internet, impact on copyright law
   broadband connectivity, impact of, 15
   commercial versus not-for-profit, 93, 95, 96, 135, 147, 158, 159, 164–66, 167–68
   digitization, impact of, 5, 8
   fairness analysis, effects on, 41, 150–51
   free, protection against, 62. *See also* Authorial incentive
   Internet as tool of, 155, 177
   maximizing works to public, interest in, 25, 51, 63, 82
   open-source licensing, rights under, 114
Distribution rights, 56, 73–78
   digital exhaustion rule, 76, 77, 78, 84
   exhaustion rule, 73–77
   moral rights, 43
   non-exclusive use licensing, 76–77
   purchaser rights, extent of, 75, 77–78
   resale of physical copies, 76
   sales notwithstanding licensing provisions, 77
   tangible versus intangible objects, 73–75
Downloading files, 15, 19, 40, 57, 71, 177
Dramatic works. *See also* Authored works
   copyright protection for, 50
   dramatico-musical works, 93
   performers' performances, and, 86
   user-generated works, of, 159–61
Dworkin, Ronald, on legal principle, 26–27, 29

Economic impact of Internet and digitization, 5
Economic interest as evolving principle of law, 27–30, 36
Equitable remuneration
   beneficiaries, 91
   infringement, recourse for cases of, 91
   Internet streaming, exclusion of, 91
   jurisdiction of rights, 91, 193
   push technology, and, 91
   right to communicate, 91, 96
   right to general performance, 91, 96
European Court of Justice, *Nils Svensson and Others v Retriever Sverige AB*, 81

Facebook, 106
Facts, lack of copyright protection for, 49, 65
Fair dealing. *See also* Contract law; *Copyright Act*, fair dealing provisions; Copyright law, international; Society of Composers, Authors and Music Publishers of Canada (SOCAN); User rights
   allowable purposes, 11, 146–47
   assessing fairness, 149–53

competition by copies, 153, 154
confidential information, and, 152–53
conventional uses vs digitalization uses, 155–56
definition of, 146
digital infringement, safeguards against, 154, 157
digital works, threshold for alternatives to, 154
exceptions to, 146,
moral rights, and, 84
non-authorial interests, advancement of, 11, 172–73
purpose of works, and, 151–52
quantitative taking, 151
reconceptualization as user rights, 11, 127
research, and, 147–48, 154, 155
technological neutrality, and, 33–34, 41, 151
Federal Court of Appeal (FCA) cases
   *BMG Canada Inc v John Doe*, 118, 120
   *Voltage Picture LLC v John Doe*, 119, 120–21
Federal Court of Canada cases
   *Davydiuk v Internet Archive Canada*, 199–202
   *Kent v Universal Studios Canada Inc*, 208
Free previews, 150, 154–55
Fuller, Lon, 16
Functionality, lack of copyright protection for, 49, 50

*Globe and Mail*, reproduction of articles in digital formats, 69
Google, 185, 199
Google Books, 11, 155, 173

Hart, HLA, 16
HathiTrust, 11, 58–59, 62–63, 173
Howell, Robert, 92

Ideas, lack of copyright protection for, 49–50, 65
Improvisation, lack of copyright protection for unrecorded, 48

Infringement, copyright. *See also* Access control right; Anti-circumvention measures; Infringers, copyright; Internet, impact on copyright law; Internet intermediaries; Internet service providers (ISPs)
authorizing, 79, 177
contributory, 181
creativity, impact on. *See* Authorial incentive, economic impact on
cross-border jurisdiction, 12. *See also* Copyright law, international; World Intellectual Property Organization (WIPO); World Trade Organization's *Agreement on Trade-Related Aspects of Intellectual Property (TRIPS Agreement)*
host sites, 11, 41, 175–76, 178, 184–85, 189
illegal copying and content sharing, 4, 9, 15, 41, 57, 61–62, 122, 150. *See also* Digitization; Downloading files; Streaming content; YouTube
implied licence from copyright owner, 116
intent, 116, 117
liability, 11, 34–35
music file-sharing, 15, 177, 203, 204. *See also* Downloading files; Streaming content
primary infringement, 116
remedies awarded for, 117
secondary infringement, 116–17
statutory damages, 117
surveillance measures, 3
ubiquitous, 12, 194, 208–12, 213
Infringers, copyright
bona fide claim, 119
copyright trolls, 120, 182
disclosure by ISPs, FCA test for compelling, 118–19
disclosure versus privacy rights of users, 119–20, 122
identifying, 118. *See also* Internet Service Providers (ISPs)

*Norwich* orders, 118, 120-21
peer-to-peer networks, subscribers to, 118
Internet, impact on copyright law, 4-5. *See also* Digitization; Dissemination; Downloading files; Streaming content
   anonymity of users, 122. *See also* Infringement, copyright; Infringers, copyright; Internet Service Providers (ISPs)
   copy dependency, 15, 22
   creativity, impact on, 5
   jurisdictional pervasiveness, 15-16
   making available rights, 90-91, 96, 204
   Web 2.0, introduction of, 15
Internet Archive Canada, 199-200
Internet intermediaries. *See also* Anti-circumvention measures; Internet service providers (ISPs); Reproductions; Supreme Court rulings
   authorization right, 179-80, 188
   cached copies, 35-36, 37, 58, 60, 178, 183
   copyright infringement liability, exposure to, 7, 11, 32, 35, 78, 178-80, 188-89, 213
   definition under Act, 175
   functions, 11
   host servers, 41, 175-76, 178, 184-85, 189
   incidental copies, 36, 37, 41, 57, 84, 96, 169. *See also* Reproductions
   infringement enablers, 175-76, 186-87
   network service providers exception, 183
   "notice and notice" regime in Canada, 11, 175-76, 181-83
   "notice and takedown" regime in US, 176, 180-81, 182, 187
   peer-to-peer sharing, 186-87, 204
   pirated content
      compensation avenues for, 175, 177
      uploading of, 175-76
   RAM copies, 58
   safe harbour considerations, 177-81, 183-86
   search engines, 175, 185-86
   transmission copies, 39, 58
Internet service providers (ISPs), 10. *See also* Authorization rights for authors; Infringers, copyright
   disclosing identity of infringers, 10, 118-19
   liability as "authorizers" of infringement, 34-35, 36, 80, 81, 177-80
Interviews (formal), copyright protection for, 50-51

Knowledge-based infringement, 4-5

Lectures, lack of copyright protection for, 48
Libraries, 79, 81
Licensing. *See also* Contract law; Copyright registration
   assignments, 105, 107, 108, 114, 115
   click wrap licences, 112
   Creative Commons licence, 113
   exclusive licence, 105, 106-8, 111, 114
   General Public Licence (GPL), 112-13. *See also* Contract law
   non-exclusive licence, 105, 106, 108
   open-source licences, 112-14, 122
   republishing photos or documents, 105

Max Planck Group, 210
McLachlin, CJC, 51-52, 127
Media neutrality. *See* Technological neutrality
Moral rights
   ability to waive, 82
   digital environment, in, 84
   economic rights, relationship with, 84
   expert opinion and public reaction as evidence, 83
   non-transferability, 82
   right of integrity, 83
   right of paternity, 82-83
MP3 stores, 77
Multimedia works, copyright protection for, 46

Musical works, 34, 85, 93–94, 97–100, 150. *See also* Performance rights; Performers' performances; Sound recordings

Neighbouring rights, 73. *See also* Broadcasts; Collective management; Equitable remuneration; Performers' performances; Sound recordings
definition of, 43, 85
Network service providers. *See* Internet service providers (ISPs)
Non-consumptive uses of works
amendments to Act, possible, 61
computational copies, 58
copyright protection, eligibility for, 59–60
digitization copies, 58
judicial interpretation, reliance on, 61–62
production copies, 59
transmission copies, 58

Originality. *See also* Copyright, conditions for obtaining
definition of, 51
skill and judgment, courts' consideration of, 53–54
"Orphan works." *See* Copyright Board; Copyright registration

Parody, 84, 147, 148–49, 160, 161
Patry, William, criticism of "old" copyright law in new digital age, 5
Peer-to-peer networks, 15, 204. *See also* BitTorrent
Performance rights, 19, 36, 71, 89, 96, 101, 102. *See also* Collective management; Dramatic works; Performers' performances; Telecommunication, definition of
Performers' performances, 86–87, 96. *See also* Collective management, musical performing rights; *Copyright Modernization Act*; Neighbouring rights; Performance rights

media producers, rights assigned or licensed to, 89
tangible mediums, right to fix as, 88
telecommunication rights, extension of, 88
Perzanowski, Aaron, 76, 77
Photos, copyright protection for, 53–54
Pinterest, 187
Pornographic content, 18, 19, 199–200
Programming code. *See also* Computer programs, authoring using
protected as literary work, 47, 50, 53
Proxy servers, 140
Public domain works, 25
lack of copyright protection for, 49, 50

Recording devices, impact on copyright claims, 51
Registrar of Copyright, 114
Reproduction rights, 31, 56–71, 84. *See also* Internet, impact on copyright; Non-consumptive uses of works; Reproductions; Substantial taking
Reproductions, 16. *See also* Broadcasts; Copyright law, international; Internet intermediaries; Infringement, copyright; Supreme Court rulings, *Théberge v Galerie d'Art du Petit Champlain inc*; Technological neutrality
as copyright infringement, 22, 23
definition of, 19–20, 23–24, 40. *See also* Statutory interpretation, dynamic intentionalism approach
quality of, as moral right, 84
Rights management information (RMI). *See also* World International Property Organization (WIPO), *WIPO Copyright Treaty (WCT)*
definition of, 140
intent requirements, 141
"IP phone home" technology, 143
protection of, 10, 123, 141–42
proximity to work, controversy in US law over, 142

terms and conditions for users, 142
US White Paper (1995) on, 140
user-generated content, posting, 141
Rome Convention, 87, 89, 90, 96
   exclusion of performances in United States, 88
Rothstein, Justice, 32-33, 37-38, 73-74, 107, 108

Satire, 147, 160
Scassa, Teresa, 158, 160
Scènes-à-faire, lack of copyright protection for, 49, 50, 65
Schultz, Jason, 76, 77
Second Life, challenge of avatars in copyright protection, 55
Separation principle, 28-29
Society of Composers, Authors and Music Publishers of Canada (SOCAN), 86, 94, 99, 148. *See also* Collective management; Supreme Court rulings
Sound recordings. *See also* Neighbouring rights
   cinematographic works, soundtracks for, 90
   definition of, 89-90
   distribution and making available rights, 90-91, 96
   first publication rights, 90
   maker, definition of, 90
   monopoly protections, 89-90
   protection under *Copyright Act*, scope of, 90, 193
   rental rights, 90, 96
Statutory damages, 10
Statutory interpretation
   approaches to, generally, 18
   broad interpretations, 18-19
   conflicting or incoherent legislation, 17
   context, 22-23
   dynamic intentionalism approach, 19-22
   incomplete legislation, 17, 95
   inferences in language, 20-21
   legislative history, use of, 19-20
   ordinary meaning approach, 18-19
   purposivism approach, 22-25
   reproduction rights, limited nature of, 39
   vague language, challenges of, 16, 17, 26, 95
   vague language and technological adaptation, 16-17, 26, 187
Statutory rules
   drafting of, 3. *See also* Copyright law interests, reconciling conflicts
   interpretation of. *See* Statutory interpretation
Stock characters, lack of copyright protection for, 49, 65
Streaming content, 15, 19, 40, 60, 62, 71-72, 92, 162, 164, 204. *See also* Broadcasts; *Copyright Modernization Act*; Equitable remuneration; Internet, impact on copyright law
Subscription-based services, 72, 80-81, 92-93, 150
Substantial taking
   appropriation, 68
   digital formats and competing copyrights, 69-70
   dissection approach, 66-67
   expansion of acceptable evidence in cases of, 64-65, 68-69
   holistic approach, 65-67, 68
   proof of copying, determining, 64-65
   quantitative taking versus qualitative taking, 65-66, 68
Supreme Court rulings
   *Agfa Monotype v Adobe Systems*, 127-28
   *Alberta (Education) v Canadian Copyright Licensing Agency (Access Copyright)*, 11, 147
   *American Broadcasting Cos v Aereo*, 92
   *Apple Computer Inc v Mackintosh Computers Ltd*, 47
   *Beals v Saldanha*, 207
   *Bishop v Stevens*, 22-23, 60
   *British Columbia Automobile Assn v Office and Professional Employees' International Union Local 378*, 47-48

Canadian Artists' Representation v National Gallery of Canada, 108
Canadian Broadcasting Corp v SODRAC 2003 Inc, 21, 26, 36–37, 38, 41, 59, 60, 63, 109, 169
CCH Canadian Ltd v Law Society of Upper Canada, 11, 24–25, 31, 32, 34–35, 51, 79, 127, 145, 146, 147, 149–50, 153, 179. See also Fair Dealing
Century 21 Canada Limited Partnership v Rogers Communications Inc, 108, 111–12, 151–53
Cinar Corporation v Robinson, 65–67, 68–69
Club Resorts Ltd v Van Breda, 196–97, 198, 199, 200, 207, 212–13
Crookes v Newton, 82
Delrina Corp (cob Carolian Systems) v Triolet Systems Inc, 48, 50, 67–68
Entertainment Software Association v Society of Composers, Authors and Music Publishers of Canada, 19, 20, 36, 37, 38, 41, 59–61, 71–72, 204
Euro-Excellence Inc v Kraft Canada Inc, 27, 29, 73–74, 107, 108
Geophysical Service Inc v Antrim Energy Inc, 171
Gould Estate v Stoddart Publishing Co, 50
Hager v ECW Press Ltd, 50–51
Harmony Consulting Ltd v GA Foss Transport Ltd, 53
Kelly v Aribba Soft Corp, 84
Kirkbi AG v Ritvik Holdings Inc, 27–29
Labrecque (O Sauna) c Trudel (Centre Bellaza, senc), 105
Metro-Goldwyn-Mayer Studios Inc v Grokster, 180–81
Morguard Investments Ltd v De Savoye, 207
Neudorf v Nettwerk Productions, 55–56
Pinto v Bronfman Jewish Education Centre, 90
Pro Swing Inc v Elta Golf Inc, 208
Productions Avanti Ciné-Vidéo Inc v Favreau, 148

Robertson v Thomson Corp, 31–32, 33–34, 40, 58, 69
Rogers Communications Inc v Society of Composers, Authors and Music Publishers of Canada, 32, 34, 37, 38, 41, 59–61, 71, 72
Sirius Canada v CMRRA/SODRAC, 71, 80–81
Snow v Eaton Centre Ltd, 83
Society of Composers, Authors and Music Publishers of Canada v Bell Canada, 11, 32, 33, 41, 148–50, 151–52
Society of Composers, Authors and Music Publishers of Canada v Canadian Assn of Internet Providers, 19, 30, 31, 34–35, 37, 38, 60–61, 79, 81, 126, 147, 169, 176–77, 179, 183, 199, 202–4
Théberge v Galerie d'Art du Petit Champlain inc, 3, 16, 23–24, 27–28, 75, 77–78, 109, 145
Tremblay v Orio Canada Inc, 107
use of technical language in, 3
Warman v Fournier, 153

Technological neutrality, 4, 9, 22. See also Fair dealing; Internet intermediaries; Reproductions
conflicts between principles of, 30–31
copyright law jurisprudence, and, 30, 80
definition of, 32–33, 36
digital facts, neutralizing, 39–41
extension of owner and user rights, and, 30, 34
functional equivalency, 31–32, 37, 39, 40
future of, 41–42
negation of material differences, 31
non-discrimination, and, 30, 31, 33, 37
non-interference, and, 30, 34–39, 41
perspectives, technical and functional, 40
statutory interpretation, and, 26
tariff setting, 38

# Index

tiered meanings, 31
Technological protection measures (TPMs). *See also* Access control right; Anti-circumvention measures; Circumvention; Neighbouring rights
  controversy of, 123
  definition of, 127
  "effective" descriptor, challenge of, 128–30
  goals of, 127–28, 129
  makers and dealers, regulation of, 133–35, 139
  private copy exceptions, and, 161
  purpose requirement, 138–39
  scope of application, 128–29
  user rights, impact on, 123
Telecommunication
  definition of, 18–19. *See also* Performance rights
  rights, 36, 56, 60–62, 71–73, 96, 183, 184, 194, 204
Trademarked logos, 28, 29

United Kingdom (UK) court cases
  *1967 Ltd v British Sky Broadcasting Ltd*, 204–5
  *Lucasfilm v Ainsworth*, 195
United States (US) court cases
  *Authors Guild v HathiTrust*, 62–63, 157, 173
  *Chamberlain Group v Skyline Technologies*, 132, 137
  *IMS Inquiry Management Systems, Ltd v Berkshire Information Services, Inc*, 130–31
  *Jacobsen v Katzer*, 113–14
  *Kelly v Arriba Soft Corp*, 156–57
  *Lexmark International v Static Control Components*, 128, 137
  *Murphy v Millennium Radio Group, LLC*, 141
  *Universal City Studios v Reimerdes*, 138, 139
  *Universal Studios v Corley*, 124–25, 138
Unregistered trademarks, extending ownership using, 28

User rights, 24–25. *See also* Anti-circumvention measures; Fair dealing; Technological neutrality; Technological protection measures (TPMs)
  educational institutions exception, 164–67
  ephemeral copy exception, 170
  incidental use and temporary copy exception, 169–70
  libraries, archives, and museums (LAM) exception, 167–68
  miscellaneous exceptions, 172
  perceptual disabilities exception, 171
  private copy exception, 161–64
  protection of, shift toward, 145
  research, and, 147–48
  retransmission exception, 170–71
  statutory obligations exception, 171–72
  user-generated content (UGC) exception, 158–61

Video games
  lack of copyright protection for players, 55
  rights regarding use in, 45
Videos, copyright protection for, 53–54
Virtual private networks (VPNs), 130, 140

Wayback Machine, 49, 199–200
Websites, protected as artistic work, 47–48. *See also* Computer programs, authoring using; Contract law
Wikipedia, 56
World Intellectual Property Organization (WIPO), 12, 123, 192
  WIPO Copyright Treaty (WCT), 61–62, 74, 87, 123, 129, 140–41, 142, 192
  WIPO Performances and Phonograms Treaty (WPPT), 87, 88, 89, 90–91, 96, 123
World Trade Organization's *Agreement on Trade-Related Aspects of Intellectual Property (TRIPS Agreement)*, 87, 88, 90, 96, 192

YouTube, 5, 92, 158, 159, 193–94

# ABOUT THE AUTHOR

DR. CAMERON HUTCHISON is a professor of law at the University of Alberta, where he has researched and taught in the areas of intellectual property law, copyright law, and statutory interpretation for the past dozen years. He is the author of numerous publications, including several pieces on the interaction between digital technology, copyright law, and legal interpretation.